LITERACY INSTRUCTION IN THE CONTENT AREAS

THE LITERACY TEACHING SERIES

Anders and Guzzetti • Literacy Instruction in the Content Areas, Second Edition

Au • Multicultural Issues and Literacy Achievement

Stahl and Nagy • Teaching Word Meanings, Second Edition

Wolf • Interpreting Literature With Children

LITERACY INSTRUCTION IN THE CONTENT AREAS

Second Edition

Patricia L. Anders
The University of Arizona

Barbara J. Guzzetti
Arizona State University

Director, Editorial: Lane Akers
Executive Assistant: Bonita D'Amil
Cover Design: Kathryn Houghtaling Lacey
Book Production Supervisor: Eileen Meehan
Full-Service Compositor: TechBooks
Text and Cover Printer: Hamilton Printing Company

This book was typeset in 10/13.5 pt. ITC Garamond, Italic, Bold, and Bold Italic. The heads were typeset in ITC Garamond, Italic and Bold.

First published by Lawrence Erlbaum Associates, Inc., Publishers
10 Industrial Avenue
Mahwah, New Jersey 07430

Reprinted 2009 by Routledge

Routledge

270 Madison Avenue
New York, NY 10016

2 Park Square, Milton Park
Abingdon, Oxon OX14 4RN, UK

Library of Congress Cataloging-in-Publication Data

Anders, Patricia L.
Literacy instruction in the content areas / Patricia L. Anders and Barbara J. Guzzetti. — 2nd ed.
p. cm. — (The literacy teaching series)
Includes bibliographical references and index.

ISBN 0-8058-4339-6 (cloth : alk. paper)
ISBN 0-8058-4340-X (pbk. : alk. paper)

1. Content area reading. 2. Language arts. 3. Learning, Psychology of. 4. Textbooks. I. Guzzetti, Barbara J. II. Title. III. Series.
LB1050.455A53 2005
428.4'071'2—dc22

2005008136
CIP

10 9 8 7 6 5 4 3 2 1

Patty dedicates this book to Karen and Paul, two young adults who have given their mother far more than they have received.

Barbara dedicates this book to Piglet, a genius potbellied pig who warmed many hearts with her clever antics.

Contents

Preface

This is a most exciting time in the history of content area and adolescent literacy. Policy makers and educators, alike, are looking for ways to support young adults' literacy development. Content area professional standards include the development of student literacy in each of the content areas. In addition, the recent research literature related to the sociocultural nature of literacy and constructivist learning theories have revived and invigorated the field, enriching our understandings of the processes of adolescent literacy development. These concurrent phenomena made writing this second edition of *Literacy Instruction in the Content Areas* an exciting and worthwhile adventure. We hope this book provides knowledge and practices that are helpful to those who are responsible for the development of students' sophisticated literacies across the curriculum.

This edition differs from the first in several ways. Having used the book ourselves for several years and having received feedback from others who have used the first edition, we rewrote to be more conversational, providing practical examples wherever possible and raising questions for teachers that are best answered by the informed professional in the context of working with both content and young people. We revised and elaborated on the "Application Activities" at the end of each chapter. These suggestions are intended to help preservice and in-service teachers apply and extend the ideas and practices of the chapter. We encourage readers to look at the application activities to help set purposes for reading each chapter. At the end of each chapter is also a section, "From Our Professional Library," and we hope that faculty and students alike will find this addition to be helpful for additional reading or elaboration on ideas presented. The major change between our former edition and this one is that we added three chapters, elaborating on ideas that were only suggested in the first edition.

One new chapter is the first, which focuses on the nature of today's adolescent. We describe some of the studies that explore and reveal young people's out-of-school experiences with popular culture, commercial and "indie" media (independent media), and such "New Literacies" as technoliteracies or digital literacies. The chapter concludes with suggestions for bridging the gap between students' out-of-school literacy pursuits and their in-school literacy instruction and assignments.

Chapter 2 is the content area literacy educators' response to the nature of adolescents' out-of-school literacy described in the first chapter. In other words, we ask, "Given the nature of adolescent out-of-school literacy, how does curriculum and instruction respond?" We begin by providing a definition of literacy, proceed to describing content area literacy historically, and conclude with reporting studies of stakeholders' perspectives of content area literacy.

We think Chapter 3 is a key chapter because it focuses on the nature of content concepts and the relationship between those curricular concepts and a teacher's beliefs. This chapter makes the point that curriculum is filtered through a teacher's beliefs, and the enacted curriculum, through instruction, is critically influential on the opportunities young people have to use their developing literacy as tools for negotiating meanings in the content areas.

Chapter 4 provides guidance for selecting and using print resources for content area learning. Both commercial textbooks and trade literature—magazines, novels and other informational books, and poetry—are discussed. We maintain that textbooks are *not* curriculum, rather reading materials the teacher supplies are resources that are meant to be resources for the construction of understandings in the various content areas.

Another new chapter is Chapter 5, which parallels Chapter 4 in that it discusses instructional resources, but focuses on the background, theory and practices related to digital resources rather than print resources. Specifically, we summarize the "New Literacies" that are available for content area instruction and we make recommendations for using them as resources for learning in the classroom. One theme in this chapter that we hope makes a contribution to secondary educators is a discussion of the differences between critical reading and thinking and critical literacy. In our experience, this is a point of confusion for many students. This chapter also includes a section on struggling literacy learners and technology, exploring both the instructional limitations and possibilities of technology for these learners. The chapter concludes with resources for teachers as they continue to develop their technological sophistication.

Chapter 6 is intended to pull together the previous chapters in terms of what they mean for planning to teach and instruction. Suggestions are made for designing lessons and units that incorporate literacy practices and content teaching. This chapter represents "tried-and-true" content area literacy practices and strategies, as well as newer practices that are based on research. We know there is no prescription for practice. We maintain that teachers use their best knowledge to plan, but they must continually revise as the instruction takes place. We respect that attribute of teaching, and throughout this volume we tried to discuss considerations that will help the "on-your-feet" instruction go more smoothly.

We are confident that the ideas presented in Chapters 1 through 6 provide the basis for good content area literacy instruction, but we realize that implementing these ideas are likely to present a challenge to many teachers, especially those who are just beginning their careers. Chapter 7 discusses some of the roadblocks that are likely to make implementing these ideas difficult, and provides suggestions for smoothing out the road to incorporating literacy and content instruction.

The final chapter is the third new chapter and is written for those who are considering leadership as a reading specialist or literacy coach in a secondary school. Principles and guidelines are provided for decision making about the structure and content of the program. Included is a brief summary of current commercial programs that a literacy coach or reading specialist might consider purchasing for a middle school or high school literacy program.

We look forward to your response, professors and students, to this second edition. We ask for your support in providing comments on features of this book that work well for you and features that can be improved. Please correspond with us or talk with us at literacy conferences such as IRA, NRC, NCTE, or AERA. We sincerely hope that this book is of value to you in your teaching and learning.

—Patty Anders
Tucson, Arizona
—Barbara Guzzetti
Tempe, Arizona

Acknowledgments

We greatly appreciate and acknowledge the contributions made by others to the publishing of this book. Like others in the academic community, we owe a great debt of gratitude to those who helped to socialize us to the profession, our major advisors. Patty worked with Professor Ken Dulin at the University of Wisconsin and Barbara worked with Professor Philip DiStephano. Ken has passed, but we hope we have done both advisors proud.

Our colleagues, especially those who are writing companion texts in this series, are wonderful people with whom to work and associate (Sheila Valencia, Kathy Au, David Pearson, Bill Nagy, Taffy Raphael, Freddie Hiebert, Shelby Wolf). We are honored to have the opportunity to work with them on this series.

The contribution of our students and other colleagues is also evident throughout this volume. We pay special tribute to Donna Alvermann and Leslie Rush, whose research on commercial secondary reading materials contributed to Chapter 8. We also thank David Betts, whose expertise and hard work contributed mightily to Chapter 5, and to Karen Spitler, a teacher extraordinaire whose spirit and practices made our text richer.

Patty is fortunate to benefit from her colleagues who also teach the "Content Area Literacy in a Multicultural School" course at the University of Arizona. This group of wonderful teachers—Terry Penfield, Frank Spencer, Debbie Anders, Dale Hicks, Kerry MacArthur, and Eliane Rubinstein-Avila—meets regularly and faithfully to inform each other about content area literacy and to support each other as we encounter challenges while teaching the course. Thank you, dear colleagues.

Finally, sincere thanks and gratitude are owed Lane Akers and his most capable staff at Lawrence Erlbaum Associates, publisher of this book and the related series. Lane's task, shepherding this and the other books in this series, is daunting, but he traverses the landscape well. We have enjoyed and benefited from his sense of humor, wisdom, and strong guiding hand.

1

Knowing Today's Millennial Youth: Discovering Students' Literacies

Kids are kids. How often do you hear that expression? We hear it a lot. Our experiences with today's young people or those born since 1981, known as *millennial youth,* show us how false this assumption is, particularly in a diverse society.

Kids, after all, are people—and people are different from each other as individuals. Each of us is influenced by his or her *multiple subjectivities* or layers, such as gender, race, ethnicity, generation, geographical location, and social class, all of which contribute to our individuality. These and other aspects of students' identities also influence their participation in particular types and activities of youth culture.

It is important for teachers to know the students with whom they work as people with literate lives outside of school. We think that it is necessary for teachers to recognize, acknowledge, and understand the range of youth culture and literacy practices in which their students engage in by choice. We maintain that it is imperative to be aware of what is important to students because teachers are not just teaching content—they are teaching students.

THE IMPORTANCE OF KNOWING STUDENTS' INTERESTS

Why is it important to become familiar with students as individuals and their outside-of-school interests and practices? Two examples illustrate why we emphasize being able to understand the language and practices of young people to truly communicate with them. The first instance is an experience that Barbara had while attending a teacher's presentation of her research for her master's thesis. A high school social studies teacher investigated her students' involvement in cooperative learning. During the presentation of her study at the university, the teacher mentioned that the cooperative groups were allowed to choose their own names. She enthusiastically praised the students for coming up with creative names for their small groups, one of which was Skunk Cabbage. Although other graduate students attending that presentation knew it, the teacher was oblivious to the fact that *skunk cabbage* is a folk term or jargon for marijuana. Unwittingly, the teacher was praising her students for celebrating and publicizing the drug culture. Had this teacher taken the opportunity to talk with and question her students to find out what *skunk cabbage* meant, she could have avoided two awkward situations—one in her classroom and one at the university.

This scenario also illustrates that students often have their own language or jargon that is reflective of their subcultures or outside interests, as do skateboarders, video gamers, and music fans. James Gee (2003) refers to students who engage in these kinds of practices or *semiotic domains* with each other and have a shared language related to those practices as *affinity* groups or *communities of practice*. Gee makes this statement:

> People in an affinity group can recognize others as more or less "insiders" to the group. They may not see many people in the group face to face, but when they interact with someone on the Internet or read something about the domain, they can recognize certain ways of thinking, acting, interacting, valuing and believing as more or less typical of people who are "into" the semiotic domain. (p. 27)

Affinity groups are illustrated in a study that Barbara and Margaret (Guzzetti & Gamboa, in press a) conducted of three European American girls from an upper-middle-class–upper-class area who created their own *zine* (pronounced "zeen"), a self-publication created as an alternative to commercial magazines. They explored the girls' involvement in the worldwide community of *zinesters* (those who create zines). Barbara and Margaret learned more than 40 terms from these girls, including *zining* (the act of creating a zine), *DIY* (do-it-yourself or the ethic of zining and punk rock) and *distros* (online distribution centers for zines). In a similar kind of study, our colleague, Eliane

Rubinstein-Avilla, investigated Hispanic and Native American students from a low socioeconomic area who created a magazine in an after-school program. She discovered a shared slang with over 20 terms such as *Yo*! for "Hey there!," *homie* for "friend," and *dubs* for "20-inch tire rims" that these students used to communicate with each other (Rubinstein-Avilla, 2003).

Although affinity groups are more common with preadolescents and adolescents, even students at the elementary grades may share a common language or common practices that set them apart from others. One example of this, the second instance that illustrates the importance of knowing students' language and interests, is illustrated by one of Barbara's graduate student's classes. In Stephanie Carpenter's fourth-grade classroom, the girls were talking and writing in *ghibberish*, a language that is structured by reversing the order of the syllables of words to disguise real words by creating variations. The girls learned and spoke ghibberish so that the boys would not know what they were saying. This shared language enabled the girls to talk without fear of being interrupted or ridiculed by the boys in their class.

In this case, the teacher was aware of and understood the girls' talk, was able to communicate with them, and, as a result, take action to help them. Stephanie was savvy to the girls' rationale for engaging in this language practice in their informal conversations and writings in the classroom. Being in touch with her students allowed Stephanie to not only recognize them and their needs as individuals, but also to make changes in her classroom structure and practices to enable the girls to speak more freely without having to resort to an invented language.

In addition to being able to understand and communicate with students, there are other reasons for teachers to take an interest in their students' language, interests, and out-of-school activities. One of these reasons is motivation. Students often see no connection between their informal literacy practices and their in-school instruction and assignments (Guzzetti, 2002; Hartman, 1997). As a result, many students feel alienated in school, and they fail to see the relevance of their assignments.

Students may very well be engaged in activities outside of school, however, that actually relate to their content area instruction, but they may not receive any acknowledgment or reward from their teachers for pursing a subject beyond the classroom walls. This situation is discouraging for students. Even high-achieving students are disenfranchised by this lack of acknowledgment. Many such students have teachers who think they like school because they are good at playing the game of school (telling the teacher what the teacher wants to hear no matter what the student really thinks) and get good grades, but these students never really feel challenged by the instruction or the curriculum. Many students, including low-achieving and Advanced Placement and Honors students, look for additional information and enrichment about a subject through their own explorations on the Internet, through television programs, movies, and videos, and through the trade books and literature they self-select (Guzzetti, 2002). By contrast, in a survey of nearly 1,000 high school students in an inner-city school and in an area school with a high socioeconomic status (SES), Barbara (Guzzetti, 2002) found that students complained about the lack of resources and stimulation in their science classrooms, leading one girl to exclaim, "This place has no atmosphere!"

Teachers who wish to motivate their students by bridging the gap between students' out-of school literacy practices and their in-school literacy instruction and assignments can benefit from becoming familiar with students' engagement with subject matter outside of school. Therefore, later in this chapter, we share the kinds of content area involvement students report or show us in their literate lives outside of school. Becoming aware of these kinds of resources that students find interesting helps teachers in acknowledging their students' own explorations of subject matter, and it assists in bringing outside resources into the classroom.

Teachers can also create more motivating and relevant instruction and assignments by becoming familiar with students' new literacies, such as video gaming, Web surfing, instant messaging, music fandom, and online journaling. By observing and interviewing young people in their engagement with popular culture, *technoliteracies* or electronic literacies (see the following paragraph), and other informal literacy practices, researchers are able to discover the elements of those practices that are motivating and interesting to students. Hence, later in this chapter, we present the findings of those studies that have implications for designing instruction that will be interesting and engaging for students.

Knowing students as individuals with their own interests and activities also assists teachers in recognizing the existence of students' multiliteracies (New London Group, 1996). These multiple literacies range from such abilities as speaking the language of a trade like roofing or plumbing to writing ghibberish. Definitions of *functional literacy*, or the skills and abilities needed to keep pace with and function in today's society, have changed with the times, particularly in the digital age (Bean, Bean, & Bean, 1999). These new literacy abilities include technoliteracies such as text messaging, online journaling, and writing html code to build a Web site. Given the new literacy demands of today's new times, traditional notions that restrict what counts as literate have constrained instruction and negated students' accomplishments (Knobel, 2001). By acknowledging that students have multiliteracies, including those not commonly recognized in school, teachers gain rapport with and the respect of their students. Knowing students as people with outside interests and abilities also assists teachers to understand the stance—the ways that students behave and respond—that students take in school (Alvermann & Heron, 2001).

NEW VIEWS OF LITERACY

The remainder of this chapter discusses the kinds of out-of-school literacies that students engage in by choice. Some of these practices are directly relevant to the content that teachers are teaching, whereas others relate to the kinds of thinking, talking, and reading abilities that enable and enhance students' learning. We also provide some examples of ways to bridge the gap between students' in-school and out-of-school literacy activities. In doing so, we review the findings of studies that surveyed or observed and interviewed students from various grade levels in their explorations of and engagement in literate activity.

By their very basis, these new investigations are different from past studies of students' engagement with text. Whereas past studies of students' comprehension of content texts were conducted from a *psycholinguistic view* (Smith, 1973) of reading as an interactive process between author and reader, these more recent studies of varying textual practices were conducted from the perspective of *literacy as a social practice* (Street, 1995). In this view, literacy is seen as a process in which students make meaning not only with their prior experiences and the author's text, but also by talking with others, writing, and by relating the current text being read to other texts. Gee (2003) explains that reading and thinking are social achievements connected to social groups. He gives the scenario of "reading and thinking in different ways when we read and think as members of or as if we are members of different groups" (p. 3). Gee gives the example of reading the Bible differently as theology, as literature, and as deserving of religious skepticism. Each of these represents different ways of reading and thinking and ways of being in the world, which depend on the group with whom we are dialoguing.

We also recognize that students have intertextual lives. The notion of *intertextuality* recognizes that "a text is a sign that communicates meaning and shows traces of past texts; that texts are imbued with the voices of others' social, cultural, and ideological practices; and that texts are constructed in a complex interplay of discursive practices and systems between the self and the social" (Kristeva, 1986 as cited in Hartman, 1997, p. 2). Hence, one text relates to or builds on another. One example might be an oral or written text that results from a game such as Pokéman, an art form such as Japanese anime, or a comparison of the Spiderman or Catwoman movies and comic books.

Douglas Hartman's (1997) observations of the intertextual lives of African American teenagers reveal the range of textual practices demonstrated within the everyday literacies of the students' lives. These included such musical texts as rap, rhythm and blues, and reggae, which often serve as backdrops for encounters with others, and the print, video, musical, audio, and dramatic texts the students experienced in church that were usually not found in the classroom. In fact, the dominant text type used in school—the printed page—was not prominent elsewhere in these students' literate lives.

We anticipate that, by highlighting studies like Hartman's investigation of students' real-world literacies, teachers' view of literacy will change. We hope to expand notions of what counts as text and demonstrate how the field has moved from traditional notions of *literacy* (reading, writing, listening, and speaking) to *literacies* (also encompassing new literacies and multiliteracies). In doing so, we offer new possibilities for literacy instruction in content areas.

Students' Engagement With New Literacies in New Times

Bertram Bruce (1997, as cited in Bean et al., 1999) identifies new literate functions—those literate abilities that include being able to effectively communicate through oral language, pagers, cell phones, computers, e-mail, the Internet, art, music, drama, film, video games, and digital aids. Text messaging, instant messaging, and Web surfing are examples of the new *sociotechnical literacies*, many of which are seeping into today's workplace. There has been an increased use of palm pilots, Blackberries, laptop computers, videophones, and portable Internet devices. These skills and technologies needed in today's global society call for a different curriculum design in content classrooms. As James Gee (2003) notes, "in today's society, print literacy is not enough" (p. 19).

Gee's point was demonstrated by a study conducted by a colleague, Thomas Bean, Bean enlisted the help of his two daughters (Kristen, in 6th grade, and Shannon, in 10th grade). The purpose of their study was to discover new textual practices that are functional literacies for many adolescents and that have implications for redefining content literacy (Bean et al., 1999). Bean suggested that functionality consists of activities that students engage in that have some valued purpose in their lives and give a sense of purpose to their actions. Young people choose these activities from a variety of options and use their time accordingly.

To discover what those activities are and the role they play in these students' lives, Bean's daughters kept a weekly tally of their activities for 2 weeks, and then they discussed those activities with their father. These textual activities consisted of reading textbooks, novels, and magazines; using computers and telephone lines; and watching videos and television. The most number of hours between the two girls were spent on television or video viewing, and telephoning. Not surprisingly, Shannon, a sophomore in high school, spent more time on the computer (an average of 6 hours per week) than did her sister in middle school, who spent only 30 minutes in 1 week engaged with computer text.

What did these girls have to teach us about technoliteracies? Shannon thought that computer online services allowed students to get information faster than traditional methods. Kristen believed that the technology she and her friends engaged with resulted in more reading for her generation than for prior generations. Both girls found video movies and video games of educational value, reporting that teachers who use these media have an increased chance of enabling students' engagement in learning.

Shannon and Kristen's report and our comments about their activities demonstrate the widespread use of new technoliteracies. Their report also suggests that the use of technoliteracies is increasing exponentially, suggesting that the definition of literacies continues to be reconstructed. Given that this study was conducted at least 5 years ago and that computer technology is even more infused since then, and given our more recent observations of today's youth, we predict that the girls' engagement with technoliteracies would be even more extensive today.

Instant Messaging. Evidence from other studies shows that other preadolescents and adolescents use *posttypographic* or *electronic text* more extensively than did Bean's daughters. For example, Cynthia Lewis and Bettina

Fabos (1999) observed and interviewed a group of middle-school girls using instant messaging (IMing) with AOL Instant Messenger. The girls in this study disguised their identities, restricted their communications to a select few, and joined chat rooms. The girls used IMing to keep them in the know socially and to increase their social currency among their peers.

Chatting online and communicating by e-mail with English language learner (ELL) students or English as a second language (ESL) learners was studied by Wan Shun Eva Lam (2000). Lam noted that research on second-language literacy demonstrates the contextual nature of literacy practices, raising questions about how literacy experiences in a nonnative language help students with identity formation.

For 6 months, Lam observed and interviewed a senior boy, Almon, who completed a personal home page on a Japanese pop singer, instant messaged online with chat mates in several countries, and wrote regularly to a few e-mail pen pals. Almon felt that it was easier to express what he wanted to say by writing it out than by speaking in front of others. He believed that, by chatting online, he was able to improve his English and, in doing so, was changed by the Internet. He evolved from having a sense of alienation from the English language in school to "a newfound sense of expressivity and solidarity when communicating in English with his Internet peers" (p. 168). Lam noted the following:

> Whereas classroom English appeared to contribute to Almon's sense of exclusion or marginalization . . . the English that Almon acquired through his Internet involvement was the global English of adolescent pop culture rather than the standard English taught in ESL classes. The English he controlled on the Internet enabled Almon to develop a sense of belonging and connectedness to a global English speaking community. Almon was learning not only more English, but also more relevant and appropriate English for the World Wide Web community he sought to become part of. (p. 176)

Online Journaling. Like Lam, Barbara and Margaret (Guzzetti & Gamboa, 2003a, 2003b) also explored students' online writing. Their study involved following two adolescent girls, Janice, a high school sophomore, and Corgan, a high school senior–college freshman, as they wrote in *Live Journal*, a personal and interactive diary on the Internet. *Live Journal* allowed the girls to augment their writings by expressing their states of mind. Each user is able to indicate the date and time and what music she is listening to as she writes.

She can choose from a list of descriptors and pictorials of facial expressions to communicate what mood she is in at the time. There is also a Communities feature, which provides online discussions groups for various interests, such as the ones that Corgan reads, "Vegan People" and "Craft Grrl."

These online journalers use *Live Journal* in different ways and to different degrees. Janice writes in her journal several times a day to her close friends about emotional events in her life. For her, writing in *Live Journal* is a means of catharsis. Janice keeps a hard-copy journal for times when she wants to write but cannot get access to a computer, transferring her entries later to her *Live Journal*. By contrast, Corgan writes primarily to people she knows only slightly, tending to either discuss events or explore writing topics and ideas by seeking feedback from others. Corgan uses her *Live Journal* primarily for its Communities feature, and she writes far fewer entries than Janice does.

Both girls, however, experience the same benefits of *Live Journal*. They both enjoy the freedom of self-expression through topic choice and genre of writing style, and the opportunity to self-select their audience. In *Live Journal*, they can choose if their writing will be read only by themselves or by others. They are able to control their audience—who will read their writing among the types of online journalers. They can narrow their audience to choose from writing to only a select few friends from their Buddies List or allow their writing to be read by anyone with *Live Journal* access.

The girls report that it is this type of freedom of choice that makes online journaling compelling. They often find it more efficient and immediate to write their thoughts and feelings online than to telephone or talk with their peers. For these girls, the Internet has delineated their social relationships and their mode of communications with their peers.

Zines. Zines, as we mentioned before, are self-publications created as alternatives to commercial magazines; they usually touch on subjects not commonly addressed by commercial and public media. In this way, they are a form of ***indie media*** or independent media. Zines are rooted in the DIY or do-it-yourself ethic of punk rock. Those who create them, zinesters, are usually middle class with the resources (i.e., time, technology, and money) to produce them. Most zinesters are also European American and adolescent females, although zines are also written by young men and by people of color.

Zines can be done in hard copy to make them accessible to everyone or done as e-zines published on the Internet. Online distribution centers for zines (distros) are one of the main ways in which zines are listed, reviewed, ordered, and acquired. Hard-copy zines can be found in some record stores, bookstores, coffeehouses, and music venues or through networks of friends and zinesters. Most are either free or available for the cost of printing and postage. Zines come in a variety of forms, including personal zines (poetry and prose), themed zines (such as skateboarding, soccer, and commercial fishing) or political zines (e.g., feminist or liberal views). Zines can be found throughout the world.

Two of our colleagues, Colin Lankshear and Michele Knobel (2002), examined several zines and characterized this form of writing:

> Zines exemplify in varying degrees diverse forms of spiritedness (gutsiness); a DIY mindset; ability to seek, gain and build attention; alternative (often in-your-face anti-establishment, although not always nice) perspectives; street smarts; originality and being off-beat; acute appreciation of subjectivity; tactical sense; self-belief; enterprise; and a will to build and sustain communities of shared interest and solidarity. . . . The writer-producers are passionate—at time to the point of obsession—about their subject matter and desire to share ideas, experiences, values, analyses, comments, and critiques with kindred spirits. (p. 168)

In addition to the passionate content of Zines, their format is often subversively creative. Backdrops, borders, and illustrations for pages are often complementary to the content of the pieces they contain. Most illustrations are self-designed or cut and pasted from other print sources such as magazines, Internet resources, newspapers, or even household items. For example, the zinesters in Barbara and Margaret's study of three adolescent girls (Guzzetti & Gamboa, in press a) used a nutrition label from a cereal box as a backdrop for a poem about anorexia. Their use of pastiche and collage with words helps zinesters to expand and enhance their messages.

Often, these messages are contrary to or in opposition to those found in commercial magazines and mainstream media. For example, two of the three zines produced by zinesters that Barbara and Margaret focused on in two separate studies (Guzzetti & Gamboa, in press a, in press b) addressed gender issues or issues of social justice. Three adolescent females in high school, Corgan, Janene, and Saundra, created the first of these zines, *Burnt Beauty*, from a feminist perspective. These girls wrote and edited three issues of their zine over the time span from eighth grade to their senior year of high school. Their zine contained not only their own writings but also those of their classmates, who were speaking out against racism, classism, sexism, and homophobia. To accomplish these goals, the girls used a writing style that exemplifies parody and satire with biting wit and sarcasm. In writing for the zine, Saundra reports being influenced by the writing style or parody and sarcasm found in *Mad* magazine and *The Onion*.

The articles speak to topics of social problems and political issues. Examples of the content of their three issues include a piece on gay marriage ("Straight People Can't Help It"), a poem submitted by an anorexic classmate about the destructive images of perfection in commercial media ("Beautiful Barbie"), a collage about assault on women ("Rape is Not a Request"), a stance against the hunting of unarmed immigrants by police on the Arizona-Mexico border ("La Resistencia: Stop the Militarization of the Border"), and Janene's contribution of recipes to promote veganism and protect animals' rights.

Corgan was motivated to learn how to write html code so that she could advertise their zine on the Internet. Her zine writing in turn was influenced by a Web site that promotes zines as a form of activism, http://www.columbia.edu/%7Ekw139/activism.htm. She also advertises her zine through a distro, Mad People Distro, at Implicate.net/mad. Corgan reads other zines on the Internet, such as one done by high school girls in Tucson at http://www.mix.eccentrica.org/buttercup and another zine created in Tucson, http://www.geocities.com/sunsetstrip/mezzanine/8229 that sometimes influence her writing.

Saundra's brother Jon, a National Merit Scholar in high school who dropped out of college after his first year to travel the world, created another zine that Barbara and Margaret investigated. Jon started writing a zine, *Testosterone*, as a rebellion against the messages he received from commercial magazines about masculinity and how masculinity should be performed. Inspired by his sister's zining, he decided to create several of his own Zines, including *Testesterone*.

Jon's writings are bitingly sarcastic and poke fun at the kinds of articles found in men's magazines of the popular press such as *Maxim*. The point of Jon's zine is to parody and mock "the beer-drinking, football watching, big-truck buying" image of masculinity portrayed in men's magazines and the media. Jon's zine contains a Letters to the Editor section in which the readership can write in about their amazing sexual exploits, a section on fake news articles along the vein of *The Onion*, and a piece titled, "Diet, Workout and Do-It-Yourself Home Liposuction Tips for Real Men." Jon's zine also contained an article on how to repulse an invading Mexican army because in Jon's words, "those magazines always have how-to articles about absurd things that nobody will ever have to do." In ways like these, Jon is enabled through his writings to express his anger at the gendered or stereotypical images of masculinity that popular culture texts attempt to assimilate into young men's images and performances of masculinity.

As we have shown by these examples, zines are outlets for young people that enable them to write and read alternative texts about issues of importance to them. They are created by youth who have something to say, and want to say it in a way that is fun and creative. Their peers who have similar views and often are zinesters themselves read them.

What implications do zines have for instruction? Like Lankshear and Knobel (2002), we do not advocate making zines an assignment in school. The zinesters tell us that to do so would take the fun out of it because in-school assignments are attached to rules, restrictions, and grades. As part of the freedom teenagers enjoy in writing outside of school, zines are often written with the use of expletives, a form of expression not tolerated in most classrooms.

Rather, we suggest that teachers become aware of zines and share their awareness with their students; they may suggest zines as alternative texts to explore outside the classroom. Teachers can also incorporate some of the spirit or ethos of zines by allowing students more freedom of choice in writing topics and styles and in choosing to share or not to share their writings or in selecting their audience (e.g., just themselves, just the teacher, or just same-gender classmates). We also advocate allowing students opportunities for creativity in the format of their writings by allowing them to use the cut-and-paste and pastiche approach of zining in some of their in-school writing assignments. Doing so will encourage the intertextual practices we have been describing, and it will expand students' literate worlds by encouraging and supporting students' explorations of various genres of texts.

Web Sites. Increasingly, students who have access to the Internet are building their own personal Web sites and visiting others' home pages for enjoyment and information. For example, Barbara and Margaret (Guzzetti & Gamboa, 2003b) discovered that Corgan constructed her own Web site by teaching herself FTP and html code. She got directions by visiting Monkey.com for tips on how to build a Web site. An Internet friend who owns Implicate.net helped her to learn this computer language by walking her through it step by step and by sending software through e-mail so that Corgan could download it.

Corgan and her friend Jeanne wrote a story that they put on their Web site. The story was inspired by a popular culture board game, *Guess Who?* To play this game, each participant asks dichotomous (yes or no) response questions about a character's appearance to guess which game character another player has. Corgan gave this explanation:

> We were just kind of sitting around and we were bored, and it was like 3:00 in the morning. So, we said, "let's play *Guess Who?* So, we played and we thought it would be really funny to write a story with characters from the board game.... We were looking at the pictures and we were like, "Yeah, that kind of looks like Pam Greer, and like a detective, and that kind of looks like so and so, and just stereotypical like.... So, it's [the story is] about two guys who won some Italian restaurants. We wrote stories based on the cards of the characters we used and put them up [on the Web site] and then wrote the story on the web site about these characters from the *Guess Who?* board game. And this girl really liked them and put them on her web site that she was making at the time. She just loves them and wants us to write more. (Transcript from interview, 3/27/02).

In addition to building her own Web site with the help she finds on others' Web sites, Corgan most often visits the Internet to obtain information. For example, she visits two news sites, particularly when doing research for school. She gets news reports on pbs.org and on CommonDreams.org. CommonDreams.org is a News Center with "Breaking News and Views for the Progressive Community" (see http://www.commondreams.org). Our visit to their home page on September 21, 2003 showed that it displayed the headline "Bush Covers Up Own Scientists' Global Climate Research," a link to the National Conference on Media Reform, a review of Common Dreams as "A Website that Could Shake the World: from *The Utne Reader*," and "Our Readers' Most Forwarded Article This Week." Similarly, our perusal of the PBS Web site on September 23, 2003 showed that it displayed five categories of features on the home page, including Science and Nature, Arts and Drama, and Life and Culture. Visitors can click on a link to become a member or pledge a donation, type in their zip codes to determine local programming, join a television program club (like a book club), or shop for a video about Ground Zero.

The experience of Corgan and Jeanne demonstrates how one of the new literacies (e.g., Web site use) spirals and intertwines with another, making it impossible to separate one of the new literacies practices from another. For these girls, Web site construction and visits led to e-mail correspondence, which resulted in readers' writing, copying, or translating the girls' words and putting them into their contextual worlds. Similarly, the girls were able to benefit from others' Web sites to gather information, pursue their common interests, and display and share their knowledge represented and formed by their literate practices.

In addition to visiting Web sites to explore personal interests like these, students also reported visiting numerous Web sites related to content instruction. Some of these were CNN.com, Discovery.com, UAthletics.com, NFL.com, and NBA.com. High school students reported visiting National Geographic.com, ChemElements.com, Phschool.com, and the NASA Web site. Elementary students reported visiting I Don't Like Science.com and Bugs.com.

Students had ideas about how to bridge the gap between their in-school and out-of-school Internet use. Teachers should

- provide lists of content-related Web sites that could be visited both in and out of class;
- talk about and share their own favorite Web sites concerning the topics that are being learned about in school; and
- offer students credit and recognition for the information they gained while surfing the Web.

Video Games. James Gee (2003) investigated various genres of video games, such as simulation games, fantasy role playing, and real-time strategy games as forms of visual literacy. He asked the question, "Is playing video games a waste of time?" (p. 13). Gee answered this question by playing a variety of games himself and by observing his elementary-school age son playing video games.

Gee (2003) found that, in certain video games, students were involved in *active learning* by experiencing the world in new ways, forming new affiliations or affinity groups, and preparing for future learning through problem solving. In addition, Gee discovered that some video games (such as Pikmin) engage students in *critical learning* by encouraging players to think of themselves as active problems solvers who persist in trying to solve problems even after making mistakes, who see errors as opportunities for reflection and learning, and who leave themselves open to abandoning their prior mastery and exploring new ways to solve new problems in new situations.

Gee provides criteria for what makes a "good" video game by linking gaming to 36 principles of learning. His book is mind expanding in that it uses the metaphor of gaming to describe learning and learning contexts. We recommend that you, our readers, delve into his recent book and also investigate video gaming in their own contexts. We anticipate that you will find in your own explorations the same kinds of thinking and literacy strategies that Gee describes.

Technoliteracies and the Digital Divide

We would be remiss in our discussion of technoliteracies or the new literacies if we simply described them and did not include a discussion of the issues that surround them. We have often heard the term ***the digital divide***, and perhaps you have, too. The digital divide refers to the "haves" and the "have nots"—those who have easy access to technology (the middle and upper classes) and those who do not (those of low SES). Barbara's investigations resulted in an illustration of this inequity. She surveyed students who were Corgan's classmates in a high SES area and found that every one of the Advanced Placement students had at least two computers at home, many of which were of higher quality than the ones provided by their school. She also surveyed adolescents at an alternative high school in a low SES area and found that fewer than half of those students had a computer at home; of those that did, many did not have Internet access.

How can teachers help to compensate for this disparity in resources? We know that schools in lower SES areas often have fewer computers and less access to the Internet. Although no strategy will truly make up for this inequitable situation, there are some resources that students and teachers can draw on for assistance.

First, teachers can help by discovering and making students aware of resources in their own communities. Community agencies and institutions often offer computer access and training that can help to compensate for the lack of access to computers in homes and schools. For example, most public libraries offer free Internet access to their patrons. In addition, city parks and recreation programs often offer low-cost classes in Internet use and in computer skills such as word processing. Agencies with after-school programs, such as the Girls and Boys Club, provide computer access and related instructional programs to young people. In addition, many low SES areas have Community Technology Centers funded by the U.S. Department of Education that offer computer access and training for students and their parents during evening and weekend hours.

Teachers can also help by seeking additional resources for classroom use. For example, the Gates foundation sponsored by Bill and Melinda Gates annually supports grants to school districts to increase students' access to technology. A list of their funded projects for prior years and an application for funding can be found on their Web site at www.gatesfoundation.com. Private companies such as Hewlett-Packard also provide grants and donations to schools in need of computers. By searching out and applying for support, teachers and school districts can help students to meet the demands of the digital age.

Students' Multiliteracies and Content Literacies

We leave our discussion of technoliteracies to focus on the kinds of literate abilities students display in their daily lives and in their explorations of subject matter outside of school. As we mentioned earlier, young people have a wide range of interests. These may include pursuits that are academic (e.g., science or history), occupational (e.g., leather work or trucking), or recreational (e.g., magazines and television programs).

Some teachers are unaware or dismissive of their students' everyday literacies. Teachers who are disinterested or ignorant of students' literate abilities in nonacademic or nontraditional forms miss opportunities to capitalize on the literate aspects of those interests that students find compelling. In the process, these teachers do their students a disservice. We agree with Michele Knobel (2001):

> Focusing solely on school literacies at the expense of literacies that students practice out of school is for many students a grave injustice because it invalidates those literacies in which they are fluent and effective out of school. This flash point brings into play analyses of relationships between school and everyday-life experiences in any consideration of what counts as an effective language and literacy education for young people. (p. 405)

Knobel based these statements on her observations of a boy in high school, Jacques, who was considered unsuccessful in school and avoided literacy assignments yet was fluent in work-related literacy tasks, such as composing a flier to advertise his lawn-mowing service or working out how many meters of gravel were needed on a road. Knobel cited economic and social theorists who agree that "the nature of work and the roles of workers are changing as modes of production and consumption change in New Times" (p. 409). These economists believe that economic success in the future will be dependent on the ability to identify and solve problems, and it will require a metalevel understanding of consumer business practices. Although Jacques was highly successful in simulation games in school during which he was able to demonstrate his mastery of business discourse, his classmates and teachers saw the simulation as just a game, rather than as an opportunity for Jacques to be a successful student.

Unfortunately, not many studies like this have been conducted. This is likely because literate practices in business or the trades have not been considered to be germane to teaching and learning in school. Knobel's point, however, is well illustrated and taken—students' out-of-school literate abilities should be recognized, celebrated, and incorporated into classroom instruction.

Hence, we devote the last part of this chapter to an exploration and explanation of the range of multiliterate practices that students engage in by choice. We focus here on students' literate abilities that complement or extend those fostered and displayed in school. In doing so, we share results of surveys of elementary, middle-school, and secondary-school students' experiences with popular culture, the media, and trade publications. In addition to identifying young people's general interests in these forms of communication, we also describe what we have discovered about students' out-of-school explorations in academic fields through these media. Where possible, we provide suggestions for ways to incorporate these literacy practices into classroom instruction.

Magazines and Comics. From elementary school to college, both boys and girls peruse magazines, often through their own subscriptions. Magazines serve a variety of functions for students at various grade levels. For example, Margaret Finders (1996) found that teen magazines were an indicator of social status for a group of sixth- and seventh-grade girls. Like the high school girls we've interviewed (Guzzetti & Gamboa, in press a), these girls used teen magazines such as *YM* and *Seventeen* as a marker for how they were progressing into womanhood. They read them as instructional manuals or references for desired experiences and appearances, sharing their comments on each page with each other.

Because magazines were not considered legitimate reading material in the classroom, there was no critical discussion of the messages the ads and articles conveyed. The girls in Finder's study identified with a traditional view of womanhood projected by the magazines and the centrality of boys to their lives.

They used the magazines' messages about romance and sexuality as sources of authority for their emerging roles in society. Finders warned, "These messages read over and over become scripts for the girls and will be impossible to revise unless they are made visible" (p. 83).

High school girls in Barbara's and Margaret's study (Guzzetti & Gamboa, in press a) read "against," that is, read critically, the gendered texts of magazines such as *Cosmopolitan* (*Cosmo*) and *Seventeen.* Some of the junior and senior girls in Advanced Placement English–Language Arts class reported reading magazines like *Cosmo* and *Glamour* for amusement or for limited reasons, such as to get ideas about clothing they would like to wear. Many of these readers reported that, even though they perused the magazines to get ideas about makeup and prom dresses, they did not have the same views as the magazine's editors, authors, and advertisers. These girls did not believe their reading of these magazines was inconsistent with their feminist identities.

The girls in this class were practicing *resistant reading*, or reading text for its covert or silent messages. Unlike many of their peers, they approached these mainstream texts with a critically literate stance. Perhaps they were able to do this on their own outside of school because their Advanced Placement teacher emphasized critical analysis or deconstruction of texts in the classroom.

These girls' comments and reactions, as well as those of the girls in Finder's study, remind us of Jon's comments about men's magazines like *Maxim.* Characterized by some as the men's equivalent of *Cosmopolitan* marketed to women, *Maxim* contains ads and articles that appeal to an audience of men and project stereotypical images of masculinity. *Maxim* was the most popular magazine read by high school boys in Corgan's upper-middle-class school district and was also reportedly read by boys as young as 14 in middle-class schools.

Other magazines commonly read by students were rather consistent across grade levels and socioeconomic levels. Boys of elementary and middle school most commonly reported reading *Sports Illustrated for Boys* and *Sports Illustrated*, whereas boys in high school most often read only the adult version, *Sports Illustrated.* Both boys and girls said they read *Time, Newsweek, National Geographic*, and *People.*

Both high school boys and girls across schools reported reading magazines marketed to appeal to an audience of adults. The two most popular magazines for junior and senior boys were *Sports Illustrated* and *Maxim,* followed by *Men's Health.* Other magazines enjoyed by high school boys included *Gamers, Popular Science, Newsweek, Consumer Reports, People*, and *Teen People*. Younger boys under the age of 13 reported reading *Boys Life, National Geographic for Kids*, and *Sports Illustrated for Kids*.

The most commonly read magazines for high school girls also included a magazine aimed at adults, *Cosmopolitan,* and a long-standing favorite of teenage girls, *Seventeen.* The girls confided that junior-high girls read *Cosmo Girl*, a magazine actually marketed for high-school girls. In addition, some girls reported reading magazines that the boys were reading, and a few boys admitted to reading magazines aimed at girls "to see what the other side is thinking."

We also discovered differences in reading habits across socioeconomic areas. Students in the middle-upper-class to upper-class school were more apt to read expensive magazines (those that cost more than $5.00). Although *Maxim* was read across socioeconomic lines, other pricey publications such as *Ad Busters, Nylon*, and *Bust* were only reported as being read by girls in the higher SES areas.

These reports have implications for instruction. Teachers can direct students to critically examine magazines by asking questions such as these: To what racial group, socioeconomic level, gender, or age does this magazine appeal? What messages do the ads and the articles convey? What does this magazine not address? How does this magazine position me as a reader? Teachers might not want to actually bring magazines with explicit sexual messages into the classroom, but they can direct students to be critical questioners and consumers of texts. As our experiences demonstrate, if students are exposed to this line of critical questioning in classrooms, they may transfer those abilities to their out-of-school reading.

Students' self-selection of educational magazines such as *National Geographic* and *Newsweek* demonstrate their curiosities about social and scientific topics and issues outside the classroom. We can well imagine how teachers could provide students with opportunities to bring into the classroom (through discussion or essay) some of the knowledge gained from their independent explorations with texts. Students themselves have suggested to us that teachers give them extra credit for their out-of-school experiences (including reading trade publications and attending plays or concerts) or allow them the opportunity to talk about those experiences during a special time set aside for sharing out-of-school literacy and cultural experiences or at appropriate times during instructional activity. As Patty's son said during his senior year of high school, "My teachers don't know anything about what I read, write, and do outside of school."

Like magazines, comics are also popular with young people (as well as with male adults). Comics can actually take two forms—cartoon strips, as in daily newspapers, and comic books. Both forms are alternative texts that are both motivational and instructional. Comics and cartoons are used as instructional materials to foster language skills, provide values clarification, and promote critical thinking. Comic books are also recommended as a way to teach students the techniques of writing found in narrative, such as *Spider Man* excerpts that can be analyzed to study foreshadowing, dramatic fiction narration, flashback, irony, symbolism, metaphor, and allusion (Palumbo, 1979).

Trade Books. Despite the advance of the digital age, the most popular resource students reported exploring outside of school was trade books. A trade book is any book that is not a textbook. Trade books can range from nonfiction (such as the Bible, a cookbook, or a biography) to fiction (such as a romance novel, science fiction, or historical fiction).

Past research examining students' choices of genre has been rather consistent. Girls of all ages tend to prefer novels about romance and relationships whereas boys of all ages tend to choose action and adventure. There has been some evidence that boys tend to prefer nonfiction whereas girls tend to select fiction (e.g., Dressman, 1997). A summary of past research on gender and reading can be found in Barbara's coauthored book, *Reading, Writing and Talking Gender in Literacy Learning*, referenced in our Library section at the conclusion of this chapter.

There is some evidence, however, that these patterns may be changing. Our recent surveys of elementary, middle-school, and secondary-school students show that today's youth appear to be crossing these stereotypical or *gendered* lines of book selection. For example, Teresa Dennison (2004) surveyed 33 sixth, seventh, and eighth graders at her school in Tucson and found that girls were reading some nonfiction (e.g., a book about Barizon modeling for a modeling class, and a self-help book, *A Girl's Guide to Life*). Boys reported reading a range of fiction, such as the *Harry Potter* series, *Holes*, and *The Fellowship of the Ring*.

In addition to this survey, Barbara (Guzzetti, 2002) received questionnaire responses from 857 students from a sample of 1,000 students at an urban high school in a low SES area and a suburban school in a high SES area. The responses revealed that girls as well as boys read books about science. The most popular books among both girls and boys at both schools were books about animals, such as *The A-Z Animal Zoo Book*. Science fiction, such as

Jurassic Park and *Star Wars*, was the next most popular choice among both boys and girls across both schools. Other popular science books included *Silent Spring*, the *Discovery* books, *Aliens*, and *The Hitch Hiker's Trilogy-Guide to the Galaxy*. Favorite authors or series included James Herriot's animal books, Rachel Carson's books about the environment, and the Roswell books about aliens. The only striking difference related to social class or gender was that the boys at the higher SES-area high school reported reading many books about computer technology, whereas the boys at the lower SES area school did not read these publications.

Students had several suggestions for teachers. Several students complained that their classrooms had no science trade books, and they thought that their classrooms should have libraries in which they could check out science fiction and nonfiction. These students also thought that teachers should recommend books to them that they might enjoy, and that teachers should share their own personal books about a particular subject matter by reading sections aloud to them. They believed that, at the very least, teachers should provide bibliographies of interesting and relevant trade books related to their content areas.

Television, Movies, and Videos. Although a medium such as television has been an issue of much concern for literacy development, there have also been positive benefits associated with viewing television programs (Neuman, 2001). Television and the media provide opportunities for students to discover new information. Through television, students learn about current events, including social issues and political stances and problems.

Our surveys of students also demonstrate that students watch television and view movies and videos not only for entertainment but also for information. Elementary, middle-school, and high school students most commonly reported watching such television programs as *The Discovery Channel*, *The History Channel*, and *Sports Center*. They reported seeing movies such as the *Matrix*, *Platoon*, and *The Client*, each of which expanded their school-acquired knowledge of topics in content areas. Secondary students reported frequently watching such science-related programs as *Bill Nye, The Science Guy* and *Animal Planet*. Science-fiction movies were the most popular kinds of movies and videos watched by high school students of both genders.

Again, students had suggestions for including the media into their classroom instruction and assignments. They suggested that teachers either show or assign episodes of science-related programs (even fictional ones such as *CSI: Crime Scene Investigation* or *ER*) and show clips of videos or movies that relate to their topics of study. They suggested this as one way to help students see the relationship between the concepts they learn in school and their ordinary life experiences.

SUMMARY AND REFLECTIONS

In this chapter, we have concentrated on describing the range of literate practices in which students engage outside of school. We have shared results of observations, interviews, and surveys of boys and girls from a variety of ages and socioeconomic levels. These investigations demonstrate that students engage in many literate practices that are typically not recognized or acknowledged by their teachers and that are seldom incorporated into instruction or assignments.

These students have provided suggestions for bridging the gap between their out-of-school literacy practices and their in-school literacy instruction in content areas. We hope that these recommendations are useful and practical, and that these reports will provide an impetus for our readers' own inquiries. Talk to your students about the kinds of literacy practices they engage in outside of the classroom, and use that information to find connections between out-of-school and in-school content area literacies. Doing so will help to motivate and interest your millennial students, and it will also help to improve their learning and literacy development.

APPLICATION ACTIVITIES

1. Design an open-ended item questionnaire to assess your students' out-of-school activities and interests and administer it to your students. Analyze the results to find ways you can incorporate some of their informal literacy practices into your classroom instruction and assignments.
2. Create a guide to help students critically evaluate the Web sites they visit for credibility and content validity. Direct them to examine the source of the Web site, its authors, and advertisers, if any.
3. Develop a bibliography of relevant trade books, Web sites, and magazines related to your content area and distribute it to your students.
4. Bring in examples of content trade books from your own library and share them with your students. Choose one in which students seem particularly interested and read it aloud.

5. Watch the newspaper or TV guide for an upcoming content-related television program, announce it to your students, guide their viewing with one or two questions, and assign students to watch the program to discover the answer(s). Discuss the program later in the classroom.

6. Create a classroom library of content-related trade books and magazines and allow students to check them out overnight.

7. Devote some classroom instructional time to allowing students to share information they obtain through outside sources and consider giving credit for those who do so.

FROM OUR PROFESSIONAL LIBRARY

Alvermann, D. E. (Ed.). (2001). *Adolescents and literacies in a digital world*. New York: Peter Lang.

Gee, J. P. (2003). *What video games have to teach us about learning and literacy.* New York: Palgrave Macmillan.

Guzzetti, B. J. (Ed.). (2001). *Literacy in America: An encyclopedia of history, theory and practice.* Santa Barbara, CA: ABC-CLIO.

Guzzetti, B. J., Young, J. P., Gritsavage, M., Fyfe, L., & Hardenbrook, M. (2001). *Reading, writing and talking gender in literacy learning*. Newark, DE: International Reading Association/The National Reading Conference.

McCarthey, S. (2002). *Students' identities and literacy learning*. Newark, DE: International Reading Association/National Reading Conference.

2

Responses to Adolescent Learners: Literacy and Content Area Literacy—Past and Present

Why do adolescents need the opportunity to continue developing their literacy? The young people described in the previous chapter show that kids can use literacy tools in contexts and for purposes of their choice—why not in your class? Why not for purposes of reading and writing in the sciences, social studies, mathematics, and other content areas? When we pose this question to our teacher colleagues, we are given two answers: First, there is a general sense, perpetuated by policymakers and those who know little about adolescent literacy, that once students have learned to read, they are able to use reading any way they want or need; second, if kids just cared, if they were motivated, they could use reading and writing as tools to understand their content area studies. Well, it is not that simple.

The youth in the previous chapter demonstrated that literacy is a valued tool for out-of-school activities, and we maintain that teachers can make literacy valued in school too. What teachers *do* in the classroom has a major impact on the literacy development and the content learning of their students. Teachers' beliefs and actions have great potential for affecting students' personal development and the opportunities they will experience as citizens, parents, and contributors to society.

However, it is more than the fact that our students need literacy to adequately negotiate meanings in the content areas; it is also that they need the flexible use of literacy tools in order to be workers, citizens, and parents. In other words, as we help to prepare young people for their participation in a democracy and a world economy, we need to provide opportunities for them to use literacy and learning strategies flexibly and strategically. That means they need to continue to develop their literacy capacity during upper elementary school, middle school, high school, and trade school or college.

So, in this chapter we first step back to provide a societal and historical context for literacy development. Then we describe teachers, both preservice and in-service, who have developed their content area instructional practices on the principles and suggestions that we write about in this book. These teachers have constructed content area literacy instruction by planning carefully; knowing themselves, their content, and their students well; and by being committed to socializing their students to the language and culture of their content specialties by using reading, writing, speaking, and listening strategies.

We know this is a big challenge. In our experience, especially from teaching this class and using the first edition of our book, we often meet resistant students or teachers who believe that their students should "already be able to read and write by the time they reach the upper grades." We agree; indeed, most of our readers' future students will be able to read and write at a fundamental or basic level. What we are trying to convey is that your future students need to continue to develop their literacy capacities. How you teach will make a difference in supporting your students' continued growth.

LITERACY BEYOND THE CLASSROOM

Citizens need to be able to read and write to be good citizens, to do their jobs, to be good parents, to enjoy the aesthetic pleasures that reading and writing can bring to their lives personally, to access needed information, and to continue to learn. In this section, we explore both what the term *literacy* means and its applications beyond the classroom.

Literacy in Society: Toward a Definition

What is literacy? What does it mean to be literate? The definition of literacy is in flux. During World War I, soldiers who could write their own names and read and write letters to and from home were considered literate. During World War II, concern for literacy increased because soldiers were challenged by the reading they needed to do to maintain and repair their weapons. As a result, the military establishment provided funds and efforts to improve the reading and writing performance of recruits. One example is the study skills program published by psychologist Francis Robinson (1941). He developed the well-known study skills program, Survey, Question, Read, Recite, and Review (SQRRR), which continues to be used by many teachers and students (we describe SQRRR in chap. 6 of this volume).

The conclusion of World War II brought about tremendous increases in the need for literacy in society. Returning soldiers and women (who had participated in the workforce during the war) wanted to go to college. As people went to college in droves, partly as a result of the GI Bill, professional and scholarly organizations (e.g., The National Reading Conference, www.readingonline.org) formed so that college teachers could better learn how to help students achieve needed reading and writing skills for college success. In addition, workers needed to read and write in more sophisticated ways than those required of their parents and grandparents. The General Educational Development Test (known as the GED) was instituted so that those who had not completed high school could do so.

In the past two decades, the definition of literacy has been complicated as researchers and practitioners extend the former simplistic definition to include situational and individual meanings. The definition of literacy has evolved beyond functional literacy, that is, the ability to complete basic life tasks such as filling out application forms or keeping a checking account, and beyond the simple application of a set of skills to read words or decipher a written text (Wells, 1990). Rather, the definition of literacy is evolving to mean a complex system of tools that people use to negotiate and construct understandings of themselves and their world.

There are four dimensions of literacy in this evolving definition. One dimension is text. There are widely and wildly different forms of text, which are used for a wide range of purposes. Some texts direct us to action (like advertisements to entice purchases, airline schedules directing travel plans, and notes to family members with messages of love and things to do); other texts transmit factual information (like reference books and business memos); and still other texts offer the author's interpretation of an experience (like history articles, scientific explanations, novels, poems, and plays). Further, texts are in all sorts of places (like billboards, on the computer screen, and in the media). In fact, text is not just graphic symbols on a page; rather, text is any set of symbols that convey meaning. A text is experienced at a play, concert, or dance performance or on the bus. Text is a symbolic representation of experience. Notice that textbook reading, which is typically found in classrooms, is just one of many types of text and is not likely to be a form of text that readers encounter in the everyday world. This observation suggests that young people are assisted in their literacy development when they have multiple, varied, and numerous opportunities to experience a wide variety of texts in the classroom—not just the textbook.

A second dimension of literacy is that literacy includes text-supported thinking and doing through critical and reflective thought, or *literate thinking*. All citizens in a democracy, and students in our classrooms, need to think critically about the texts they are engaging. To think (and read) critically means to question why an author is promoting a certain perspective or point of view and to ask questions of power relationships. A critical reader, for example, might ask these questions: Who benefits from these ideas? Is there a hidden agenda in the way this text is organized, presented, and promoted? Why am I being asked to read this material? Who is the author of this material? Why is the author advocating this particular information or point of view? In addition, then, to providing adolescents with a broad range of text types, this dimension implies that students should be challenged to think beyond the text, to question the text, and to think critically about what they are reading. This requires reading against the text, or resistant reading. Those who read against the text examine how a text positions a reader, and they evaluate a text for its silences as well as its overt messages (Darder, 1995).

The third dimension of literacy is that it encompasses reading, writing, speaking, listening, and viewing—multiliteracies. In other words, literate citizens are able to use these multiliteracies to express themselves and to better understand themselves and others in the world. This is a big change from the definitions of literacy that are limited to basic skills like those that are found on various kinds of assessments or in some programs that teach these so-called basic skills. This consideration goes beyond answering the questions of a teacher, textbook, or test maker. It pushes us to realize that we use these various literacies to make meaning. It is legitimate to question the validity of literacy instruction and assessment that does not include a reader's purpose for communicating. This is important to keep in mind when we are selecting teaching materials and programs. A common misconception is that some teaching materials teach children and youth how to read and that those materials do not need to be meaningful or designed for a communicative purpose. Literacy educators, ourselves included, strenuously object to this reasoning: We believe and promote literacy processes as first and foremost a matter of engagement in meaning making.

Finally, the fourth dimension of literacy is that it is collaborative and a social practice. It is not individualistic; admittedly, an individual reads, writes, speaks, listens, and views, but those activities are done with the individual as a participant in a social network. As a reader reads what an author has written, a dialogue takes place between at least two humans: a reader and a writer. An individual does not ordinarily speak in a vacuum; rather, a speaker speaks to one or several others in an effort to communicate. In the same way, a television program, movie, record, or software program represents ideas of one or more authors that are being shared with whoever happens to view or listen. Literacy is part of the social fabric that holds the world together and contributes shared meanings and understandings (Street, 1995).

Let's extend this notion to your classroom; we propose that literacy can very well be the glue that holds your classroom together. As students participate in literacy activities, they learn from each other and grow in their understandings of themselves and their world. Literacy helps your classroom to be a place that is valued by young people and is enriching for you as well.

These four dimensions of literacy are profound and are radical influences on what educators need to offer their students. Shirley Brice Heath (1991), a renowned educational anthropologist, elaborates on these dimensions:

> People often think of literacy as if it were some nonrational feature, like having red hair or healthy skin, or at best as if it were—to use a disastrously infectious word—a "skill," like being able to ride a bicycle or swim. I doubt whether any elements in reading and writing involve much skill, in the strict sense, but in any case, the major elements certainly involve understanding, not just doing something. Computers can, in some sense, be programmed to read and write; but how thin this sense is—how much is missing from what we hope human beings do in their reading and writing—is, in general terms, clear enough. We want our children not just, like machines, to perform strokes and letters, or to enunciate the syllables represented by "the cat is on the mat," but to express their thoughts and feelings in writing, and to understand those of others in reading. Literacy, so far from being a single skill or even a set of skills, is inextricably bound up with understanding, with choice of words, with grasp of syntax, grammar and diction, and—what is all too often omitted—with a certain attitude toward the whole business. (p. 28)

We like Heath's notion of "an attitude." We think that attitude speaks to our call for critical thinking, a type of thinking that is enabled by instruction in reading, writing, speaking, listening, and viewing that is integrated in the ideas and curriculum in which we invite our students to engage.

This is easier said than done. Sometimes teachers are thought of as "insiders" and students as "outsiders" (Delattre, 1983). That is, there is a popular myth, sometimes shared by educators, that students don't want to read, that their backgrounds are too limited to participate in literacy engagements, and that reading is too boring in this day and age of instant gratification and rapid-fire television and video games. This could be. It could also be, however, that students simply do not view school literacy activities as being worth their time and effort. Teachers could change that. Delattre (1983) claims that students become insiders to school literacy in the following way:

> [This happens by teachers'] telling fascinating stories, providing toys and manipulatives that raise questions, teaching how to read a chessboard or a pool table and moving by analogy to books and works of art, solving a problem by using a manual, finding engaging places to visit by securing written information about local geography and history, reducing grocery costs by reading unit prices, examining catalogs to discover the best available bicycles or skates, reading directions of how to assemble and fly a kite or a model rocket. Offering worthwhile and engaging invitations takes imagination, patience, time and for youngsters who are outsiders only because of their youth, very little else. (p. 53)

The notion of insiders and outsiders to literacy is intuitively seductive and is confirmed by Frank Smith (1988) in his book, *Joining The Literacy* Club. Smith's intended audience is those who teach children, but we find his arguments relevant for adolescents as well. He argues that we each belong to various clubs, or affinity groups (Gee, 2003)—formal and informal organizations of like-minded folks—and that those who are literate share a common bond and belong to the literacy club. He is concerned that too many teachers focus on materials and methods and not enough teachers think about and plan experiences in their classroom that invite learners to join the literacy club. In fact, he thinks socializing learners to want to belong is more important than the actual skills taught or the materials used.

It is certainly true that each of us is at times an outsider. Rigg (1985) reminds us that we are all illiterate at times and in some situations. We hire others to do our reading for us when we consult with attorneys and accountants. White (1983) agrees: "Who, for example, can read and understand an insurance contract or a pension plan? An OSHA or IRS regulation? Yet these documents that govern our lives are even said in some sense to have the standing of our own acts, either directly, as in the contracts we sign, or indirectly, as in the laws promulgated by officials who represent us" (p. 139).

These four dimensions—the *multidimensionality* of text; the *multiliteracies* of reading, speaking, listening, and writing; the collaborative, social nature of literacy; and the necessity for users of literacy to be critical—represent the complexities of literacy. As educators we recognize that schools are part and parcel of society, and so we are obligated to engage in school literacy practices that parallel and reflect the demands of society. If all the functions of literacy are used in school, students should continue to develop the tools of literacy that will stay with them throughout their lives.

Literacy in the Workplace

The business and labor community is continually calling on schools to do a better job of preparing young people for the literacy demands of the workplace. Attend any business and education meeting and hear the laments of business people about job applicants who purportedly cannot read directions on a simple application form. Go to the federal government Web site on vocational education (see, www.ed.gov/about/offices/list/ovae) and read the depressing statistics about youth's lack of preparation for the world of work. It is hard for educators to not feel attacked by these statistics and laments.

We would be mistaken if we pointed to the statistics (i.e., Programme for International Student Assessment; see www.pisa.oecd.org for international comparisons of student's scores in reading and math) and noted that the highest scoring 17-year-olds in the United States are competitive internationally and that is good enough. It is not. On this same international comparison, the lowest scoring students in the United States were among the lowest scores in the world. This is commonly called the *achievement gap*, and educators are trying to both better understand why this gap occurs and provide instruction and programs to lessen the gap.

Diehl (1980) studied the amount of time various workers spent engaged in on-the-job reading. These workers represented 100 occupations, ranging from lawyer and vice president to assembly-line workers and stonecutters. Diehl found that, across occupations, the average amount of time that workers spend in job-related reading per day was about 2 hours. Literacy activities are central to the most common positions of the workplace. Diehl also describes a study comparing secretarial employees' and trainees' perceptions of the on-the-job literacy demands. The trainees underestimated the amount of time they would spend on reading job-related material, and practicing secretaries thought the reading and writing they did on the job to be far more important to their job success than did the trainees. The marketplace requires the use of increasingly more sophisticated and multiple literacy tools, and the graduates of our schools need to be able to use those tools. Mikulecky and Kirkley (1998) add technology to the mix of literacy requirements:

> Technology and the restructuring of work to compete in the global economy have increased the breadth and depth of workplace literacy demands. Multiple job roles, quality monitoring, team planning, print communication, and regular reeducation are increasingly parts of jobs that have not left the continent or been automated. To maintain the same relative pay status, middle- and low-level workers are expected to do more, using a much higher level of literacy, communication, and problem-solving skills. (pp. 318–319)

Educational programs can do better to prepare youth for the workplace, but employers must realize that, despite the best efforts of educators, they will need to continue to educate their workforce. Literacy demands at work increase and change at such a pace that schools cannot prepare students with the skills they need for a lifetime; teachers can, however, prepare students to be lifelong learners, problem solvers, and literacy users. We can do this by integrating literacy activities, practices, and instruction with content area, or subject matter, instruction. As students are engaged in developing the ideas and skills needed to negotiate the curriculum, they can learn to be sophisticated literacy users. Weisz (1983) provides a striking example of what we mean:

> A happier experience involves my association with a fine and successful research team whose members represent many of the disciplines, including physics, chemistry, engineering, economics, and others. This team has especially distinguished itself by developing new catalysts that can be placed in a chemical reactor to form new chemicals selectively. Other accomplishments of the team include the development of a solid catalyst to form gasoline from petroleum and the innovation of another solid catalyst called ZXM-5, which is used to make polyester.
>
> Once a month members of the team contribute to a newsletter, which reports new insights or findings encountered during the month. This kind of regular reporting can easily become a nuisance, but our effort has become one of the most important and creative parts of the research process itself. The

> newsletter emerged from our objective to reexamine our findings enough to convey their significance in plain English which any scientist, engineer or manager can understand. This exercise in writing has provided the most effective way to recognize clearly what we really know, as opposed to what we think or feel we know. . . . Equally important is that the newsletter is an example of a small "institutional" mechanism for building those bridges between disciplines that seem to me so important. (p. 132)

What does a mature research scientist's comments about an interdisciplinary project have to do with teachers and teaching? How can teachers reconsider curriculum and the school day so that students can participate in similar experiences? Middle schools and ninth-grade teams are increasingly organizing the curriculum around themes that draw on each of the content areas. Students in those teams could develop their own newsletter showing the linkages between the ideas they are studying. Students could solve real-life problems by using the ideas being learned in their studying and report those in a newsletter that went to the business community, the local newspaper, and the school community. These are but examples—each of us needs to think of ways that we can make learning and literacy authentic and relevant to students.

THE HISTORY OF LITERACY INSTRUCTION IN THE CONTENT AREAS

These complexities and challenges are daunting. How did we get here? How have previous generations of teachers helped to prepare their students for literacy demands? What has literacy instruction in the content areas been like historically? What current thinking informs what we should be doing to meet these literacy challenges in ways that honor the complexities?

Content Reading in the 1900s to 1910s: Early Foundations

As far back as the early 1900s, educators realized the importance of developing students' reading in the content areas. One of the first educators to write about such needs was Edmund Huey (1908), author of the classic book, *The Psychology and Pedagogy of Reading.* Huey advocated instruction that encouraged students to read entire works of real literature (p. 373), to read in the "central subjects" (p. 371), and to read widely (p. 382). Thorndike (1917) concurred, emphasizing that "Perhaps it is in their outside reading of stories and in their study of geography, history, and the like, that may school children really learn to read" (p. 282).

Huey and Thorndike made these comments in light of the prevailing reading instructional practices and theory of the day: Reading was thought to be the accurate reproduction of an author's words and so students were instructed by having them read aloud. It's not surprising, then, that these early psychologists emphasized the contrary concept of silent reading, suggesting that reading was more a *thinking* process than a reproductive process. This is a point worth thinking about even today. Many teachers continue to ask their students to read their textbooks aloud. This practice has a number of detrimental effects. Most students can read faster silently than they can orally; hence, oral reading slows down the reading and thinking of students; oral reading in the classroom takes time away from other activities that require teacher guidance; and oral reading reinforces slow word-by-word reading, which limits comprehension and critical thinking. Some texts should be read aloud, such as plays, poetry, and some math problems—but that is very different because meaning is carried in the oral language of those forms of texts, and that is not the case in other genres. We have, however, encountered teachers who report having to read the textbook out loud to and with their students because the information in the text is so abstract that students need the teacher to explain the meaning of the text. If such is the case, the text is inappropriate and better explanations could and should be found. Having said that, however, we wonder what would happen if the teacher were to use content area literacy strategies, like the ones we describe throughout this book. Research and experience suggests that students would be better able to negotiate the meaning of the text.

Content Reading in the 1920s and 1930s: Directives for Practice

During the 1920s and 1930s, more reading educators and researchers joined in the call for attention to reading in the content areas. In 1922, Judd and Buswell, prominent psychologists of the time, believed that the reading process varied according to the reader's purpose and the content and difficulty of the material. Another key figure in the early development of content reading was William S. Gray, professor emeritus of the University of Chicago, who was perhaps the best known proponent of content reading. Professor Gray published several essays and edited two monographs on reading instruction in content areas. He also allocated attention to content reading instruction in his second annual summary of reading research, published in 1927.

The call for content reading instruction grew more popular at this time, and the slogan "Every teacher a teacher of reading" gained popularity. Chairing the National Committee on Reading, Gray was instrumental in developing the report for the *36th Yearbook of the National Society for the Study of Education*, in which all teachers were directed to include reading instruction in their curricula. With similar directives, James McCallister (1936) published *Remedial and Corrective Instruction in Reading*, a text that included procedures for reading instruction in the content areas. The close of this decade saw an established need for content area reading instruction, and the time was ripe for establishing a research base and for developing instructional strategies.

Content Reading in the 1940s, 1950s, and 1960s: An Emerging Research Base

During the 1940s and 1950s, reading researchers conducted investigations in content reading that laid the foundation for the field, but the foundation did not include the dimensions of literacy discussed in the previous section. Rather, most investigations explored the relationship between general reading ability as measured on standardized tests and achievement in content areas. For example, Eva Bond's (1941) doctoral dissertation revealed that ninth graders' reading comprehension was related to their achievement in subject areas like science, Latin, algebra, and English. She concluded that students need specialized reading instruction to meet the requirements of different subjects. Teachers were advised to teach reading and study skill techniques in each subject.

Research during this period not only theorized that reading in the content areas was different than (although related to) general reading ability; studies also emphasized unique differences between reading skills in each content area. For example, Shores (1943) found that some reading skills were related to the ability to read historical material, but these were not related to the skills needed to read science materials. He concluded that, by the time students reached ninth grade, their ability is specific to the content field in which their reading is done. His study advised teachers to be concerned with teaching reading in science and history. In similar investigations, Artley (1942) and Krantz (1955) compared scores on a standardized general reading test with scores on content reading measures or content area subject matter achievement. Although the correlations obtained were very high in both instances (which would indicate a holistic view of the reading process across content areas), the researchers concluded that certain reading skills were specific to particular content areas.

This differential skills model of content reading was popularized both by authors of the research and by authors of methods texts for teaching reading. For example, Bond and Tinker (1967), in their classic text on reading diagnosis, stated that these studies "provided plenty of evidence to support this (skills) view" (p. 397). Similarly, Bond and Bond (1941), in their methods text on developmental reading in high school, stated that "each subject demands specialized and rather highly complicated groupings of reading skills which must be developed in the study of the particular subject itself" (p. 55).

This model or view of content reading as a differential skills process was consistent with the popular view of general reading at the time. Reading educators posited that the reading process was composed of a progression of distinct and measurable skills (Gray, 1948, 1960), as Fay (1956) demonstrated:

> Hidden in the reading of a person with good general fluency are a large number of mechanically applied skills. The degree to which these skills operate automatically with high accuracy is one of the best indicators of a reader's over-all efficiency. Involved are: (a) All the skills used in the perception of word forms—the word form itself, its sound structure, its pronunciation and meaning structure, clever use of context and, for independence, the dictionary pronunciation key. (b) Those skills that result in a rapid and flexible reading . . . and (c) Those skills that result in an accurate reading of the text—to insure that the text is not distorted by changing, adding or dropping words. (p. 6)

Given this theory of reading, it was logical to assume that content reading was the differentiation of skills by subject areas, and that research in content reading would be interpreted to fit this paradigm. That is exactly the path that content area reading research took.

Research that could be considered contrary to this skills model was either interpreted to fit within the popular paradigm of general reading, or it was disregarded. For example, Esther Swenson (1942) studied eighth graders' reading achievement in general reading compared with their achievement on three tests of science reading. She found that a good reader on one type of measure was also a good reader on another. She also discovered more evidence of similarity than of dissimilarity between general and science reading materials, and that the only deviations from the striking concomitance of reading abilities were found among different types of reading skill (say rate vs. vocabulary) rather than among the reading materials (general narrative vs. science material). Although the results of this study supported a holistic view of the reading process, reading researchers disregarded the findings because group comparisons were used. This study and others with similar findings were refuted by leading researchers of the time because the results indicated only general trends and did not reveal the extent or the amount of the relationship for individual students in different content areas, which was the dominating question of the day (Bond & Tinker, 1967).

The model of content area reading as specific to the content with unique skills was the dominant perspective of these decades. Methods textbooks in college classes and research-to-practice monographs presented sections devoted to the needs of readers in particular subject areas like social studies, science, mathematics, and literature (Bond & Bond, 1941; Fay, 1956; Strang, 1938). For example, Bond and Bond identified particular difficulties that readers encounter when reading specific content areas. Mathematics, for example, presented unique challenges, such as distinguishing between relevant and irrelevant facts, giving irrelevant words more attention than important words, relating previous material to that being read, and understanding math-specific vocabulary (pp. 185–189). Science, in contrast, presented other difficulties, such as following directions, locating materials, noting essential details, and seeing relations among facts and forming accurate generalizations (pp. 189–193). Lists of skills like these were generated and described in methods texts for several decades, and some present-day authors continue the tradition (Manzo & Manzo, 1990; Roe, Stoodt, & Burns, 1991; Rubin, 1992).

Close on the heels of the theory and research was the creation of prescriptive materials and programs. Two well-known names during these decades were Nila Banton Smith and Ruth Strang. Both of these reading educators were given Citation of Merit Awards from the International Reading Association (www.reading.org) for their efforts. Strang is credited with promoting developmental reading programs in the secondary school. She promoted content area reading, but she also wanted educators to understand that reading was a developmental process and that students continued to learn to read as they progressed through the grades. Smith is best remembered for her recently republished *Be a Better Reader* (1963) series. These materials offer students guidance and practice in reading content area texts. Her materials are designed to help students identify patterns in writing style and to classify paragraphs into definition, enumeration, classification, comparison and contrast, generalization and proof, hypothesis and evidence, problem and solution, or sequence of events (Smith, 1946a,b). As we shall see, these are the rhetorical patterns that are used in expository, or explanatory, text in the content areas.

Content Reading in the 1970s and 1980s: A Reexamination of Theory

Research in content reading took a dramatic turn in the early 1970s with the publication of Harold Herber's *Teaching Reading in the Content Areas* (1970). Herber maintained that reading was a holistic process rather than a process of differing skills for different content areas. Herber believed that the reading process did not vary across content areas, and to compile lists of skills peculiar to each of the content areas was "a waste of time" (p. 122). In a keynote address at the 1980 annual meeting of the International Reading Association, Herber called for increased and intensified empirical research to explore the two differing theories of content area reading.

Herber's call helped to focus attention to studies conducted during the 1970s that had been heretofore unnoticed. For example, Carlson (1971) had analyzed the reading miscues (oral reading deviations from the text) of average fourth-grade students reading aloud two basal reader stories (basals are commercially prepared materials to teach children to read), two social studies selections, and two science passages. Results indicated that all readers tend to use the same types of cues to gain meaning, regardless of the content area. In a similar study, Kolczynski (1974) also refuted the theory of separate reading skills for various content areas. She used miscue analysis to analyze the reading processes of sixth-grade students reading passages from science, social studies, literature, and mathematics. In a comparative analysis, findings showed no significant differences in readers' strategies across content passages.

Other kinds of research have also supported a holistic view of reading across content areas. Dole (1978) used a multitrait, multimethod matrix to assess the validity of separate reading skills in different content areas. She found no evidence that different skills were needed in different content areas. Building on these studies and having heard Herber's challenge, Barbara reexamined the nature of the reading process in content fields (Guzzetti, 1982, 1984). She replicated Carlson's and Kolczynski's studies by analyzing the reading strategies of high-, average-, and low-ability fifth-grade students as they read aloud and retold passages from social studies, science, and literature. Results indicated that readers at all ability levels consistently used syntactic (grammatical) and semantic (contextual) cues to construct meaning. These readers' strategies did not vary with the content of the reading materials, and she concluded that it is the reader's prior knowledge and interest in content material that influences comprehension.

This view of reading—a holistic perspective—is consistent with the holistic view of the reading process that developed during the early 1970s, expanded in the 1980s, and is influential, albeit controversial, today. Two theorists, Kenneth Goodman and Frank Smith, are credited with developing and articulating the assumptions undergirding the holistic theory. Goodman's (1976) landmark paper, "Reading: A Psycholinguistic Guessing Game," and Smith's (1971) *Understanding Reading* and *Psycholinguistics and Reading* (1973) markedly changed the way the reading process was understood. The shift was from reading as the acquisition of a series of discrete skills to a transactive, unitary, and holistic process of meaning construction. This theoretical shift affected how teachers taught reading, in terms of how to read and reading to learn in the content areas, the materials used, and the ways that a student's achievement is measured.

This shift provided impetus for pioneering research and practice in the specialization of content reading. The first teacher education course devoted solely to content reading was initiated by Harold Herber at Syracuse University in 1968. It was officially approved by the Curriculum Committee in 1969, and it became a permanent part of the secondary teacher education program and also a focus of doctoral research from the 1970s forward (H. Herber, personal communication, June 29, 1993). Herber and his graduate students advanced the research in content reading by using a federal government grant to produce four monographs reporting investigations of topics in content reading (Herber & Baron, 1979; Herber & Riley, 1979; Herber & Sanders, 1969; Herber & Vacca, 1977). As these and other Syracuse doctoral students (such as Donna Alvermann, Thomas Estes, Judith Thelen, and Richard Vacca) graduated and became teacher educators at other universities, they, in turn, developed courses in content reading. In this way, content reading courses snowballed, evolving nationally as a required part of the curriculum for prospective and practicing content teachers.

The impact of these teacher education programs and materials in content reading on secondary schools affected both of us. Barbara was a reading specialist in Jefferson County, Colorado (the second largest school district in Colorado, encompassing the western suburbs of Denver). Barbara explains the program like this:

> The district had 32 secondary schools, with both reading teachers and reading specialists in each. Secondary reading teachers taught remedial, developmental, and advanced reading classes. We specialists taught reading classes, but we also had periods free to plan and teach with the content teachers. We assisted content teachers in individualizing instruction for their students, in assessing the readability and appropriateness of reading materials, and in ascertaining students' reading abilities in the content texts. Our main focus was to provide in-service education for content teachers within and outside their own classrooms; we taught teachers by "doing" the methods of content reading in their classrooms so that they could adopt the methods.

Judith Thelen, a professor at Frostburg State College and a former student of Herber, was a consultant for Barbara. Professor Thelen visited Jefferson County and was a frequent in-service presenter. The model the district followed in implementing content reading reflected Thelen's (and Herber's) position that "the teacher knows the content and the reading teacher knows the reading and thinking processes needed to learn the content—by collaborating, students will successfully understand."

Patty was a secondary reading specialist in Racine, Wisconsin. Before Patty was hired, there was no secondary reading program in that district, but plans were to start at one high school and to use that high school as a model for the others to follow. Patty describes her experiences like this:

> This was an awesome task. There were nearly 3,000 kids and over 150 teachers in the building. Just like in most high schools, the kids ranged from being very poor readers to readers who won National Merit Scholarships. Many teachers were resistant to the idea of integrating reading instruction because they figured that the kids should already be able to read before they got to high school. The school had a tradition of "tracking" students and so the newest teachers would get the lowest kids. I was committed to working with the teachers, much like Barbara was, but needed to find a way to provide support for the most struggling of readers. With no additional resources on the horizon for reading teachers, I instituted a tutoring program. I recruited teachers and principals to donate 2 hours a week to the program, and I also got future teachers from the

> neighboring university and retired teachers to become tutors. As the tutoring program was developing, I also worked one on one with individual teachers and in departments to help teachers learn about content area reading. Over a 3-year period, nearly every teacher came on board and we accomplished a lot to improve the reading in that school.

A recent report (Anders, 2002) reveals that, during the late sixties and early seventies, there was an informal national network of reading specialists in secondary reading programs. The secondary reading specialist was an important response to the challenges of providing for adolescent literacy development. For example, schools were undergoing desegregation orders and teachers were faced with teaching students they had never seen before. School literacy programs, like the ones established by Barbara and Patty, helped teachers to learn about teaching students with different needs and experiences. Frankly, many secondary reading programs of the day provided a safety net for both kids and teachers who were experiencing tension and stress as the process of desegregating schools was underway. Both federal and local funds were available and dedicated to these efforts. During the past 20 years, support for programs like these has waned; nonetheless, there is legislation pending in the U.S. Congress to once again provide funds for adolescent literacy programs.

Content Reading in the 1990s: An Expanding Definition

In addition to an expanding research base, the field of content reading was extended to include speaking and writing. Until the 1990s, the term *content area reading* dominated the field. In the 1990s, however, the term *content area literacy* drifted into use. Why did this occur? One reason was the sense among content area reading specialists that reading was part and parcel of the language arts—that learners use writing and speaking with reading to negotiate and construct the ideas in the content areas. Pushing this idea a little further, some suggested (e.g., Pearson & Tierney, 1984) that reading and writing were actually two sides of the same coin. That is, authors comprehend what they compose and that to compose one comprehends. Likewise, when readers read, they compose a meaning in their heads. When the processes are conceptualized that way, it makes sense to conjoin them.

One consequence of this broadened perspective was to encourage research and practice in the writing process. Donald Graves (1990) and colleagues influenced elementary-level teachers to institute "writing workshops" in their classes—that is, students were invited to engage in the writing process like "real" authors. Instructional strategies provided children with opportunities to go through the various steps that most authors employ, from brainstorming to gathering information to drafting to editing to rewriting and to publishing. Secondary teacher educators and teachers began to adopt and adapt these strategies to use in content area classrooms. Judith Langer and Arthur Applebee (1984) conducted a study in Oakland Public Schools (California) that demonstrated the power of process writing in the secondary classroom. Doctoral students worked with various content area teachers, teaching students to write in different genres in the content areas. The findings suggested that, when students write in different genres, their thinking is expanded and shaped in ways that are different than those that occur when students do not do that writing; see *Writing Shapes Thinking* (Langer & Appleby, 1984). Davis et al. (1992) substantiated these findings by investigating the types of writing activities that characterized high- and low-scoring fourth- and fifth-grade classrooms. In low-scoring classrooms, teachers had fewer explicit expectations of the students in their writing of whole texts. Conversely, in high-scoring classrooms, students wrote as part of a series of activities that culminated in writing whole texts. High-scoring classrooms incorporated formal student–teacher conferences, which seemed to contribute to students' understanding of the purpose of their writing. In high-scoring classrooms, students also had greater choice of topic in their writing and did more rewriting than did students in low-level classes.

Research conducted by Odell, Goswami, and Quick (1983) also lends support to the theoretical assumptions of process writing. They called for teachers to use less instructional emphasis on editing rhetorical style and more emphasis on critical thinking and the exploration of content issues when helping students to write. They interviewed undergraduates and legislative analysts, and they compared what these two groups told them about their writing experiences. They found that the questions undergraduate students asked themselves about their writing were less sophisticated conceptually and less inclined to call for critical thinking about the text they were composing than the questions legislators asked while writing. For example, legislative analysts queried themselves about the consequence of the material and their assertions, whereas undergraduates asked questions about the completeness and correctness of the text they composed. One recommendation from this study was that teachers complete their own writing assignments and assess

BOX 2.1. Possible Journal Responses to Promote Thinking

•This is very interesting, please tell me more. •Hmmmm, I have never thought of that before. •What makes you think so? •I am not convinced. Can you provide some examples that would convince me? •That must have been very (appropriate adverb). How did you cope? What would you recommend to someone else faced with the same challenge? •What do you think the author would say to this? •The assignment you are writing about is structured in an unusual way; did you think about that when reading-studying? •Is this confirmed by your experience? How so? •I am confused here. You seem to be discussing two contradictory ideas. How could you clarify? •How do you think you could use this information?

the kinds of questions they need to ask to write meaningfully. A second recommendation was that teachers conceive of assignments as having authentic and meaningful purposes, not just something that has to be done for a grade.

Martha Ruddell (1993) maintains that students need to see their teachers write and recommends instituting "sustained silent writing." That is, during a specific time each class period or week, the teacher and the students would each write without interruption and without critique. This would be an authentic activity if students were responding to content being learned. They could ask questions, write reflections, and describe their confusions and their developing understandings. The teacher could set up a system so that each week she or he responded to some of the journals. Responses would take the form of clarifications, answers to questions, and comments about the quality of *thinking* (See Box 2.1 for a sampling of teacher responses to student journal writing). These journals would be "process" journals; that is, students would receive credit for doing them, but they would not be corrected for grammar, spelling, or style. One of the principles behind process writing is that students need both the space and the time to get their ideas on paper. Editing comes with rewriting. Sometimes writing is simply thinking on paper and is not meant for publication. When writing for publication (or a grade), students need opportunities to rewrite, edit, and to rewrite again.

Like writing, speaking, or orality, is also related to literacy development and to learning in the content areas. Deborah Tannen (1983) suggests that speaking and listening strategies may underlie text comprehension (p. 21) and that strategies needed for good conversation may actually be efficient for both writing and reading (p. 91). For example, she points out that successful writing requires a sense of audience and a desire to respond to the needs of that audience. The ability to imagine what a hypothetical reader needs to know is an interactive ability. Likewise, reading comprehension involves a close listening to the author, an ability to question the author and to empathize with the author for an adequate understanding and response.

By way of providing a historical background, the term *orality* is used to characterize societies that rely on the use of oral communication (Havelock, 1991). Orality and literacy are interrelated. For example, among Native American speakers of indigenous languages, the oral lives and works alongside the written text. In cases in which the indigenous language is not written, speakers of the indigenous language read and write a second language, such as English, and when the indigenous language is written, members of the community use both languages to communicate as appropriate in the context of the situation (M. E. Romero, personal communication, June 3, 2004).

To foster students' oral language in the content areas, it makes sense for teachers to make interactive discussion an integral part of the methods used in the classroom. Alvermann, Dillon, and O'Brien (1987) distinguished typical classroom recitation from interactive discussions. Recitation generally consists of the teacher asking a question, a student or students giving a brief answer, and the teacher asking another question. This mode of discourse is common and prevalent in many classrooms. Deborah Dillon (2000) found that teachers with whom she worked thought of discussion as consisting of activities like reviewing, drilling, and quizzing students. This is not what we mean by interactive discussion.

Rather, we agree with Alvermann et al. (1987) that discussion should satisfy three criteria:

- Class members should put forth multiple points of view and be prepared to change their minds about their thinking on the topic being discussed;
- Students should interact with each other in the discussion, as well as with the teacher; and
- The interaction should exceed the typical two- or three-word phrases common to recitation.

The ability to accomplish this sort of a discussion requires that it be thought through and intentionally developed. We have sat in classrooms where a student said something in a discussion and the teacher had a hard time

BOX 2.2. Questions that Respect Students' Perspectives

•I think your idea has potential; tell us more. •How many of you agree? Why? •How many of you disagree? why? •What do you think the author would say about our discussion? •Who would disagree with the position we are suggesting? Why? •Interesting; tell us more. •I never though about it that way; can anyone else add to this? If not, where is the disconnect for the rest of you? •Interject conflicting or confirming information and ask for students' responses.

making a connection between what the student said and the topic being discussed. Sometimes kids do say wild and crazy things that do not connect, but most of the time, students want their ideas to be honored, acknowledged, and accepted in the discussion. Francine Falk-Ross (2001) investigated teaching preservice teachers about classroom discourse routines and found that, with intentional effort, one could implement discussion in interactive ways. The participating preservice teachers were particularly impressed by the increased participation by students whose cultural and linguistic backgrounds were different from the majority of students. Kathy Au (2005), in a companion book to this one, discusses the same point at length. Teachers can help by asking the type of questions listed in Box 2.2. These are just a few examples of the "language manners" teachers who are committed to having good interactive discussions in their classes reveal in their practices.

As a result of these expanded foci on writing and speaking, the term *content reading* is now subsumed by the phrase *literacy instruction in the content areas*, the focus of this book. Each of the language processes interrelate and reinforce the other, facilitating students' learning and engagement of concepts—the ideas you, our readers, are responsible for teaching in the content areas.

These language processes play a part in content areas that traditionally have not incorporated reading or writing. For example, recommending an appealing trade book (like a biography of a famous sports figure) to a student in a physical education class may motivate and interest a student in a sport being studied. Asking students to complete guides challenging them to consider questions about the meaning and themes of a sports-related video may assist students in learning the vocabulary and "big ideas" of a sport. Adaptations like these can be made for various content areas to help mediate and scaffold the ways in which students are able to engage concepts and behaviors in a content area.

In addition to expanding the emphasis on language processes in content area literacy, content area literacy educators recognize contributions from theorists grounded in sociocultural perspectives. Research in social psychology, cognitive psychology, and anthropology is converging to support the premise that all learning takes place in settings that have particular sets of cultural and social norms and expectations and that these settings influence learning and transfer in powerful ways (Bransford, Brown, & Cocking, 1999). This view compliments and extends the cognitive and linguistic model of content reading by including the contextual interactions of gender, ethnicity, history, and culture in our understanding of students' comprehension of concepts.

How does this relate to content area literacy instruction? It is relevant because it acknowledges that we live in a pluralistic society and that classrooms mirror our multicultural society. Our students are not likely to understand dominate meanings of some concepts or may interpret concepts differently because of their expectations, backgrounds, and roles within their cultures. We will go a long way toward teaching all our students and providing equal opportunity for them when we use teaching methods and multiple literacies and establish a classroom climate that acknowledges, accepts, and honors these differences. Doing so means that we work hard to find connections between and among students and ideas rather than exclude students' experiences and limit their engagements with the ideas in our content areas. In case this is too abstract, let us be blunt: When teachers hold narrow conceptions of knowledge and experience, they are likely to not adequately honor and incorporate experiences and knowledge that is different from their own. When

we use the term *literacy*, we do so intentionally. Literacy means that differences are acknowledged and honored and differences in power relationships and opportunities are interrogated as part of the reading, writing, speaking, and listening experiences in the classroom.

The Beginnings of a New Century

Directions for the field of content area literacy continue to be in the areas of research and improved classroom practice. Alvermann and Swafford (1989) examined instructional research in content reading by investigating the empirical support for recommended strategies. After comparing 54 strategies recommended in six content area reading texts and the research base for those recommendations, they concluded that empirical support was variable and in many cases lacking. Blanchard (1989) compared the strategies recommended in methods textbooks, such as this one, and found that the research base for recommended practices was mentioned for only 13 studies. As educators, including policymakers, continue to emphasize the importance of establishing and depending on a research base for classroom strategies, content area literacy specialists need to continue to improve their research base.

The National Reading Panel (2000) brought this point home. The panel was congressionally mandated, and Congress charged the Panel to analyze the research base for reading instruction. They chose to define research narrowly and selected only studies that used classic experimental designs. The panel concluded that there were few studies in the area of content area reading that met their strict criteria. We argue that classic research designs are not the best ways to investigate content area literacy; nonetheless, it is clear that research is desperately needed in content area literacy. As we write this chapter, research money is being made available for literacy studies with adolescents as their focus.

It will be interesting to see what happens in content area literacy during the next ten years. It seems to us that the field is at the crossroads of a paradigm shift. As we already discussed, content area reading researchers and teachers are moving toward replacing traditional notions of reading with notions that are more inclusive and are more appropriately encapsulated in the terms *literacy* and *multiliteracies*, implying the social context in which reading, writing, speaking, and listening influence the meaning constructed with the many forms of text.

This emphasis on the social nature of literacy is a sea change from the previous individualistic perspectives of learning skills and strategies to use reading and writing to learn. The theoretical foundations for a social cultural perspective on literacy have been around for many years (see, e.g., Vygotsky, 1978), but a sense of what that means in school and in content area literacy has taken a while to emerge. This social cultural perspective is currently expressed in terms of *situated learning*, *critical pedagogy*, and the *new literacy studies*. Along with these theories, technological advances including the media and computer-assisted learning have opened whole new avenues for exploration and practice.

Situated learning, as expressed by Jean Lave and her students and colleagues (Chalkin & Lave, 1995; Lave, 1988; Lave & Wenger, 1991; Wenger, McDermott, & Snyder, 2002), presents the idea that learners affect each other in a community and that others in the community are highly influential on individuals in the community. If we take this principle to content area classrooms, the implications are profound and sensible. Consider, for example, a community of scientists and a community of literature experts; what are their differences? One major difference is the methods used to advance the knowledge in each field. The scientist uses methods of observation and experimentation that have been developed over time and with which the community at large agrees. The literature community, in contrast, uses various types of text analyses to construct understandings and critiques of the literature. Another difference is the ways that members of each respective community communicate their findings to other members of their community; they use accepted standards of form as reflected in their writing and speaking. Each content area classroom represents a community, albeit a naïve and immature community, which is led by the content area teacher. The science teacher, literature teacher, math teacher, and so on are each responsible for socializing students to a content community by teaching the language, culture, and ways of knowing represented by each content area.

The central concern of critical pedagogy is the issue of power in the teaching and learning context. It focuses on how and in whose interests knowledge is produced and passed on. Henry Giroux is one of the leading contributors to our understanding of critical pedagogy. In his book, ***Disturbing Pleasures: Learning Popular Culture*** (1994), he defines critical pedagogy as signaling "how questions of audience, voice, power, and evaluation actively work to construct particular relations between teachers and students, institutions and society, and classrooms and communities" (p. 30). The challenge to content area educators is to help students understand the power relations that are inherent within the content being taught as well as to teach in such a way that students are able to be participants in the class rather than merely receptacles of knowledge that the teacher controls. This suggests that facts in the content areas are not merely propositions to be learned but are parts of systems of belief and action that have aggregate effects with the power structures of society. For example, Giroux and McLaren (1994) give this explanation:

> [Critical pedagogy] asks about systems of belief and action, who benefits? The primary preoccupation of Critical Pedagogy is with social injustice and how to transform inequitable, undemocratic, or oppressive institutions and social relations.... Indeed a crucial dimension of this approach is that certain claims, even if they might be "true" or substantiated within particular confines and

> assumptions, might nevertheless be partisan in their effects. Assertions that African-Americans score lower on IQ tests, for example, even if it is a "fact" that this particular population does on average score lower on this particular set of tests, leave significant larger questions unaddressed, not the least of which is what effect such assertions have on a general population that is not aware of the important limits of these tests or the tenuous relation, at best, between "what IQ tests measure" and "intelligence." Other important questions, from this standpoint, include: Who is making these assertions? Why are they being made at this point in time? Who funds such research? Who promulgates these "findings"? Are they being raised to question African-American intelligence or to demonstrate the bias of IQ tests? Such questions, from the Critical Pedagogy perspective, are not external to, or separable from, the import of also weighing the evidentiary base for such claims. (preface).

Each content area teacher can think of his or her own field and find questions to ask about power relationships. These questions often are related to issues of social justice such as differences between men and women, differences between people who are wealthy and those who live in poverty, and differences among religions, ethnicities, and race in the content area specifically and society generally. Helping students to understand these issues leads students to think more deeply about the world in which they live. Understanding power relationships and their consequences contributes to better informed citizens and more sophisticated members of the content area community.

The account of the young people zining in our first chapter is an excellent example of the new literacies, a view of literacy that foregrounds the present and recognizes that literacy is linked to continuous change, which Leu, Kinzer, Coiro, and Cammack (2004) say is the essence of reading and reading instruction. The advancement of thinking about new literacies includes aspects of situational and critical literacies already described along with new forms and functions of literacy and texts, including emerging technological and multimedia tools such as gaming software (Gee, 2003), video technologies (O'Brien, 2001), Internet communities (Chandler-Olcott & Mahar, 2003), instant messaging (Lewis & Fabos, 1999), Web pages, and many more yet to emerge. Observations of young people and their new literacies (e.g., Bean et al., 1999; Guzzetti & Gamboa, 2004) reveal the functional importance of these literacies, and the remarkable possibilities they offer for communication, information exchange, and development.

Federal research dollars and think tanks across the United States are pretty much ignoring these trends by calling for studies and teaching practices that narrow the field; they are back from a literacy perspective to a model of skill acquisition with an emphasis on decoding, vocabulary, and basic comprehension skills—a model similar to the pre-1960s models. Nonetheless, we hope to build an argument and provide practices that can be used to counter the current reductionist emphasis. We are convinced that narrowing the curriculum to basic measurable skills is a regressive and potentially damaging trend that affects the quality of education and ultimately democratic thinking and citizenship. We recognize that our readers are in the midst of learning about these and other exciting perspectives on literacy but are also struggling with staggering impositions on their academic freedom and professional judgment. We care passionately that teachers in general, and literacy leaders in particular, teach in ways that are critical and generative of new knowledge. As a result, we challenge you, our readers, to confront the current trends by aspiring to provide your students with opportunities to engage in communities of critical thought by incorporating new literacies in your curriculum.

PERSPECTIVES FROM STAKEHOLDERS

Formal investigations and informal observations of instruction and conversations with former students in methods classes demonstrate the utility of literacy instruction in the content area classroom. For example, Barbara (Guzzetti, 1989) conducted a follow-up study of her former students in content reading classes by interviewing and observing six secondary teachers from three content areas. Her observations focused on the adaptations, modifications, or innovations these teachers incorporated as they implemented content reading methods across varying contexts (differing grade levels and subject areas). Interviews centered on the contextual conditions that facilitated or inhibited these teachers' adoptions of content reading methods. She found that the most frequently implemented strategy was to ask students in the content areas to think in ways concerning evaluation, application, and synthesis about the content being learned. These teachers used reading guides with three levels of questions (literal, interpretative, and applied) as described by Herber (1970). We also provide directions and examples of three level guides in chapter 6 of this book.

Adaptations of strategies were found to fit particular content areas, like music and mathematics. A middle-school choral music teacher constructed three levels of questions for each song sung in an interschool competition.

Literal questions asked students to remember words to lines of the piece; interpretative questions required students to paraphrase by putting the lyrics into present-day language; applied questions required students to relate the words to a personal or vicarious life experience. The teacher believed that, in the process of completing the reading guide, students approached the song more sensually, understood the need for particular dynamic level or pause, and incorporated the song's concepts into a personal perspective. The teacher stated, "The secret of our success (in competitions) is working at the applied level" (Tim Bullara, personal communication, June 30, 1989).

In a similar way, a senior high school mathematics teacher found that using three levels of questions to guide students' reading was the only way to motivate her students to read the text and to do the required homework. Her three-level questions were part of her point system for evaluating and monitoring students' performance. Hence, both of these teachers found that using comprehension strategies increased students' performance.

An elementary school teacher reported her experiences in implementing a literature-based approach to teaching social studies (Kowanliski, 1992). As a teacher in Barbara's content reading course, she implemented a literature-based reading curriculum. The course, which presented ways to incorporate literature into content teaching, inspired her to begin teaching social studies by using trade books. The inquiry approach, which became almost entirely student directed, incorporated language, writing, mathematics, reading, and art into a social studies unit. The result was that "students no longer were unmotivated, but anxious to work together to learn more about the world" (p. 7).

Although the conditions these teachers experienced permitted and facilitated implementation of content reading methods, this is not always the case. Competing demands on teachers was the main reason former students of literacy instruction were unable to implement content reading strategies (Guzzetti, 1989). Curriculum content and format overwhelmed beginning teachers, particularly when they were forced to teach a content they were less prepared to teach. When this happened, process gave way to content as the teachers spent their preparation time attempting to learn the concepts themselves. We believe, however, that the teaching of process—incorporating reading, writing, speaking, and listening instruction—in the content areas will help teachers teach better and students to learn better.

Patty and her colleague Virginia Richardson (Anders & Richardson, 1992) found that teachers were reluctant to adopt and incorporate process strategies when they were under severe pressures of accountability. The teachers in their study were cautious about "research based reading instructional practices" because students might do less well on the tests.

In addition to listening to and recording the voices of teachers, we have also gathered students' reactions to content reading and writing strategies. At Benchmark School in Media, Pennsylvania, students have been taught the language of literacy instruction and have become metacognitively aware of their own needs related to learning from text. This deliberately taught learning strategy was apparent to Patty as she observed students attempting to work cooperatively to solve a physical science problem. These eighth graders were required to explain and draw how to retrieve a vase from a gully while standing at the top of an overhanging cliff. In an informal interview, one student named David confided that "I don't have enough background knowledge to know how to figure out this problem. I'm not sure if we are supposed to use a lever or a pulley to get the vase up. I have to read about levers and pulleys to find out which one I should use. I have to read to get the prior knowledge I need to come up with a solution" (David, personal communication, March 3, 1991).

In another example, a senior high student in Phoenix used reading guides that had three levels of questions and think sheets (records of students' questions and their prereading and postreading ideas—strategies that are introduced in upcoming chapters) for the first time while reading the novel *Ethan Frome*. She remarked that these reading guides gave her a focus and directed her attention to major themes in the novel. Comments like these from students reinforce in an experiential, realistic way the results of experimental research that concludes that content area strategies are effective in promoting learning from text (Guzzetti, Snyder, Glass, & Gamas, 1993).

Elizabeth Sturtevant, a professor of education in Virginia, has also followed her content area literacy students into the classroom. She was particularly interested in the sense that mathematics teachers made of the principles and ideas in content area literacy for their discipline. In one study (Sturtevant, 1996), she developed five case studies of men, retired from the military, who were pursuing a career in education. She found that personal experiences were highly influential in the methods they chose to use in their secondary classes. For example, all the men used methods that involved student collaboration and group work because they had seen the benefits of "teaming" in former jobs. Contextual influences also played a major role in the methods they adopted. These included cooperation among teachers, curriculum and textbooks, departmental regulations, student characteristics and behaviors, paper work and other administrative details, and conditions such as lack of time for teaching and planning. This study affirms the importance of the personal and the contextual for constructing meaning. All learners make sense by relating their personal knowledge and experiences to the social contexts in which they practice.

SUMMARY

This chapter has provided a definition of literacy that reflects notions of what it means to be literate. The definition we provide of literacy includes using different texts for different purposes, thinking critically about texts, using other forms of symbolic communication—like music, media, and computers—and collaborating between authors and readers. We also recognize that being literate is personal, social, and situational. Examples of literacy demands in the workplace demonstrate these aspects of literacy.

We have traced content area reading and how literacy how developed and expanded through the decades. This historical base allows us to study successes and failures of past generations, giving us insights into how the study of reading has evolved and progressed to its present form. When pertinent theoretical and practical threads of information are monitored from their inception to their practical implementation in classroom learning, a more global view of reading is attained (Readence, Rickelman, & Moore, 1982, p. 10). The historical perspective also advises us as to what might be worthwhile choices for both research projects and for classroom practice.

Finally, this chapter has shared teachers and students' experiences and opinions about content literacy. We provide these examples to encourage others to consider the potential that the ideas in this book have for practice. The previous chapter discussed students and what they bring to the content area classroom; this chapter provided an overview and introduction to the field of content area literacy. The next chapter introduces two central points: teacher's beliefs about content area literacy and the construction of content area ideas.

APPLICATION ACTIVITIES

1. Compare the philosophy of content reading that is evident in current content literacy textbooks. Contrast the way textbooks present instructional

strategies for content areas. If possible, compare current methods books with methods books from previous generations of textbook authors.

2. Formulate and articulate in writing your view of content literacy.

3. Reflect on an experience you had in which reading or writing made a difference in learning a subject.

4. Create a writing assignment for a content topic. Analyze and list the questions that have to be addressed. Ask a high school or middle-school student to do the assignment; complete the assignment yourself and compare and contrast your own questions with those asked by the student.

5. Collect articles from the Web and popular press that demonstrate both the new literacies and the back-to-basics movement. Analyze these in light of your current thinking about content area literacy. Project what this debate means for your own practice.

6. This suggested activity is taken from an article by David Donahue, "Reading Across the Great Divide: English and Math Teachers Apprentice One Another as Readers and Disciplinary Insiders." A humanities teacher teams with a science or math teacher. Each teacher selects a challenging text in his or her subject area and reads it over the course of one month. During the month, each teacher writes a response journal about what is being read and exchanges the journal with his or her partner. At the end of the month, each teacher has a week to read the other's text, and then each set of partners discusses each other's texts. The following questions are addressed in the discussion: What have you learned about reading in your own subject area? What have you learned about reading outside your subject area? How will you use this learning to help your students make meaning from the texts you assign in your class? The article reports the results of this conversation in Professor Donahue's class.

FROM OUR PROFESSIONAL LIBRARY

Alvermann, D. E., Hinchman, K. A., Moore, D. W., Phelps, S. F., & Waff, D. R. (1998). *Reconceptualizing the literacies in adolescents' lives.* Mahweh, NJ: Lawrence Erlbaum Associates.

Darder, A. (2002). *Critical pedagogy reader*. New York: Taylor & Francis.

Gore, J. M. (1993). *The struggle for pedagogies: Critical and feminist discourses as regimes of truth*. New York: Routledge.

Guzzetti, B. J., Young, J. P., Gritsavage, M. M., Fyfe, L. M., & Hardenbrook, M. (2002). *Reading, writing, and talking gender in literacy learning*. Chicago: National Reading Conference.

McCarthey, S. J. (2002). *Students' identities and literacy learning*. Chicago: National Reading Conference.

Moll, L. C. (1990). *Vygotsky and education: Instructional implications and applications of sociohistorical psychology*. London: Cambridge University Press.

Moje, E. B., & O'Brien, D. G. (Eds.). (2001). *Constructions of literacy: Studies of teaching and learning in and out of secondary schools.* Mahwah, NJ: Lawrence Erlbaum Associates.

Street, B. (1984). *Literacy in theory and practice*. London: Cambridge University Press.

FROM OUR COMPUTER FILES

www.ed.gov/about/offices/list/ovaewww.ed.gov/about/offices/list/ovae
www.pisa.oecd.org

3

Literacy and the Teaching and Learning of Ideas

Most of us become teachers because we enjoy working with young people and because we have wonderful ideas and experiences that we want to share with them. These wonderful ideas are represented by the term *content knowledge*. Content knowledge is the basis for curriculum in subject areas.

The public is very interested in teachers' content knowledge. The press commonly features articles and editorials asking if teachers know enough about their disciplines to be effective teachers. In most colleges and universities, the requirements for a teaching major have been increased, and teachers regularly participate in in-service and professional development programs to upgrade their content area knowledge. The content knowledge teachers are expected to teach is also found in state and professional standards, district and departmental curriculums, and textbooks.

Content is not simply transmitted to students. Teachers don't just "cover" content and hope that students somehow absorb it. The idea of covering material does not make sense because to cover something means to hide it from view. That is not what teachers hope to do with their content. Rather, teachers arrange experiences and activities so that students engage, think about, and apply the content they learn. The choices teachers make regarding these activities and experiences are what educators call *pedagogical knowledge*. A teacher's particular way of mixing content knowledge and pedagogical knowledge with and for students results in a *curriculum*. A thoughtful teacher chooses among infinite options for making just the right mix of content and process so that students will grow in their understanding of themselves, others, the discipline, and ultimately the world.

This may seem to be straightforward, but the curricular choices we make are influenced by our individual beliefs about teaching and learning, ourselves as teachers, and our students. What are beliefs? Goodenough (1963) explains that beliefs are "propositions that are held as true, and are accepted as guides for assessing the future, are cited in support of decisions, or are referred to in passing judgment on the behavior of others" (p. 151). We maintain that these propositions are highly influential on the decisions teachers make while "on their feet" in the classroom. Some teachers are unaware of the influence of beliefs on their practice. For example, a teacher might teach the way he or she was taught by a favorite teacher, but be unaware that the propositions learned as a child affect instructional decisions today. A new idea that is inconsistent with the way in which a teacher was taught doesn't make sense and so it is resisted. It may well be that the new idea is not worth accepting, but without the insight of understanding the reasons for resisting the idea, the teacher is unable to make an informed and well thought out response.

This is what Dewey (1938) meant when he called on teachers to be reflective. He claimed that, to advance our capacities as teachers, we must turn ideas back onto our belief systems, to examine root beliefs that affect our decisions, and, if need be, to employ practices of dialogue and inquiry to challenge or to elaborate on those beliefs. Notions of reflective practice have gained substantial popularity in recent years (Richardson & Anders, in press). Teachers are being called on to examine their beliefs about teaching and learning and about how their content area is enacted in the classroom (Shulman, 1987). We support this trend and encourage weighing and evaluating of the ideas in this book in light of the beliefs and theories that you, our readers, hold.

The purpose of this chapter is to look deeply at two related ideas. First, we explore teachers' beliefs and their relationship to literacy instruction in the content areas; second, we consider the nature of ideas in a discipline and how those ideas might become curriculum. We conclude the chapter with a discussion of the relationship among beliefs and theories, ideas, and practices. We begin by sharing our own literacy memoirs, or literacy autobiographies. The notion of the autobiography or memoir is grounded in genre studies and, according to an Internet search, is widely adapted by literacy teacher educators to help teachers discover the experiences that lead to their theories of literacy (Dillon, 2000). The difference between a memoir and an autobiography is that the memoir tends to focus on one event with an elaboration of the event; the autobiography tends to be more of a broad-brush description of one's literacy development. Barbara writes an autobiography and Patty writes a memoir to demonstrate that the experiences written about in the activity bring beliefs to consciousness and make them available for self-reflection. For the purposes of this chapter, we relate our experiences to beliefs about principles of learning that are grounded in research and central to the view of content area literacy being presented in this book.

TEACHER BELIEFS

To write this essay, we ask teacher education students to think of events related to language, literacy, and culture that stand out in their memories, and to describe the events in light of their meaningfulness for literacy development within cultural settings. We find this assignment valuable and meaningful in our content area literacy classes because the activity sets the wheels in motion for reflection and practical application.

Box 3.1 My Literacy Memoir
(Patty Anders)

I always loved to read. I don't remember learning to read, although I do remember the "Dick and Jane" books and the teacher telling us how to sound out words. One day, in about second grade, I was embarrassed because I couldn't pronounce the words *squirrel* and *owl* in a story I was reading out loud during reading group. But overall, I was very successful in school, especially in any classes requiring reading.

I'll never forget Mrs. Laxton. She was my teacher in the one-room country school I attended from Kindergarten through Grade 3. One day she asked me to stay in during recess to work on my math. I cried and was discouraged because I had made so many errors on my work. She picked me up, put me in her huge lap, and assured me that everyone makes mistakes now and then, and that I would be able to do anything I wanted because I could read well.

Finding time as a child and young person to read was very difficult. I lived on a farm, was the oldest of several children, and always had tons of chores to do. I can remember trying to sneak in some reading while I was supposed to be doing chores like pitching ensilage down from the silo to feed the cattle, pulling weeds, or helping to bale hay. In the house, I had a special hiding place in my closet where I would sit to finish a really good book instead of doing housework. I was yelled at a lot for reading instead of doing my work!

I also wanted to write, but had no idea how to go about it. When I was a really little girl, I found my Dad's old beat up typewriter and spent several hours typing letters at random. When my uncle stopped by, I proudly but shyly showed him the piece of paper. I didn't claim ownership; rather, I told him I had found this piece of paper, and asked him what it said. He replied that it looked like someone practicing their typing but that it didn't say anything. I was disappointed.

Later, in about fourth grade, I wanted to write a story and labored long and hard, trying to make up a mystery that sounded something like the "Nancy Drew" stories I loved so much. I planned for my sister to be the illustrator. I wish I could find that story now.

School was pretty easy for me. I don't think I was ever really challenged—at least not until college. I took a college-prep course in high school, worked several hours a week, helped on the farm, and was involved in extracurricular activities. I loved classes in which I could read and argue, like social studies and literature. I didn't like the sciences and math as much, but I did well enough to get into college.

College was the shock of my life. At the end of the first semester, my grades amounted to all Cs and one D—PROBATION! I couldn't believe it. I had studied all the time and did as well as I could, but obviously not well enough. I was very frustrated and had no idea what to do.

I had enjoyed my religion class, and for reasons unknown to myself, I stayed after class to talk with the professor, Dr. Cone. I told him that although I was getting a C, I had enjoyed his teaching and felt I had learned a lot. He smiled a quiet and understanding smile and asked me why I was getting a C. I blurted out that I had no idea why and, in fact, that all my grades were a disaster. He listened, nodded, and smiled. I blabbered on.

When I paused to take a breath, he asked me about my history as a student. After recounting my growing up experiences (mostly farm work and not too much value placed on education) and characterizing my high school (a place that demanded little serious scholarship), he asked me why I was in college. What did I want to do? Well, that threw me.

What I (secretly) wanted to be was a minister, but I was a girl (this was in 1966) and girls were not considered suitable for the ministry, so I had never told anyone. I had admitted to my dad that I wanted to be a lawyer, but both he and the school counselors advised against that. My dad was afraid no one would marry me if I had that much education! I knew I would be a good teacher. I had played school ever since I could remember and I was always helping little brothers and sisters with their schoolwork, and so I told the religion professor that I wanted to be a teacher. (It wasn't that I didn't want to be a teacher; it just seemed like I should have had more options, but I didn't know what they were, and if any one else knew, no one was telling me.)

By this time Dr. Cone and I had talked about an hour, and he asked me *how* I studied. I said that I spent *all* my time studying, that I had read the assigned readings several times, highlighted the readings, copied and highlighted lecture notes, and reviewed everything before the tests. What he said after I described my methods surprised me. He said I was spending *too* much time studying and not making my study time really count. He reminded me that I had always been a very active person and that I needed to maintain a balance in my life. The balance needed to be one that reflected who I really was—I shouldn't be trying to make myself over because I was now in college. I needed to participate in meaningful activities outside of studying. I also needed to let myself have fun.

He also said I needed some better strategies than just highlighting, rereading, and reviewing before the tests. He suggested that I go to the Learning Skills Center to get specific strategies, but to remember that the most important thing was to care desperately about what I was studying and to *work productively*, at it, not just assume that putting in time would give me the results I was after. (I did attend the Learning Skills Center and learned some of the strategies that are included in this book.)

Now thirty-five years later, having spent my professional life teaching, studying, reading, and writing, I admit to never regretting that I am a teacher. I do wish, however, that I had learned about studying as a young person in public school. Most would-be students do not find a professor or a teacher who will spend hours talking about studying and goals. Many young people have their dreams dashed early on (or maybe they don't even realize what their dreams are), simply because they don't yet possess the tools or know how to use the tools of reading, writing, and studying—tools that allow students to be all that they can be.

Today my life is filled with reading and writing. I need to read and write as a professor, but I also read and write to better understand myself, to stay abreast with current events, to inform myself of topics of current interest, and to read for pleasure and entertainment. One long-standing interest is gardening, but more recently I have become enamored with reading about the history and field of glass blowing. I also belong to a book club, which at present is reading and discussing books by Latino and Latina writers. In addition to professional literature, I always have one or two popular books that I am reading, including adolescent literature. I read everything written by certain authors—Marge Piercy, Sarah Paretsky, and Michael Crighton, to name just a few. I also write in a journal every day about both professional and personal issues. I find it helpful to reread the journals when I am dealing with recurring personal issues and when I am trying to remember what I have thought about with regard to professional topics. The Internet has drastically changed my life in the past few years. It is easy to stay in touch with family, friends, and colleagues over e-mail and to do a rapid search to find out about topics in which I am interested.

Just recently, my experiences have been confirmed by the personal experiences of my nephew. His story is much like mine, except I don't think he ever had a teacher like Mrs. Laxton and I sincerely hope he meets a Dr. Cone. He is going off to college this fall on a wrestling scholarship, but he has no idea how to study and has few experiences with challenging courses. I will spend part of my summer working with him, but I know that he too will need to care passionately about what he is studying and then apply strategies as tools to negotiate the meanings of his studies.

Box 3.2 My Literacy Autobiography
(Barbara Guzzetti)

My earliest memories of my literacy development are of my father reading to me. He would sit with his arm around me with, a book in his other hand, and read aloud books like *The Three Little Pigs*. He would read aloud a page several times, and then I would read it. He didn't know that he was doing "assisted reading" with me! Because my father read to me so much, I was reading by the time I went to kindergarten.

My parents put me in a private school in Chicago because of my young age. I wanted to go to school so badly that I would sneak out the door and follow my older brother to school. He would have to turn around and take me back home. The public schools would not take me because I needed to be 5 years old before September 15 but I didn't turn 5 until November. So, my parents' only choice was to enroll me in a private school. I came to school knowing how to read as well as most first graders, and I could write the alphabet.

But, by the fourth grade, I had fallen behind in reading; I was in the "B" reading group. It was finally discovered during an eye exam in school using the Snellen Chart that required reading its large and small letters at a distance that I needed glasses. Once I got my glasses in fourth grade, I quickly caught up to my classmates. I remember their applause when the teacher announced that I would be joining the "A" group in reading.

I also remember that reading instruction consisted of sight words on flash cards and phonics drills. I recall my first-grade teacher telling my parents how good I was in phonics. We also had the typical basal readers with short stories about Dick and Jane.

Looking back on my experiences, it seemed that my in-school reading had little to do with my out-of-school reading. At home, I read voraciously, picking up other family members' reading materials like the newspaper. I still have a photo of me reading my brother's *Mad* magazine. My favorite book was *Black Beauty*, that sad tale of a horse's hard life. I read that book over and over again from fifth through eighth grade.

We had very few writing assignments in elementary school. At home, however, I kept a diary. I wrote entries in my diary every day. It had a lock and I kept the key hidden so that no one could read it. I was especially worried that my older brother would find the key and discover my secret thoughts. I also remember doing a lot of note writing and passing to my friends in school. When I graduated from eighth grade, I was very proud to have been chosen by my eighth-grade teacher to write and read aloud the class prophecy at the graduation ceremony. It was a humorous account of what we would all be doing as adults. It gave me enormous satisfaction to make people laugh through my writing and to be able to express my sense of humor through the written as well as the spoken word.

I don't remember much about my reading in high school aside from the magazines I read. Each month, I would eagerly await my subscription to *Seventeen* magazine. I recall paging through it to get the latest hairstyles—my hair was naturally curly and wavy, and it was humid in Chicago. Yet, all the models in *Seventeen* had straight hair. Those images compelled me to start ironing my hair on an ironing board with a regular clothes iron. I would go to school with burns on my arms because I wanted to live up to the images in those magazines! (This was in the days before large rollers, so my friends and I slept on hair rolled around orange juice cans.)

My favorite class in high school was political science. We each had our own subscription to *Time* magazine that we read at home and then discussed in class. I enjoyed that class so much that I would use my free period each day (when others went to the Senior Lounge) to attend that class a second time. I wanted to participate in the discussions and not miss anything. My teacher finally told me to stop coming to his class twice a day because I was dominating those discussions and knew all the answers from the period before.

As I transitioned to college, my recreational reading was put on hold. All I remember reading aside from course texts was the *Red Cross Life Saving and Water Safety Manual*. I taught swimming and life guarded at the YWCA as a part-time job, so I needed to study the Red Cross manuals for certification along with my classes in lifesaving and water safety. I remember how proud I was to earn my WSI (Water Safety Instructor) certificate from the Red Cross. I still remember quotes from that book, including "Each one teach one" (to swim), the motto of the author.

After college, I got a teaching position and immediately started my master's degree in education with a specialization in reading instruction. I remember doing so much reading about reading that I had very little free time to read anything else. This was, however, a time in my life when I wrote to and got lots of letters from friends and family. That seems to be a lost art today with the advent of e-mail. I also recall discovering the pleasure of children's literature as I attempted to find interesting and motivating books to read aloud to my inner-city fifth graders.

My professional reading increased when I moved to Colorado and got into a doctoral program. I was both working as a Secondary Reading Specialist and taking classes on a full-time basis. I commuted an hour each way to the university, and studied on the weekends. That schedule left me with very little free time for recreational reading. I do remember a bit of avocational reading at the time, however. I devoured Steven King books and exchanged children's literature with a friend. One of these books was so humorous that I still recall it—*Blackula*, the funny and imaginative story about a vampire rabbit.

Since becoming a professor, my recreational reading seems to be more tied to my professional research interests. I am currently studying the out-of-school literacies of adolescents. That focus had led me to collecting zines (self-published alternatives to magazines created by adolescents and young adults). Now when I travel locally, nationally, or internationally, I distribute the zines done by three young women who were my informants, and

I collect others' zines of various genres (personal, political, and special themes). For example, I have in my collection a zine done by a young woman in Chicago who publishes accounts of women who were raped and survived, a zine by a young woman who writes about commercial fishing, and a zine about skateboarding.

Access to the Internet and e-mail has resulted in electronic communications' and posttypographic text's dominating my professional and personal reading and writing. On a personal level, I belong to four electronic mail lists that discuss Havanese and Bichon Friese dogs. Because I do rescue work as a volunteer, I am on e-mail lists for Bichon and Havanese rescue, as well. Most of my correspondence with out-of-town friends is on e-mail. On a professional level, I review manuscripts for journals, submit manuscripts for publication, and access our university library online. I have used the Internet for research (e.g., investigating adolescents' literacies and the Web sites these kids visit) as well as for shopping and making travel arrangements (e.g., hotels and airline tickets). I spend a large part of my day at my computer. I would not want to be without its convenience of communication.

Writing this reflection, I realize that electronic text has taken over the space in my life that traditional forms of print once occupied. For example, Patty Anders recommended highly that I read a series of books set in Scotland before going to Scotland. I traveled to Scotland, but I never read the books. I have one of them on my nightstand so I intend to read it, but have not made the time to do so. Instead, I tend to take printouts of e-mails or journal articles sent electronically to bed with me. I never seem to get past quick reading materials like the plethora of catalogues I get in the mail each day.

This literacy autobiography makes me realize that I need more of a balance between my professional reading and my personal reading. That seems to be the power of authoring a literacy autobiography—self-realization through self-reflection. It has proved to be a powerful tool in my "Gender, Culture and Literacy" seminar as my graduate students reflect on their lives in very personal and intertextual ways. Following our examples, Patty and I invite you to write your own literacy autobiography or memoir and see what you discover about yourself in your journey back to and from time past.

BELIEFS AND RESEARCH-BASED PRINCIPLES AND PRACTICES

What do these memoirs say about each of us? For Patty, one basic belief is resoundingly clear: *learning has to be meaningful*. Barbara's autobiography illustrates this point when she recalls that her out-of-school reading and literacy practices were not connected to her in-school literacy instruction and assignments. When we are continually faced with tasks for learning that are meaningless, we forget that what we are about in school (and life) is to make meaning. Some people theorize that kids who have trouble in school, many of whom are identified as learning disabled, are victims of meaningless instruction (Cambourne, 1988).

What makes curricula meaningful to students? *Meaningful curricula are related to students' interests.* Reading, writing, speaking, and listening about topics, if one has little interest or reason for doing so, is very difficult. Interest, however, is not as straightforward as it seems. For example, one time when working with teachers of Navajo students, Patty was disconcerted by Anglo teachers who reported, "these kids are only interested in drugs and rock and roll." Having spent time with young Navajos, Patty knew this to not be true. The students knew and were interested in lots of topics (e.g., weather, geology, poetry, and genetics). The problem was that the teachers, coming from urban backgrounds and having lived a lifestyle very different from the Navajo, did not recognize the students' interests. Luis Moll points out the same finding when he discusses his concept of *funds of knowledge* (Moll & González, 1994). Moll and his colleagues do household interviews in the barrio to discover the interests and sources of knowledge found in Latino communities. He finds that children have a large base of experience with many topics, but that Anglo teachers do not recognize their Latino students' interests because of different backgrounds. Patty's and Barbara's experiences and research, and chapter 1 of this volume, demonstrate the necessity to know students and their outside-of-school literacy practices.

Other research (Osako & Anders, 1983) suggests that some students are accustomed to suppressing their interests when doing schoolwork. Candy Bos and Patty (Bos & Anders,1993) observed that high school students labeled as learning disabled did not expect their personal lives to be connected to what they studied in school. One student who resisted the strategies being taught in the study by Bos and Anders reported being shocked that the experiences and interests he had outside of school had anything to do with ideas being taught

(The Fourth Amendment to the U.S. Constitution). When he successfully completed the study and said, "This was great!," Patty and Candy asked him, "Why? You gave us so much grief while we were doing this." He answered, "Cuz it was the first time I ever read something that was like real life." That was a profound statement for a tenth-grade student to make!

Students' interests are connected to prior knowledge and experiences. The research related to reading comprehension of the eighties and since convinces us that a reader's prior knowledge is directly related to the quality of the reader's reading comprehension. Here is a classic "experiment" that demonstrates the influence of prior knowledge. Please read the following passage from Anderson, Reynolds, Schallert, and Goetz (1977) and envision what is happening:

> Rocky slowly got up from the mat, planning his escape. He hesitated a moment and thought. Things were not going well. What bothered him most was being held, especially since the charge against him had been weak. He considered his present situation. The lock that held him was strong but he thought he could break it. He knew, however, that his timing would have to be perfect. Rocky was aware that it was because of his early roughness that he had been penalized so severely—much too severely from his point of view. The situation was becoming frustrating; the pressure had been grinding on him for too long. He was being ridden unmercifully. Rocky was getting angry now. He felt he was ready to make his move. He knew that his success or failure would depend on what he did in the next few seconds. (p. 369)

How do you interpret this passage? What do you think it is about? Richard Anderson and his colleagues asked college students majoring in either physical education or music to read and interpret this passage. Most of the music majors interpreted the passage to be about a prison break. The physical education majors interpreted the passage to be about wrestling. Chances are you interpreted this passage in a way that is connected to your prior knowledge, too. Patty's memoir relates to the impact of prior knowledge in at least two ways:

> First, I think I was feeling out of place in college. I knew my background was weak in high school, and I believed that college was an entirely "a new game," and I did not know the rules. I did not know that studying involved connecting prior experience to new learnings and making meaningful connections. Nor did I have confidence in my prior experiences. Now that I was in college, I thought I had to study all the time to somehow or another get this new information in

> my head. I did not believe that school and learning were supposed to be related to real life. Because school was hard, I thought I should not take time to play or participate in outside activities. These "disconnects" worked against my best efforts.

Students who come from homes where going to school is the norm find that what we do in school is commonplace and natural. This was evident in Barbara's autobiography. Her family members were educated; college was assumed. For others, like young people who come from homes where the parents were not successful in school, or those for whom English is not the first language, or for those labeled as learning disabled, the content and conduct of school is alien and therefore difficult for them. A teacher who believes students' interests and backgrounds are critical to teaching and learning will use activities in the classroom to learn more about her or his students. Here are some ideas.

1. Having decided on the topic or concept around which upcoming instruction will focus, create, along with students, interview questions to ask of each other about the topic. Have students meet in pairs or small groups and then report to the other class members. This will provide all students with an opportunity to learn where interest and background knowledge and experience lie.
2. Develop a sentence completion exercise, asking students to complete sentences that are relevant to the topic or concept to be learned about. Analyze students' answers so as to get a sense of students' interests and prior experience.
3. Ask the whole class to brainstorm all the words they associate with a central topic. List all of the words that students give you on the board. Analyze the list of terms. Which ones do not belong and may be misconceptions? How can the words be grouped so that they show how much accurate prior knowledge students have about the country, its people, its climate, its products, and so on? Use the list to predict and plan for how much prior knowledge and what kind of prior knowledge you will need to build or extend with your students.
4. Lead the class in a PREP procedure (see Box 3.3 for directions).

Patty's memoir also seems to suggest that *the purpose for studying or learning a topic should be clear and evident*. She reported spending all her

BOX 3.3. The Prereading Plan (PREP; developed by Judith Langer, 1984)

I. Provide a stimulus such as a poem, picture, or vignette, and ask students what comes to mind.

II. Ask students "what made you think of that?" Lead a discussion of their recollections and thinking.

III. After the discussion, ask students, "Has this discussion made you think of anything else?"

IV. Analyze the quality and quantity of each student's responses, using the following criteria:

- If a student's associations are nonsense words, simple associations, or personal experiences, it is likely that the student has *little prior knowledge* about the topic.
- If a student provides describing characteristics, other attributes, or explanations at a detail level; it is likely that the student has *some prior knowledge* about the topic.
- If a student provides analogies, generalizations, themes, or superordinate concepts, it is likely that the student has *much prior knowledge* about the topic.

time studying, but Dr. Cone pointed out that she was probably wasting a lot of time. He told her that study time had to be purposeful. Teachers can help students to have a sense of purpose in their studying. Instructional time in the classroom should be spent before each reading assignment, helping students to determine their purpose or purposes for reading an assignment or for writing. Perhaps Barbara would remember more of her high school reading if teachers had spent time helping her to develop purposes for her reading.

We acknowledge that mature readers shift purposes while reading. For example, how many times, when searching for a particular recipe, have you decided to prepare something else? We are not saying that students should not ever shift purposes. What we are saying is that purpose for reading should at least be a discussion in content area classrooms. If, per chance, a student does shift purpose, the teacher can talk with the student about that. Why was it appropriate or necessary to shift purposes?

This sort of conversation with your students will help to promote *metacognition.* Metacognition is "thinking about your thinking" and is part of being a successful student. That is, mature and independent learners monitor their learning. They are confident of their learning abilities, are able to recognize when they are confused, and have a repertoire of "fix-up" strategies when they find themselves struggling. Some fix-up strategies include rereading a text, adjusting rate to purpose (such as reading a math problem to solve it more slowly than reading a novel for pleasure), asking questions as you read, anticipating the information or story line to come, and reflecting on reading. Many of these and other instructional strategies we present in this book can be translated into learning strategies, but usually a teacher must work with students to help them learn how and when to apply the strategies.

Teachers help students become independent learners by creating a classroom culture that devotes time, concern, and energy toward explicit instruction of how tasks might be accomplished and why certain strategies might be effective for certain tasks and other strategies might be less effective. The teachers at Benchmark School (Gaskins & Elliott, 1991) developed just such a curriculum for their intermediate-grade students by helping students to monitor their studying behavior and by providing opportunities to discuss appropriate strategies. For example, both Party and Barbara each visited Benchmark at different times and observed the students. Patty saw a fifth-grade class that was at the beginning of a unit on immigration. To activate students' prior knowledge abut this topic, the teacher asked the students to talk about their experiences moving from one place to another. These were summarized in phrases on the chalkboard (e.g., Mark moved from Anchorage, Alaska to Media, Pennsylvania). After the students' experiences were listed, the students and the teacher looked at a map of the world and traced the paths that students had taken to their present homes. The teacher introduced the term *migration* and then the term *immigration* by writing the two words on the board and asking the students to look at the similarities and differences between the two words. She asked the students to pronounce the words and to write them in their notebooks.

What was impressive about the teacher's presentation and the students' response was that the teacher explicitly told the students that they were doing this activity *to activate and organize their prior knowledge*. She also explicitly told them that the term *immigration* was the focal point of the unit they were beginning. Later, when Patty interviewed the students as to why the teacher had done the activity, the students confidently and knowledgeably reported that they were "activating and organizing their prior knowledge to prepare for a new unit on immigration."

Students at Benchmark were also able to recognize occasions when they needed to ***build their prior knowledge*** to understand a passage. For example, Barbara observed sixth graders attempting to solve a problem about pulleys in science class. One of the boys in the class, David, told Barbara that he did not have enough prior knowledge about levers to answer the question. He said he would have to find a text that explained levers and pulleys to read in order to get the information he needed before he could finish the question.

A high school English teacher, Ellen Spitler, has marvelous success with her students as she applies systematic strategy instruction to help the students in her classes become more metacognitive. In both Advanced Placement classes and classes for students who are at risk of failing high school, she implements the same methods. She begins the semester by asking each of her students to write an essay about the strategies they each employ when asked to read something challenging. The assignment asks students to describe (a) the strategies used when encountering "difficult text," (b) the specific "difficult texts" that have required the use of each strategy, and (c) which strategies are the most helpful and the least helpful, and why they are helpful or unhelpful. The essay is graded according to a rubric (see Box 3.4).

Throughout the semester she teaches students about and requires that they use particular learning strategies like *Anticipation Guide*, *Word Splashes*, *Sketch-to-Stretch*, *Dialectic Journals*, *Reading Logs*, *Think Aloud/Along Strategies*, and the *Book Walk* (these strategies are described in chapter 6 in this volume). During the semester, she regularly asks students to reflect on the quality of each strategy; Box 3.5 shows the template she provides students for their reflections. At the end of the semester, she again asks students to write the same essay they wrote at the beginning of the semester. Over three semesters, she has seen tremendous growth in her student's metacognitive awareness and a substantial increase in students' success in school. It's interesting to ponder what these students' literacy autobiographies will be like.

Another idea closely related to having a purpose for reading is *selection.* Naïve learners have a difficult time selecting the most important information to pay attention to in a text, lecture, or other types of presented material. This is one of the key problems with the Internet: So much information is available, how is a naïve student supposed to know which information to pay attention to? No doubt, Patty was having a difficult time with selecting what to study—she thought she had to study everything. We know students who take statistics twice, because the first time through they were learning

BOX 3.4. A Rubric for Scoring a Student's Strategy Use (developed by Ellen Spitler, 2004, personal communication)

The student essays are scored on a continuum from 1 to 5, with 1 being the lowest score and 5 being the highest score:

1. Student names no strategies and seems to have no personal strategies for reading something difficult and challenging.
2. Student is able to describe at least one strategy but does not name it and provides little or no explanation about when and why the strategy is helpful.
3. Student names at least one strategy and describes when and why the strategy is helpful.
4. Student names three or more strategies used when reading something that is very hard or challenging. In addition to naming the strategies, the student discusses the context in which each strategy is likely to be of use and provides examples of when each strategy has been helpful. Student infers why each strategy is helpful.
5. Student names five strategies used when reading something that is very hard or challenging. In addition to naming the strategies, the student discusses the context in which each strategy is likely to be of use and provides examples of when each strategy has been helpful. Student explains why each strategy is helpful.

what the topic was about, and the second time through they could select the appropriate material to study and learn. This is perhaps one of the most important roles for a teacher to play: A teacher can guide students as to how to "distinguish the forest from the trees." To become experts, naïve learners must learn to distinguish between and among different trees and relate

BOX 3.5. Student Strategy Reflection Guide (developed by Ellen Spitler, 2004, personal communication)

I. List the strategy or strategies used to comprehend this text.
II. List reasons for selecting the strategy.
III. On a scale of 1 to 3 (1 = not helpful, 2 = somewhat helpful, and 3 = very helpful), evaluate the helpfulness of the strategy and describe why the strategy was helpful or not helpful.

those to the forest. Each topic in a content area is made up of little ideas that relate to big ideas. Choosing which little ideas to pay attention to, relating those ideas to each other, and making connections to the big ideas is the essence of constructing an understanding of the topic and ultimately of the content area. As a result, beginning a relatively new area of study is challenging and naïve students need a knowledgeable and thoughtful teacher as a guide.

In psychology, this selecting notion is often identified as *selective attention*. The research to date on selective attention is of two types. The first focuses on the processes involved when a learner distinguishes among features of letters or other relatively simple graphic stimuli. The second focuses on the types of rewards (both intrinsic and extrinsic) that learners respond to when distinguishing among those features or when having been involved in a learning task (Gibson & Levin, 1975). Among the conclusions drawn from this research is that learners develop in their abilities to distinguish among features and that prior knowledge interacts with what is being paid attention to.

One of the best ways teachers can guide students in being selective is through the use of instructional strategies such as a graphic organizer. The teacher can lead the construction of a graphic organizer, or, as students become more independent, he or she can have the students do graphic organizers cooperatively or individually. Graphic organizers can take many forms, but they are often in the form of a map, diagram, or chart that shows the relationship between and among ideas being studied. Maps take many shapes; the central idea may be positioned in the center of a page with subordinate ideas connected to it by lines, or the central idea may be placed at the top of the page with subordinate ideas connected by lines under the central idea. Mapping provides a concrete opportunity for the learner to think about the important and less important ideas and their relationships. This is not to suggest that all students' maps would be the same. Maps differ because of each student's prior knowledge, purpose for reading, and the organization of the text. Hence, the map that is produced is not as important as the process of constructing the map. As an example, a map of this chapter is included as a model (see Fig. 3.1).

The composing process also facilitates selection and is another strategy that helps students engage in the selection process. As the student writes a representation of the ideas being studied, the more important and less important ideas must be sorted out. As a student composes, gaps in understanding become readily apparent, and purposes for further study become clear. This

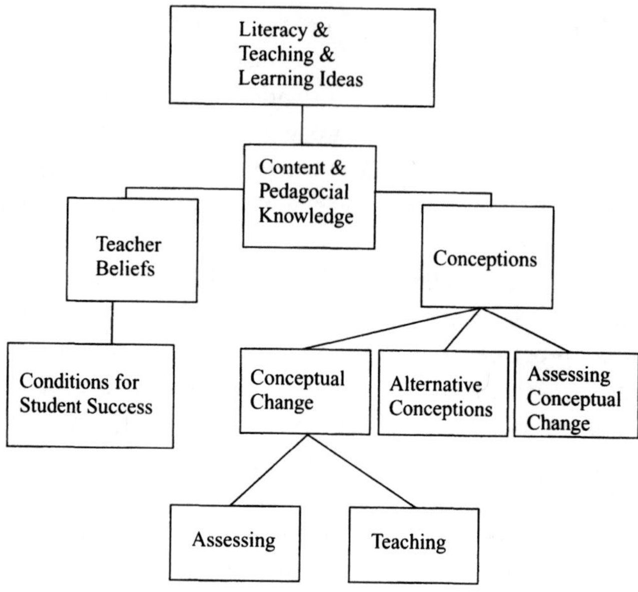

FIG. 3.1. A "map" of chapter 3.

is perhaps one reason why asking young people to write more than a one- or two-sentence answer is important. The only way students can become capable of successfully selecting what to pay attention to is to do it, and writing requires that sort of mental activity. In other words, learners write to know what they know.

Another advantage to using graphic organizers or writing is that doing so requires students to create new mental networks of knowledge. As students draw or write, connections are made between prior knowledge and new information being learned; they are consciously creating and constructing new schema, which becomes future prior knowledge. Recalling the basic ideas learned from Piaget, we can say that new learning, knowledge or schema construction, takes place when the mind makes accommodations in previous understandings or assimilates new information with prior information. These processes take place in the content areas when students actively and intentionally reconstruct their understandings. These reconstructed understandings become long-term memory when students *create a personally meaningful organization.*

One way expert learners create personally meaningful knowledge is to regularly *review* what has been learned. Many students wait until just before the test to review, which limits opportunities to do well on the test and, more importantly, limits the amount of information that is retained in long-term memory. The information stored in long-term memory is the critically important prior knowledge that is needed for later learning; hence learners cannot afford to only get by on tests—learning has to be for the long haul. Regular review results in developing long-term memory when the personally organized information is used and reviewed regularly over a long period of time.

Rewriting notes, drawing maps, and talking about the ideas being studied are worthwhile strategies. As difficult ideas are discussed, written and drawn ideas are reaffirmed in the learner's mind; the more sensible the ideas become, the more likely they will be remembered and stay in long-term memory. Excellent students tend to "hang out" with others who are outstanding. The conversations among successful students tend to be obsessive about the ideas being learned in whatever they are studying. As a graduate student, Patty shared a car with three others who were taking the same courses she was taking. The group drove 4 hours round trip each week and talked about what they were studying during most of the trip. That conversation would not have been very interesting to someone not taking the same courses—but it was an excellent strategy for studying and reviewing.

Barbara's autobiography makes "meaningful organization" clear—if we read between the lines, it seems to us that Barbara organizes her life and study to her love of animals and commitment to her career. For example, she belongs to an organization that is committed to searching for and rescuing lost animals, which requires that she *apply* what she reads. Successful students do this, which makes us aware of the threats to a successful literacy life of those who do not have the space and resources to make a meaningfully organized literacy and learning life. It is a commonly accepted fact of life in the United States that poverty is correlated to poor literacy development. There are lots of reasons for this, but one reason is certainly that those who are poor have limited opportunities to meaningfully integrate and organize literacy activities in their day-to-day activities.

Constructing a meaningful organization, as already described, is related to the idea that successful students *synthesize, integrate*, and *consolidate background knowledge with new information.* These terms are synonyms, meaning that new information is transformed and integrated with a learner's prior understandings to create a new knowledge structure, which becomes the background knowledge a student relies on when broaching the topic again. Knowledge is synthesized when a student engages in the language processes of reading, writing, talking, and creating. Students need time and opportunity during instruction to engage in these sorts of activities. Too often, students are not asked to engage or demonstrate this sort of thinking until the final exam. An example of one activity to push the brain toward this kind of thinking is the following modified cinquain:

Studying
Active, Constructive
Purposeful, Related, Useful
Challenging, Rewarding, Frustrating, Empowering
Learning

This modified cinquain is a five-line poem incorporating students' understanding of the content and their response to the content. Guidelines for writing are the following: (a) Line 1 is a one-word title; (b) Line 2 is two words that describe the title; (c) Line 3 is three words expressing an action; (d) Line 4 is four words expressing a feeling; and (e) Line 5 is another word (a synonym) for the title.

Literacy as a social practice is throughout both Barbara's and Patty's essays. We can hardly imagine a reader who would disagree; however, examples abound of this principle being violated in the classroom, where students are required to work independently and the social nature of learning and literacy is seen as a problem. There are probably two reasons why "the social" is not appropriately incorporated into content area instruction: a teacher's concern about discipline or a teacher's philosophy being closer to a transmission model of learning than a constructivist model. The first issue is out of the purview of this book, but we are confident that discipline is less of a problem when these principles are engaged in the classroom. The second issue is within the domain of this book: Teachers who adhere to the transmission model say to themselves, "if these students would just do what I ask and pay attention to what I teach, they would do well on the test." In other words, these teachers see their students as blank slates on which the content is written. We want to disabuse anyone of such a notion of learning and teaching. One hundred years of research and all of our experience teaches us that learning uses constructivist principles and that teachers who incorporate opportunities for students to make these principles come alive in their lessons contribute to the successful learning of their students.

To reiterate, then, here are the principles that research and experience suggest most significantly contribute to student success:

- Learning has to be meaningful;
- Students' interests are connected to their prior knowledge and experiences;
- The purpose for studying or learning a topic should be clear and evident;
- Metacognition, the act of thinking about one's own thinking, is critical to becoming an independent student;
- Prior knowledge has to be activated, elaborated on, and organized;
- Select information that is related to purposes for reading and learning;
- Create a personally meaningful organization;
- Synthesize, integrate, and consolidate background knowledge with new information; and
- Take advantage of literacy as a social practice.

These principles are the foundation from which instructional decisions are made for selecting and incorporating strategies into content area instruction. Using these guidelines as the standards for selecting appropriate instructional strategies provides students with the scaffolding they need to successfully negotiate meanings in your class. In other words, select instructional strategies that provide space and opportunity for these principles to become visible and alive in your class. These principles do not stand alone; students do not practice these principles and then become learners. Rather, students apply and operationalize these principles when they use strategies under a teacher's tutelage within the context of ideas—concepts and processes that are fundamental to the content being studied. We return to strategies you might adopt and adapt throughout this volume. In the next section, we explore the nature of ideas—the content we want to teach.

CONCEPTIONS: THE CORNERSTONE OF CURRICULUM

Teachers are very special folks. They typically care a great deal about the future generation and want to share ideas about a subject they love with young people. The "stuff" of a course is the curriculum—a systematic collection of ideas, which are gleaned from lots of sources: the courses taken in college, textbooks, personal experiences, colleagues and students, curriculum guides published by school departments, districts, and the state. Here we make suggestions about ways that teachers might think about the ideas they share with their students, which is an important component of the planning to teach process.

We begin by examining the scientific basis of concepts, and we offer definitions of what a concept is and some of the other terms associated with the notion of concept development. Vygotsky, as interpreted by Dixon-Kraus (1996), is one source we draw on. Another source is Herb Klausmeier (1984), an educational philosopher, whose research over many years focused on the development of concepts. We also synthesize research that science educators have conducted about the ways students develop conceptualizations about science.

The next part of the chapter addresses misconceptions. Sometimes students come to the classroom with invented ideas that do not jive with accepted knowledge. Teachers can and should prepare to use instructional interventions to help students challenge these misconceptions and change their intuitive knowledge to scientific knowledge.

Concepts and Conceptions

We emphasize concepts, or conceptions, because they are the ideas that teachers want to teach and students, if given the opportunity, want to learn. Literacy instruction should be embedded in the teaching of conceptions and concepts. There is no better place to begin planning than with a clear idea of the concepts and conceptions around which you want to plan your unit and lessons.

Vygotsky (1978) distinguished between *spontaneous concepts* and *scientific concepts*. Spontaneous concepts are those that are learned from concrete experiences in everyday life. These concepts are acquired naturally. The classic example is Piaget's description of how a child might generalize that all four-legged furry creatures are dogs, and then, through experience, the child begins to distinguish between and among the different features of four-legged furry creatures and learns about cats, cows, and pigs in addition to dogs. Scientific concepts, in contrast, are ideas that are learned in school, are abstract, and are shared by other educated members of a particular culture. He noted that words are critical to thinking about concepts and that "abstract synthesis" (definitions of words) occurs when a learner is able to describe certain traits about the object or event being studied, synthesize those traits, and represent them in a symbol or sign like a word. Words represent scientific concepts, which embody a system or systems of attributes.

A naïve learner is not likely to be able to think in abstract ways (conceptually) about a content area topic or event because the words related to that topic or event are likely to be what Vygotsky termed *heaps*. Teachers know students are at the heaps level if word meanings are not well established, if students have difficulty using the word grammatically, and if the terms are easily forgotten. It is only through engagement with the term or terms in different contexts, genres, and modes (reading, writing, speaking, and listening) that abstract synthesis and long-term learning takes place.

Klausmeier and his colleagues (Klausmeier & Sipple, 1980) studied concept and conceptual development for many years, and their ideas complement Vygotsky: They suggest that long-term learning occurs when concepts are engaged in three ways: concretely and descriptively (in terms of defining attributes), organizationally (in terms of categorization), and formally (in terms of creating an abstract sign; see Klausmeier, Ghatala, & Frayer, 1974).

Both Vygotsky and Klausmeier suggest that a concept is not simply an idea or a word; rather, it is a system of relationships between and among ideas. Science educators (e.g., Strike & Posner, 1985; 1992) distinguish between *concepts* and *conceptions* to refer to concepts that are interrelated and plural in their nature and represent complex units of thought. A concept (as we refer to it in our everyday talk, but not in the Vygotsky or Klausmeier sense) may be a "simple idea," but a conception denotes a sophisticated network of ideas that are central and organized in thought. For example, a conception in social studies could be an individual's view of a subculture or culture; in mathematics, a complex conception could be a set of related principles that explain a theorem or postulate; or in any field a conception could be a statement that represents a major assumption, thesis, or "universal truth" of that field.

For our purposes, then, we see that the definition of a concept is much more elaborate than how the term is used in everyday language. Science educators use the word *conceptions* to help distinguish between the common uses of the word and the complex meaning being suggested here. Vygotsky and Klausmeier would agree; their perspectives are not different from the perspective of science educators. For example, teaching students that camels store food or fat (not water) in their humps is fundamentally different than teaching evolution and refuting creationism, a concept at variance with the scientific conception of evolution. The first concept is a simple idea, one that merely corrects a case of a mistaken fact. The latter concept, however, is a complex conception (which may also be an entrenched belief), supported by related notions. As a learner engages in the complex conception, the schema changes. Accommodation, in the Piagetian sense, takes place; schema is elaborated on and instantiated and learning occurs—all of which may have implications for the learner's future actions. Conceptions, then, are the substance of a learner's schema. It makes sense for teachers to select, organize, and share content with their students in ways that support the development of schema.

To recap, then, we propose that content area literacy instruction takes place as teachers engage students in the process of discovering, interacting with, and negotiating the meaning of complex conceptions. Literacy is not learned and then used in the content area; rather, literacy is used to engage complex conceptions, and as a teacher guides student engagement, students increase their literacy capacity. Teachers help students, through the activities they provide in their classes, to use literacy tools to engage conceptions. This suggests that the content area teacher begins planning for instruction by first articulating and then deconstructing the complex conception. The discussion that follows about mapping conceptions is a helpful tool for beginning to plan.

Mapping Conceptions

Conceptions have a minimum of three related categories (Klausmeier et al., 1974). The first is termed a *superordinate concept*, which English teachers usually identify as a theme in literature and a thesis statement in composition. Like a thesis statement, it is written in a complete sentence (see Box 3.6 for examples of superordinate concepts).

BOX 3.6. Sample Superordinate Concepts

1. Justice is a relative term, which evolves as a culture changes.
2. Native American history, literature, and are are integral to the history, literature, and are of the United States.
3. Communication is relayed through written, verbal, and nonverbal avenues.
4. Vectors and matrices are systems with some of the same properties as the real-number system.

Embedded within the superordinate concept are *coordinate* concepts, which are categories of ideas that are related to the superordinate. The coordinate concepts are put on the map in either a word, phrase, or focus question. Using the first superordinate concept in Box 3.6, a teacher might think of terms like *legal system*, *courts*, *history*, and *cultural changes* as possibilities for the coordinating ideas. Teachers who organize their instruction around inquiries often use focus questions as coordinating concepts.

Embedded within each coordinate concept are subordinate concepts, also referred to as heaps. (Dixon-Kraus, 1996) of ideas that relate to one of the coordinate concepts. These ideas are usually represented in one word or in a phrase and represent the technical or detail vocabulary of the conception.

We provide our conceptual hierarchy map for this chapter in Fig. 3.2. One caveat: As you might imagine, conceptual hierarchy maps are not necessarily the same from one teacher to another. Why? Each teacher's construction of, or understanding, of the author's message is likely to vary according to background knowledge, interest, and purpose for reading.

The conceptual map is a tremendous planning tool. A problem that many of us have when we teach is choosing the activities and resources we want to share with our students. We typically lack criteria for making decisions. For example, a new video comes in and the librarian thinks it might fit in the unit you are doing. How do you decide if you should spend the time showing the video? Does it really relate to your unit? Having mapped the conception of your unit provides a critical framework to view the video and to make a decision about its relevance or appropriateness.

The map is also helpful because teachers can "play" with the ideas by mapping them, either by working from the top down or from the bottom up. The direction chosen is not important. If you have a high degree of expertise in the topic, begin with the superordinate concept; if you are less expert, it may be easier to begin with the details (the heaps). If working from the top down, begin with the superordinate concept, formulate categories, and list the details related to each of the categories. If working from the bottom up, begin by making a list of relevant details, categorize the ideas, and then create or choose an appropriate superordinate concept. This playing with ideas and discovering or making clear the relationships between and among them deepens and makes clearer your own understanding of what you want to teach.

As each of us has become more facile at developing and using conceptual maps, we can't imagine planning to teach without them. The map-making

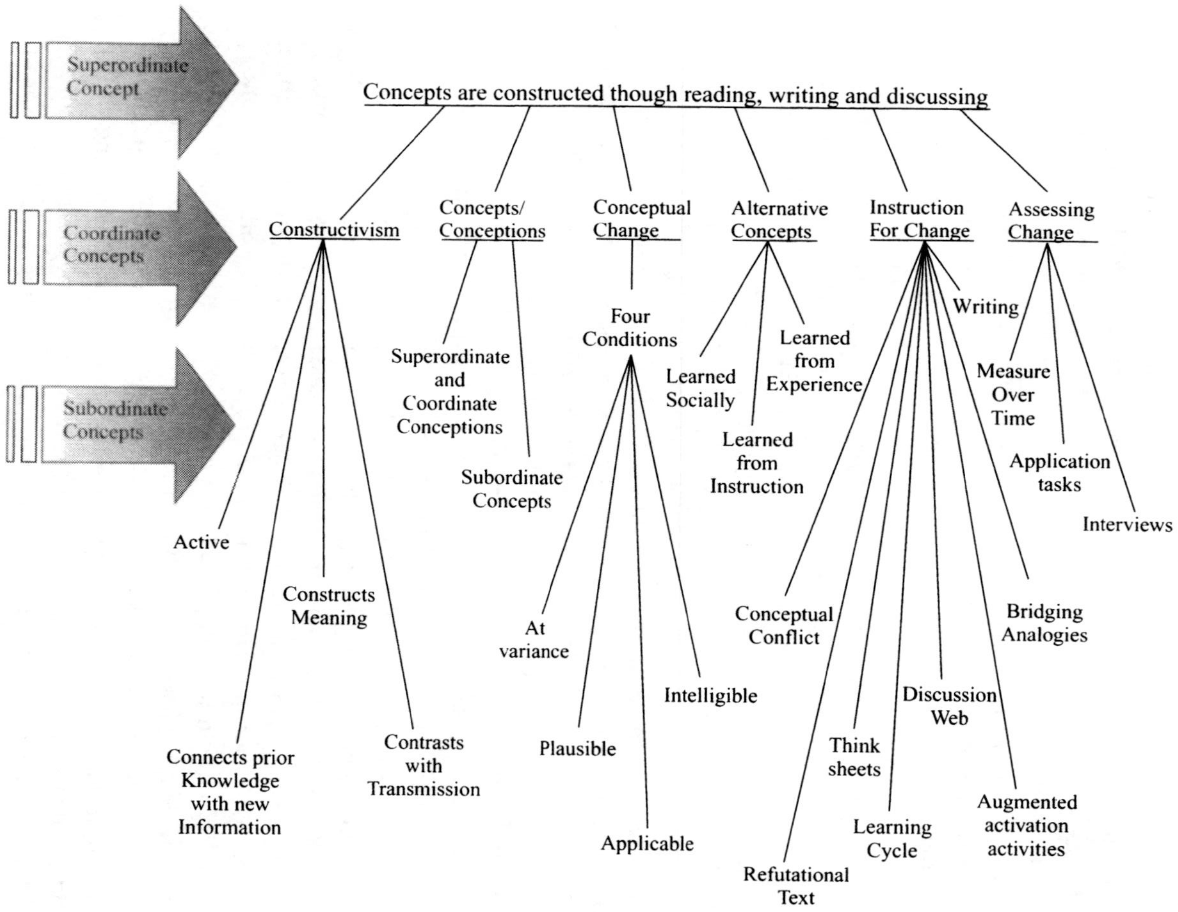

Superordinate Concept
Coordinate Concepts
Subordinate Concepts

Concepts are constructed though reading, writing and discussing

- Constructivism
  - Active
  - Connects prior Knowledge with new Information
  - Constructs Meaning
  - Contrasts with Transmission
- Concepts/ Conceptions
  - Superordinate and Coordinate Conceptions
  - Subordinate Concepts
- Conceptual Change
  - Four Conditions
    - At variance
    - Plausible
    - Applicable
    - Intelligible
- Alternative Concepts
  - Learned Socially
  - Learned from Instruction
  - Learned from Experience
- Instruction For Change
  - Conceptual Conflict
  - Refutational Text
  - Think sheets
  - Learning Cycle
  - Discussion Web
  - Augmented activation activities
  - Bridging Analogies
  - Writing
- Assessing Change
  - Measure Over Time
  - Application tasks
  - Interviews

FIG. 3.2. Conceptual hierarchy for Chapter 3.

process is exciting. As conceptual maps are developed, teachers end up rethinking what they plan to teach, and content they thought they knew well becomes new again; never before thought of possibilities for activities, resources, experiments, and assignments emerge. There are other reasons why the conceptual map is such a powerful and generative planning activity.

One reason is that creating the map requires the teacher to think in a structurally coherent framework for the unit being planned. The superordinate concept is written in a complete sentence. The grammar of a sentence provides a subject (what the unit is to be about), a verb (what action is called on to engage the subject), and an object or objects (these will most likely be the coordinate concepts). Coherent units are likely to be more easily engaged by students. The complete sentence provides a launching pad for providing coherent activities, resources, and assignments.

The conceptual map also provides a template for evaluating the quality of instruction during the unit. If, as the unit progresses, students' activities and work emphasize one aspect of the superordinate concept more than another, then activities can be designed or resources selected to broaden their perspective. Similarly, if, on reflection and self-evaluation, the teacher recognizes that there are limited resources or activities regarding a particular aspect of the conceptual framework, adjustments can be made to the daily lesson plan. The teacher might add materials (if they can be found), downplay the importance of that particular concept, or turn that branch of the map into an area for student inquiry.

The conceptual framework also provides a means for checking to be sure that discussions and activities provide ample opportunities for students to work at all levels of the conception. A common complaint among teachers is that students get stuck on details and do not relate details to categories or to big ideas. The template provided by a conceptual map provides direction for guiding discussion and other activities toward all aspects and components of the superordinate concept.

Some teachers, when learning about using conceptions as an organizing framework for units of instruction, are concerned that the map might be limiting. They ask: Aren't we encouraging convergent thinking rather than divergent and creative thinking? We don't think so. The map is merely a planning tool. New concepts or alternative ways to organize concepts are likely to emerge as students and teacher interact around the ideas. The map can always be changed as new ideas and resources are discovered. Teachers who value student inquiry place questions in the coordinate level of the map and articulate the key conceptual vocabulary in the subordinate part of the map that they expect their students to learn and use while conducting their inquiries to answer the questions.

Teachers use the map to get a clear picture of their own construction of the ideas they want to teach. A conceptual map is not cast in stone. Two colleagues teaching the same topic are likely to create two different maps about the same body of knowledge. This is the nature of cognition. Likewise, authors are likely to construct the same body of knowledge in ways that are different than either those of the teacher or the students. It isn't surprising then, that the resources we ask students to read or view are constructed in conceptually different ways. Chapters 4 and 5 look at the resources we ask students to read—that is, textbooks, trade books, digital texts, and the media. Comprehension and learning is made easier when teachers are skilled at selecting concept-related reading resources with their students.

Learning as Assimilation and Accommodation: Conceptual Change

Piaget (1950) taught the lessons of *assimilation* and *accommodation*. Assimilation occurs when a learner already has ideas related to the new conception, and all that is needed is for previous ideas to be linked with new ones. It is quite likely, however, that students will have existing knowledge that is at variance with the new conception and accommodation will be needed.

Accommodation occurs when the learner restructures or changes his or her preconceptions, resulting in a conceptual change (Hewson & Hewson, 1983; Posner, Strike, Hewson, & Gertzog, 1982). Conceptual change is difficult; it is the hardest teaching you will ever do. Several studies have shown that learners hang on to their previous understandings with great tenacity (Pfundt & Duit, 1991). Because student's existing conceptions are so resistant to change, it is worth our while to consider conditions for conceptual change.

Conditions for Conceptual Change

Science education researchers are on the forefront of considering what is necessary for conceptual change to occur (Posner et al., 1982) and posit that there are four conditions that must be met for conceptual change to occur. First, the learner's existing conception must be shown to be at *variance* with the scientific or accepted conception. The learner must become dissatisfied with his or her prior understandings. The new concept must be seen as *dysfunctional*, because students do not accommodate new concepts (change their structures when needed) when assimilation (merely adding ideas to their prior knowledge) is still reasonable.

Second, the new conception must be shown to be ***intelligible***. Learners can begin to explore a new concept only if it makes sense to them. Interference with learning occurs when the new concept is incomprehensible to the learner. Often students do not understand a new concept because they are unable to visualize what the world would be like if it were true, or what the new conception really implies.

Third, the new conception must appear to be *plausible*. The learner must see the new conception as a possible version of the truth. This is more likely to occur if the new conception is consistent with the learner's other well-established beliefs, and if the new conception is shown to have the potential to solve problems.

Researchers used to (and sometimes still do) call students' ideas that are inconsistent with commonly accepted or scientific conceptions *misconceptions*. We recognize, however, that concepts change as knowledge evolves, and what may be considered an acceptable conception today may be considered a misconception tomorrow. Furthermore, misconceptions can represent an individual's attempt to explain an observation, or they often represent knowledge that is at least partially acceptable, and so other less pejorative terms are used. These terms include *alternative conceptions*, *alternative frameworks*, *naïve theories*, *preconceptions*, or *intuitive theories*.

In this text, we use the term *misconception* to refer to simple cases of mistaken belief. We use these other terms interchangeably when we refer to restructuring complex conceptions, or when the term *misconception* does not seem accurate. By providing examples, in these next sections we show how common cases of alternative conceptions or misconceptions are in all content areas, and we discuss ways to teach and test for conceptual change.

Alternative Conceptions

Researchers in fields such as reading education, science education, social studies education, and mathematics education know that many concepts (and conceptions) have associated alternative conceptions (Pfundt & Duit, 1991). Two common examples include one from social studies—the view that the

Tea Act was simply an unfair tax by the British versus the view that the Tea Act was intended to save the British East India Company and benefit the colonists—and one from science—Newtonian mechanics (objects move by outside forces) versus impetus theory (objects move by internal forces). Alternative conceptions like these are very common among students in all content areas and in all grades. Frequently, they persist into adulthood.

How Alternative Conceptions Affect Learning. Students' alternative conceptions are important to pay attention to for several reasons. First, researchers have found that having the wrong prior knowledge is more debilitating to learning than having no prior knowledge at all (Alvermann, Smith & Readence, 1985; Lipson, 1984). It is more difficult to change an existing conception than to acquire new information. Physical education teachers, for example, know that it is a much greater challenge to teach someone a tennis stroke if that person has been doing the stroke incorrectly prior to formal instruction. Perhaps you can think of a skill, a process, a concept, or a strategy that you learned incorrectly and how difficult it was for you to "unlearn" it. Alternative conceptions have the same detrimental effect. Alternative conceptions are also extremely tenacious and resistant to change, despite ordinary kinds of instruction (Champagne, Gunstone, & Klopfer, 1983). Instructional strategies like lecture, recitation-discussion, oral reading from the regular textbook, and question-answer worksheets have been shown to be ineffective in affecting students' conceptual change. In short, researchers know that traditional methods of instruction do not affect the *unlearning* of alternative conceptions.

Origins of Alternative Conceptions. Researchers find that students' misconceptions or alternative conceptions can be acquired in three different ways (Pfundt & Duit, 1991). First, they can be acquired *physically*, through an individual's interactions with the environment. For example, a student may observe that grass grows faster in the summer. He or she may try to explain this observation by reasoning that plants grow faster in warmer environments, or that plants eat more minerals in the summer, which makes them grow faster. Naïve theories like these represent a student's attempts to make sense and to form personal theories of real-life phenomenon.

Another way alternative conceptions may be acquired is *socially*, through interactions with peers, family, and the media. For example, the misconception that ostriches bury their heads in the sand is reinforced by a magazine advertisement for a life insurance company that uses a photograph of an ostrich burying its head in the sand. Roadrunner cartoons that show a pursued victim running off the edge of a cliff, continuing in a straight line, and then falling straight down reinforce a common alternative conception in physics contradicted by Newton's laws of motion.

A third way that alternative conceptions can be acquired is *instructionally*, through inaccurate texts or teachers. Textbooks, for example, may be out of date, biased, or simply incorrect. Often the illustrations in textbooks are inaccurate because graphic artists do the artwork and have no background in the topic (Iona, 1990). Students will most likely remember misleading diagrams long after they have forgotten details from the text (Iona, 1990). In the model of learning in which teachers act as transmitters of knowledge (rather than as coinquirers or constructors of knowledge), teachers can pass on alternative conceptions to their students if they are unsure of the correct conceptions themselves.

It is important to be aware of the sources of students' alternative conceptions because their origins may make a difference in how easy or how difficult it is to change them. For example, if a young child's father tells her that ostriches bury their heads in the sand, but her teacher denies this, the child may be more inclined to believe her parent and therefore less ready to give up the alternative conception. In contrast, a child may refute a parent who provides the accepted conception in favor of the authority of the teacher who mistakenly stated an alternative conception.

Examples of Alternative Conceptions. A plethora of naïve theories or misconceptions exist in all fields. Recognizing this phenomenon, we asked our students (preservice and in-service content area teachers) to list the misconceptions they know of in their discipline. Our students had no trouble coming up with many misconceptions they had heard. We were surprised to find that these alternative conceptions consist not only of preconceptions about substantive concepts within the discipline but they also include misconceptions about the content area itself. In other words, students have preconceptions about topics within a discipline, but they also have naïve conceptions about the nature of the discipline. These misconceptions often represent value judgments, not facts (e.g., a career in art is only for those who have innate talent; science and math is a field for men; or history consists of memorizing facts and dates). We consider these to be misconceptions because these beliefs can affect the way people function in and relate to a discipline.

To help demonstrate the pervasiveness of alternative conceptions, we list some common examples by content areas in Box 3.7. In some cases, we include the accepted conception in parentheses. As you read these, reflect on whether you have ever heard of these misconceptions, and see if you can add to the list.

BOX 3.7 Common Misconceptions by Content Area

Science

- Science is a process of passive observation and memorization of facts. (Science is an active process in which knowledge changes and evolves.)
- Plants get their food from water and minerals in the soil; they "eat" through their roots. (Plants manufacture their own food through photosynthesis.)
- Popular fiction, including movies and television, frequently depicts encounters between dinosaurs and cave men. (Cave people did not live at the same time as dinosaurs.)

Social Studies

- American political parties are provided for in the constitution. (The Constitution does not have any provision for political organizations.)
- The battle of Bunker Hill was fought at Bunker Hill. (The battle was actually fought on Breed's Hill, a smaller mound nearby. Breed's Hill was, unfortunately for the Americans, much more vulnerable to attack.)
- The Liberty Bell was rung when independence was declared on July 4, 1776; it rang so hard and long that it cracked. (There is no evidence the bell was rung when independence was declared. In any case, it would not have been rung on July 4 because independence was declared on July 2.)

English

- Poetry must rhyme. (Many famous poems do not rhyme.)
- Every production of a play is the same every time it is produced. (Different directors will interpret the author and present a play differently than others.)

- A newspaper article is true and accurate. (Reporters are not necessarily authorities or experts on the subject they write about; articles are often wrong, as was the case when the papers printed "Dewey Wins" when in actuality Truman was victorious.)

Physical Education-Exercise Science

- You must not swim for 1/2 hour to 1 hour after eating a meal. (The American Red Cross has deleted this rule and now states that it does not matter if you eat before you swim.)
- Muscle will turn to fat if you stop exercising. (Muscle cells cannot be converted to fat; rather, muscles will atrophy when not used.)
- Physical fitness is hereditary and fixed. (Physical fitness can be improved through regular exercise.)

Art

- Impressionism is pictures of dots. (Impressionism is a study of how light affects objects and color.)
- Artistic talent is innate. (Talent can be acquired through practice and investigation.)
- Illustration is not art. (all art illustrates.)

Music

- Nero played the violin while Rome burned. (In fact, the violin was not invented during the time of the Roman Empire.)
- The initials m.m. in front of the metronomic marking on a score stands for "metronomic marking." (They stand for "Maelzel's metronome," the inventor of the metronome.)
- Violinists only play classical music. (Violinists play a wide variety of music; e.g., the Kronos String Quartet does a rendition of Jimi Hendrix's Purple Haze and Charlie Daniels plays country violin.)

Home Economics-Human Resources and Family Living

- Home economics is just cooking and sewing. (The field encompasses other areas such as child care and finance, and it has been renamed to reflect this broader scope.)
- A watched pot never boils. (Try watching sometime and see.)
- A tomato is a vegetable. (A tomato is a fruit.)

Foreign Language

- The Spanish alphabet has the same letters as the English alphabet. (The Spanish alphabet has no *w* and uses it only in writing a foreign language.)
- French spoken in Canada is the same French as the French spoken in France. (This statement does not account for regional dialects.)
- German is a Romance language, as is English. (English is a Germanic language.)

Mathematics–Statistics

- A line is always straight. (Lines can be crooked.)
- You can subtract infinity from infinity and get zero. (Infinity is not a number.)
- The chances of getting a head in a coin toss are greater after several tails in a row. (Odds do not "improve" like this.)

Discovering Students' Alternative Conceptions and Preconceptions. Experienced teachers are usually well aware of common alternative conceptions associated with the concepts they teach. There are, however, methods for discovering common naïve theories or related acceptable preconceptions.

We have already described suggestions for ascertaining students' prior knowledge. Those same ideas work well if, as the activity is conducted, you keep a special ear tuned to student's statements that suggest a misconception. Most likely, it is not appropriate to correct misconceptions during the preassessment activity; rather, make note of the alternative conceptions expressed by students and make plans to provide experiences and information to replace the misconception during instruction.

Conversations with students also reveal common alternative conceptions. As you talk with students about the topic being studied, such as "Why do you think so?" and "What makes you think that?," Probe the students' answers further by asking for evidence that supports those suppositions or by asking for logical applications of the alternative conception.

Other methods of preassessment will occur to you; the important point is to get a sense of what students already know and have experienced related to the concepts being engaged. Those students with lots of prior knowledge will be able to carry their concept development further than those with little prior knowledge. Those with misconceptions will need specific and explicit instruction to change their understandings.

INSTRUCTIONAL IMPLICATIONS OF ALTERNATIVE CONCEPTIONS

We've said before that traditional methods of instruction (such as listening to a lecture and reading the textbook) are ineffective in changing misconceptions. There are, however, types of text and text-based strategies (which compensate for inadequacies in ordinary text) that are effective in changing students' alternative conceptions. In this next section, we describe and give examples of those effective strategies.

Effective Instruction for Conceptual Change

Educators in all content areas are concerned about addressing students' alternative conceptions. Barbara and her colleagues examined instructional studies that were done on science topics to address alternative conceptions (Guzzetti et al., 1993). They chose science as the area of focus because most studies of conceptual change use science topics, and because investigators from several scientific fields conducted these studies, they provided a broad perspective. The members of her team were researchers in reading education, science education, and educational psychology, and they explored the effects of a plethora of instructional strategies on students' alternative conceptions.

Specific instructional strategies that are effective in promoting conceptual change in science were identified by meta-analysis (Guzzetti et al., 1993). Meta-analysis is a way of synthesizing all past research on a topic by using the statistics from those studies to determine an average effect for each strategy (Glass, 1976). Results show the relative efficacy of an instructional strategy (in comparison with a control group or another strategy) and show how the efficacy of the strategy might differ in different circumstances (like for students at various grade levels).

Four strategies from reading education and three instructional approaches from science education were found to be effective in promoting conceptual change. All the effective strategies had one common element—*cognitive conflict*. In other words, each effective strategy was designed to cause the learner to become dissatisfied with his or her prior belief and take the new conception into account.

Effective Strategies From Reading Education. One instructional strategy that shows the most consistent and long-term effects in promoting conceptual change is *refutational text*. Refutational text is a passage that identifies the misconception or alternative conception and directly refutes it by explaining the accepted conception. Students who read refutational text tend to maintain their learning over time (Guzzetti et al., 1993; Hynd, Qian, Ridgeway, & Pickle, 1991).

Why is refutational text effective? There are several possible reasons. First, researchers (Dole, Niederhauser, & Hayes, 1990) speculate that the power of refutational text may be that it helps readers to identify when text ideas are different from their own preexisting ideas. This may cause students to become dissatisfied with their alternative conceptions (cognitive conflict), and it may motivate learners to test the plausibility and applicability of new conceptions. Second, Barbara and her colleagues found that students prefer refutational expository text for learning complex concepts (Guzzetti, Hynd, & Williams, 1995). Students may be more able to learn from text they prefer. Third, the author of a refutational text attempts to interact more with the reader by taking his or her ideas into account. Hence, refutational text enhances the transactive process of making meaning between reader and author. Finally, refutational text also provides an especially authoritative view of "correct" information that the reader may find more credible than nonrefutational text.

Refutational text may be varied in its structure. It may be a *narrative* (story) structure, or it may represent an *expository* (informational without dialogue) structure. Most textbooks are written as *nonrefutational expository* text and contain no mention or refutation of common misconceptions. *Narrative refutational* text is effective with elementary students, but it is unnecessary at the junior and senior high school levels. Secondary students can change their conceptions by reading refutational material without altering the text to reflect a story structure (Guzzetti et al., 1993; this is not to say, however, that secondary students do not appreciate or learn from narrative text; in fact, we encourage teachers to use narrative text in content areas). The most common way of writing refutational text is to cite the alternative conception, and then the refutation, but the refutation may appear first, followed by the alternative conception. The order of the refutation appears to make no difference (Maria &

BOX 3.8. Sample Refutational Text in Social Studies

A common misconception students have is that Lincoln's Emancipation Proclamation freed the slaves. A social studies textbook by Kisjord (1986) refutes this alternative conception:

> Beginning January 1, 1863, he [Lincoln] declared, the slaves belonging to persons in rebellion against the United States were free. The Proclamation did not free slaves in the border states or even those in parts of the South, such as Tennessee, that were under Union control. Lincoln still felt he did not have constitutional authority to free slaves belonging to loyal planters.
>
> Since it could not be enforced in the South, Lincoln's Proclamation did not actually free any slaves. It was a war measure, designed to hurt the Confederacy by encouraging slaves in the rebellious states to escape and deny their labor to the southern war effort. The proclamation also gave a moral tone to the war. For many northerners the conflict became a crusade to rid the nation of slavery. (p. 286)

MacGinitie, 1987). Some examples of refutational text are given in Boxes 3.8, 3.9, and 3.10.

Examples like these illustrate how easily refutational text can be constructed. Because other methods are also effective, is it worth it to look for or to write refutational text? Are students more likely to read refutational text than their ordinary textbooks? What do students think about refutational text?

These are the questions Barbara and her colleagues asked high school students (Guzzetti et al., 1995). Students were asked to read three passages on one topic. One passage was selected from their regular textbook, representing nonrefutational expository text. Another passage was constructed as refutational expository text. The third passage was written as refutational narrative text.

When students compared these texts, they overwhelmingly reported that they preferred the expository refutational text. Readers preferred the refutational expository text because it presented both sides of an issue; it helped them think through to the right idea; it gave them some historical background; and it presented the major concepts in a straightforward way. Students liked having the alternative conception pointed out to them with an explanation of why it was wrong, either because they themselves had the

BOX 3.9. Sample Refutational Text in Physical Science

A common alternative conception in physics is that objects have an internal force that causes them to move. Researchers (Hynd, McWhorter, Phares, & Suttles, 1991) wrote this passage to refute that naïve theory:

Newton's Ideas About Motion

Every time we experience an event, we may develop ideas that help us predict what will happen the next time we experience it. We may have an idea about the motion of objects that we learn from our daily lives. We may even use the idea to predict what will happen to other objects in the same situations. But scientists have found that many people have the wrong ideas about the motion of objects.

The wrong ideas are like the theory of impetus people believed in before the time of Sir Isaac Newton. People who believed in impetus theory thought that motion must have a cause. When they couldn't see any reason for an object to keep going, change its direction, or stop, they decided that there must be a force inside of the object which is put there when the object was set in motion. They called this inner force impetus.

Newton showed us that impetus theory was wrong. According to Newton, an object that is carried is in motion, even if it appears to be at rest in relation to the person carrying it. That is why when a car slows or comes to a stop, the objects inside the car continue to move forward.

It is incorrect to think that a rolling object stops or that an object moving through the air falls because of the loss of inner force. Newton explained that a moving object comes to a stop or begins to fall because outside (external) forces act to change the speed or direction of the object's motion. A ball rolling across the floor is slowed by friction, a force that acts in the opposite direction of the ball's motion.

Finally, according to Newton, after an object is put in motion, it moves in a straight line when no force is acting on it. For an object to change directions, an outside force must act on it. For a ball to move in a circle, an outside force such as a string must act on it. The string pulls on the ball and keeps it from moving in a straight line. (Conference Handout)

alternative conception, or because it enabled them to explain to someone else who had the alternative conception why it was faulty. Students also thought that knowing the alternative conception and why it was wrong would enable them to avoid being convinced of the naïve theory by someone else later on.

BOX 3.10. Sample Refutational Text in Physical Education

A common preconception students have in swimming is that the flutter kick is used both in the freestyle and in the backstroke. A student in content literacy (K. Smith, personal communication, September 14, 1992) wrote this refutational text to refute this misconception:

> Many people believe that in swimming the kick used in freestyle called a "flutter kick" is the same kick used in the backstroke. This is not true. The actual kick used in the backstroke is called the "back crawl kick." The difference between these two kicks has to do with the "flick," when you have your leg bent or straight. For the back crawl kick, the leg is straight as it thrusts downward into the water, and it bends and flicks up toward the surface. The opposite motion is used for the freestyle flutter kick. Many people can improve their backstroke by using the proper kick.

A second instructional strategy is an *augmented activation activity*, which is a demonstration designed to cause surprise or incongruity in the mind of the learner (Kintsch, 1986). The strategy causes the learner to question his or her prior beliefs by showing the alternative conception to be inapplicable and by showing the applicability of the accepted conception. The demonstration is supplemented by a verbal refute of the commonly associated alternative conception, and a direction to the correct information in the text. Augmented activation activities should, of course, also be supplemented by a guided discussion between students and between the teacher and the students.

Augmented activation activities do more than just activate the learner's prior knowledge. They also assist in correcting preconceptions that are at variance with the accepted conception. These demonstrations produce cognitive conflict by simultaneously showing the inapplicability of the naïve conception while demonstrating the applicability of the accepted conception.

Examples of augmented activation activities from two content areas are provided in Boxes 3.11 and 3.12.

A third instructional strategy is to provide students with a *Think Sheet*. A think sheet is a prior knowledge monitoring activity that helps students contrast their preinstructional ideas with ideas from the text (Dole & Smith, 1987). It is intended to serve as a prereading, guided reading, and postreading activity. Discussion between students and between the teacher and students

BOX 3.11. Example of Augmented Activation Activity in Home Economics–Life Management

> Debra Waitze Gray (personal communication, October 6, 1992) gave this example:
>
> To change the naïve theory that there are "men's jobs" and "women's work," a home economics teacher we know regularly brings in guest speakers or photos of and interviews with women who hold such positions as physicians, heavy equipment operators, pilots, garbage collectors, fire fighters, police officers, etc. Guest speakers and interviews also include examples of males who are day care operators, kindergarten teachers, nurses, and homemakers. Students' preconceptions and stereotypes are discussed in light of the experiences of these non-traditional role models.

may conclude the activity. A think sheet is partially constructed by the teacher and partially constructed by the students. Here are the procedures:

- Formulate a central question about the concept under study (When the method is used in an inquiry approach, students generate their own central question.)
- Record the question at the top of a sheet of paper.
- Divide the remainder of the sheet into three columns. In the first column (labeled "My Questions"), students record questions they have that are stimulated by the central query. In the second column (labeled "My Ideas"), students record their preinstructional ideas about the central question. These two columns are completed before students read the text.
- In the third column (labeled "Text Ideas"), students read the text and record ideas from the text that answer their questions and confirm or deny their prereading ideas.

Think sheets contain the element of cognitive conflict common to effective strategies that produce conceptual change. This strategy helps to make students aware of their preconceptions and contrasts those preconceptions with correct conceptions in the text. Areas of discordance can be revealed, and then they may be corrected through activities such as discussion, experiments, observations, and so forth.

Examples of think sheets from two content areas are provided in Box 3.13 and Box 3.14.

BOX 3.12. Example of Augmented Activation Activity in Chemistry

Many students have the alternative conception that as pressure increases volume increases. In fact, there is an inverse relationship between pressure and volume on a given mass of gas when temperature is held constant. This principle is known as Boyle's Law.

The associated alternative conception results from students' personal experiences in blowing air into a balloon and watching it inflate and grow larger. Students think that the amount of air and its pressure inside the balloon increases, causing the volume of the gas to increase. They do not think about the air pressure outside of the balloon.

Two augmented activation activities were designed by a chemistry teacher to overcome this naïve conception (Guzzetti, 1990). To create incongruity with the naïve conception, the teacher placed a balloon inside a glass jar and vacuumed out the air inside of the jar. The balloon grew larger as the air pressure decreased. Then the teacher conducted a similar demonstration with a can of shaving cream by placing the can inside the glass jar and vacuuming out the air inside the jar. The gas inside the can of shaving cream expanded, causing the contents to explode out of the can and filling the glass jar as the air pressure decreased.

The students' reactions of surprise were discussed in light of their alternative theory. The teacher directly refuted the common preconception and drew attention to the accepted conception (Boyle's Law) by referring to information in the text. The demonstration caused the students to become consciously aware of their naïve theory and become dissatisfied with its predictive power and applicability.

The *discussion web*, the fourth instructional strategy, is a structured discussion that uses a graphic to record students' positions around a central issue or concept from the text (Alvermann, 1991). Starting with the central concept, students work in groups of two to determine a pro or con stance in agreement or disagreement with the statement or question about the central concept. Students are required to support their opinions with evidence from the text. Individuals are asked to record the reasons for their opinions on the graphic.

Once a group of two students has formed an opinion, they are asked to join another group of two. Their task is to convince the others in the group

BOX 3.13. Think Sheet for Literature

Tara Wyatt (personal communication, October 6, 1992) used this sheet:

Central Question: What are the Essential Attributes of True Love According to Shakespeare?

My Questions	My Ideas	Text Ideas
What is true love?	True love is good sex. True love is marriage. True love is appearance.	True love is loyalty and sacrifice (Othello). True love is developed between mature people (As You Like It).

of their positions and to reach a consensus among the group members. Following their decision, group members are asked to join another group of four and, in turn, convince those group members of their stance and reach consensus among the larger group. Because the discussion "webs" in this way, it is called a discussion web. Finally, the group of eight members elects a group spokesperson who reports their position and rationale to the total class.

The teacher's role in the discussion web is to provide the central concept from the text, to assist students in forming and supporting their opinions, and to facilitate discussion. The teacher moves among the groups during their deliberations, asking leading and directing questions. These probes from the

BOX 3.14. Think Sheet for Physical Education

Kathy Smith (personal communication, October 6, 1992) used this sheet:

Central Question: What is the Proper Technique for an Underwater Swim?

My Questions	My Ideas	Text Ideas
How many breaths do I take before diving? Do I hold my breath the entire distance? Do I breathe out through my nose as I swim?	Take two or three breaths before swimming underwater.	Take only one deep breath and hold it the entire distance.

BOX 3.15. Discussion Web for Physics

When an object is put in motion, is there a force behind it?		
	Reasons	
Yes		**No**

teacher assist students to locate information in the text that either supports or refutes their positions.

The discussion web is different than other types of discussion in several ways. First, the web requires and facilitates structured discussion, not only between students and the teacher but also among students. Students are required to persuade each other to take their positions. Second, the strategy makes students aware of any preconceptions they might have that are at variance with the accepted conception by requiring support for their answers from the text. In this respect, the discussion web includes the element of cognitive conflict common to strategies that are effective in producing conceptual change. Finally, the discussion web transcends mere recitation of answers by encouraging debate and critical thinking.

An example of a graphic for a discussion web in physics is taken from Alvermann and Hynd (1989) and is shown in Box 3.15.

Concept-oriented reading instruction is a fifth instructional strategy. Guthrie, Van Meter, Hancock, Anderson, and McCann (1998) promote reading instruction that is integrated with content concepts. Their studies focus on children in Grades 3 through 5, but they follow the same principles we have already discussed. The first step is for the teacher to choose a theme or concept, and then lots of trade books and textbooks are laid out on tables for children to peruse. After looking over the materials, the children and teacher make a graphic representation of what they have read, labeling illustrations of the text and creating models based on the information gleaned. Next the students generate questions, which are then answered through continued reading, experimenting, or observing. The remarkable contribution made by Guthrie and Cox (2001) is that their research shows that students who engage in this type of instruction become significantly better readers and also learn significantly more and better concepts.

Effective Strategies for Conceptual Change From Science Education

Science education researchers also suggest strategies to promote conceptual change. We share three of these strategies and suggest that they can be easily adapted to other content areas. For the *Learning Cycle* was first introduced as a way of teaching science (Atkin & Karplus, 1962; Karplus & Thier, 1967; Lawson, 1967). It has also been used in English (Lawson & Kral, 1985) and social studies, including economics and history (Fuller, 1982). This lesson plan has a good research base (Lawson & Thompson, 1988; Lawson & Worsnop, 1992) and may be expanded to other content areas.

The Learning Cycle consists of three stages. In the first stage, *exploration*, provide students with materials and settings to allow for manipulation and inquiry with the concepts under study. Involve students in initial experiences to present new information that causes dissatisfaction with their prior conceptions.

Next, *introduce the concept or key terms*. In this phase, introduce the new concept, thereby providing a new way of thinking about the experiences students had in the exploration stage. This phase includes introduction of new terms or vocabulary, the language students need to articulate their changing conceptions.

The final phase is *concept application*. In this stage, additional experiences are presented that to provide students experiences that enable self-realization and extrapolation of the new concepts. Refutational expository text may be incorporated to serve as confirmation of students' ideas.

The Learning Cycle is most effective when the cognitive conflict is emphasized, which is another reason to include refutational expository text in the approach. Students may predict outcomes, record their predictions, and compare results of their experiences to their predictions through the course of the activities. By doing so, students are made aware of their preconceptions that are at variance with the scientific conception, thereby creating cognitive conflict. Refutational text following these companions assist students in clarifying their observations.

An example of the Learning Cycle applied to biology addresses the naïve theory of spontaneous generation, which is life produced from no life (A. Lawson, personal communication, October 20, 1992). In the exploration stage, students are asked to articulate their theories of what happens to organisms when they die. Typical answers include responses such as "They rot" and "They fall apart." Students are then asked to predict conditions that would influence this breakdown. Common responses include variables like heat, water, alcohol, salt, and sunlight.

To test these hypotheses, students conduct experiments to test the effects of at least three of these conditions on the decay of a cooked piece of fish, using water in one experiment. Students' resulting data are then recorded on the whiteboard by listing the conditions varied, and recording a plus (to indicate an increase in breakdown), a minus (to indicate a decrease in breakdown), or a zero (to indicate the condition had no effect on decay). Results reveal that water produces more breakdown, salt impedes a breakdown, and heat increases the breakdown.

During their experiments, students may observe flies or maggots on the dead fish. Some students will think they came from the dead fish. This raises the possibility of *spontaneous generation*, or *abiogenesis*, terms the teacher introduces to help students explain their hypothesis. This represents the concept or term introduction phase of the Learning Cycle. At this point, the teacher can raise questions like, "If the maggots did not come from the dead fish, where did they come from?" Some students will speculate that flies came in and laid eggs on the dead fish, producing the maggots. This hypothesis produces the possibility of *biogenesis* (life from life), a term the teacher introduces to help students articulate their predictions.

In the *application phase*, students test their hypothesis by conducting a classic experiment. In this example, students are given two hunks of cooked fish. One piece is covered with cheesecloth, but the other is exposed to air. The prediction for those holding the naïve theory of spontaneous generation is that maggots will appear on both pieces of fish. Those who maintain the conception of biogenesis will predict that maggots will appear only on the exposed piece of fish. When flies and maggots appear only on the exposed fish, students who held the naïve conception are shown that their idea has no predictive power or applicability. The experiment offends the student's intuition, and causes dissatisfaction with the naïve conception, which leads to revising the naïve concept.

Bridging Analogies is another powerful instructional strategy (Brown & Clement, 1987; Clement, 1987, 1991) that uses analogies to bridge the gap between a known conceptual example and an unknown example. The point at which they are introduced and the way in which they are used distinguishes these analogies as so-called bridging analogies.

This approach is described by using an example from physics. To begin, students are tested to determine which application problems tap knowledge of a particular concept students misunderstand (in this example, mechanics). These "target problems" become the focus of the lesson. For example, one problem requires students to describe the force exerted by a table on a book that is resting on that table. Most students will answer that a table exerts no force on the book. The associated naïve theory is that a static object is a rigid barrier that cannot exert a force other than its own weight.

Once target problems like these are identified, other problems are presented to students to discover beliefs that are in approximate agreement with scientific theory. These correctly answered problems are called "anchoring examples," and they are used to help students make sense of the material in terms of their own intuitions. For example, most students believe that a spring pushes up on a person's hand when the hand is pushing down on it. This scientifically acceptable intuition is used as a starting point for teaching the target concept.

The beliefs that a spring exerts force but a table does not are incongruous. The teacher addresses this incongruity by using bridging analogies, types of analogous cases in the form of thought situations (application problems) or analogies. For example, a bridging analogy for the physics principle is the idea of a book resting on a flexible board. Bridging analogies are used as intermediate cases between the intuitive belief (anchoring example) and the scientific conception (illustrated by the target examples). These examples produce dissatisfaction with the intuitive belief. A discussion should follow that challenges students to provide their rationales for how this bridging analogy is similar or dissimilar to the anchoring and target examples. The teacher may provide other bridging analogies. Finally, the teacher stimulates discussion of additional examples from the students' own experiences.

Many studies in science education tested the effects of instructional approaches that Guzzetti et al. (1993) identify as "conceptual conflict." These approaches were based on the proposition that when a student's prior conception is at variance with the scientific conception, the prior conception must be shown to be unacceptable. As a result, these investigations used methods designed specifically to produce conceptual conflict by causing dissatisfaction with an existing conception.

The first step in this approach is to determine students' alternative conceptions. Results from the assessment expose the learner's alternative conceptions. Use these results to design questions, materials, or activities to challenge students' alternative conceptions. Examples of these strategies include interactive discussions that emphasize conflicts between students' thinking and the scientific conceptions and experiential demonstrations that are semiguided by the teacher. Although a variety of instructional activities may be used, the common goal of each strategy is to reveal the inadequacy of the alternative conception, to result in dissatisfaction with existing beliefs, and to assist students in formulating the appropriate conception.

Some research has investigated writing as a way to affect conceptual change. Christine Gordon (1991) conducted a case study of a sixth grader learning earth science concepts by using response journals (together with interactive discussion of models and diagrams, and reading refutational text) as a way of altering his naïve conceptions. Gordon concluded, as did Langer and Applebee (1984), that engaging in the process of writing contributed as much to the restructuring of thoughts as did reading and talking. Kate Maria (1993) had similar findings when she investigated a primary-grade child's conceptual change. This study replicated Gordon's study, and showed the power of writing to affect the quality of learning and to measure conceptual change.

From these investigations, we can see that writing responses to instruction has potential as another means to reinforce the conceptual conflict that leads to conceptual change. The act of writing requires students to think reflectively and to commit their ideas to a written record. Because an analysis is required for this more formal means of expression, students may become aware of any inconsistencies between their preconceptions and the correct conception.

Measuring Conceptual Change: Assessing Learning

How can teachers know when students have changed their preconceptions? It is no secret that students might lead teachers to believe that students have the accepted conception, when, in fact, they have not. "Playing school" is common. Recent research shows that teachers need to measure complex conceptual learning over time to determine long-term conceptual change. Dole et al. (1991) observed that, although students could correctly answer textbook-type and applied questions about concepts immediately following their reading, they were unable to answer related applied questions on delayed posttests. Not only did the good readers in their study fail to retain the information, they returned to their prior knowledge 1 month later.

In addition to assessing learning over time, developing different kinds of measures is also important when we are measuring conceptual change. Several researchers believe that application tasks more accurately measure students' learning (Dole, 1988; Guzzetti, 1990) than do multiple-choice test questions. Application tasks assist teachers in distinguishing between students' assimilation and accommodation of concepts.

Application measures could include open-ended questions and scenarios. For example, Guzzetti and Taylor (1988) created application problems in the form of scenarios to test students' knowledge of Boyle's Law (the inverse relationship between pressure and volume on a mass of gas when temperature is held constant). In addition to answering true–false and multiple-choice items, they asked students to predict what would happen to the volume of their car tires when driving down a tall mountain into Los Angeles and what would happen to the flame of a Bic lighter when used in the mountains. An open-ended question was also used to assess students' knowledge of Boyle's Law by videotaping a balloon that continually increased in size. Students were asked to give a scientific reason why the balloon would grow larger. Comparing students' responses to each type of measure distinguished those who knew the concept only in a rote way from those who had learned the scientific conception.

Interviewing students is another way to gain insights into students' learning. For example, Barbara (Guzzetti, 1990) interviewed a sample of students who had doubled their pretest–posttest scores and their confidence of response ratings. She asked them to examine their tests and to talk about how and why they had changed their responses. Several students who were unable to generalize the new concept to the scenarios the researchers provided were able, however, to generate their own real-world scenarios that illustrated the concept. One insight gained was that asking students to create their own applications of a concept might be a better measure because it draws on students' own experiences.

Using multiple measures like these will reveal more information about students' learning. Application problems and open-ended queries can be used in addition to traditional multiple-choice and true–false items. Multiple assessments demonstrate the ways that complex conceptions have been integrated into the learner's schema (Valencia & Stallman, 1988).

SUMMARY

This chapter opened with descriptions of the pedagogical and content knowledge necessary to be a successful teacher. In the first part of the chapter we focused on the fundamental process of reflection. We wrote essays describing each of our literacy histories and asked you to do the same. Then, by reflecting on those essays, we discussed what we believe to be key principles for successful learning. We suggest that these principles be used for choosing and designing instructional strategies to help your students learn in the content areas.

We then turned to what content area teachers believe their students should learn, and provided the notion of concepts and conceptualizations. We described the importance of concepts for a teacher's planning, instruction, and assessment and for students' learning. We compared the "common sense" definitions of concepts, and we introduced the notion of conceptions to represent more complex and abstract ideas. We provided a framework for concepts that is useful for planning. Also included in this chapter were examples of students' alternative conceptions, ways to determine students' preconceptions, instructional activities for changing those naïve theories, and methods to assess students' conceptual change. Another overview of these instructional strategies to address students' alternative conceptions about counterintuitive ideas can be found in Guzzetti (2001).

A critical consideration in teaching concepts is to address students' prior knowledge, whether it is right, partially right, or wrong. We have made the point that it is critical to ascertain, build, and sometimes challenge and attempt to change students' prior knowledge. If we agree with schema theory, we know that prior knowledge is critical to the development of a schema. Hence, instructional accommodations must be made to support students' rejection of inappropriate prior knowledge, and to advance students' construction of new knowledge. Teachers and students rely on print and digital resources for constructing knowledge. The next two chapters provide insights to better understanding these reading and viewing resources.

APPLICATION ACTIVITIES

1. Write your own literacy autobiography or memoir; make connections between your writing and the principles of learning described in this chapter. Are there principles you believe are more important than others? Why? Recall the principles you have learned in learning theory classes. Is there agreement between those in learning theory and in this chapter?
2. List the naïve theories you are aware of in your content area. If you are able, poll students to determine if they have heard of these naïve conceptions and to discover if they hold them.
3. Compose a refutational text for a particular alternative conception that you know is common in your area.
4. Design an augmented activation activity that will cause students to experience incongruity between their prior conception and the commonly accepted conception.
5. Conduct a discussion web by using a central query you formulate based on a complex concept.
6. Create and use a think sheet for a central concept that is presented in a content text.
7. Think of some bridging analogies you could use to bridge the gap between students' existing knowledge and a new conception.
8. Design a lesson or unit for a topic by using the Learning Cycle as an instructional approach.
9. Create application problems you could use as measures for one particular concept.
10. Construct a conceptual map for your content area.

FROM OUR PROFESSIONAL LIBRARY

Evans, K. S. (2001). *Literature discussion groups in the intermediate grades: Dilemmas and possibilities*. Newark, DE: International Reading Association.

Goodman, Y. M. (2003). *Valuing language study: Inquiry into language for elementary and middle schools*. Urbana, IL: National Council of Teachers of English.

Guzzetti, B. J. (Ed.). (2002). *Literacy in America: An encyclopedia of history, theory, and practice.* Santa Barbara, CA: ABC-CLIO.

Guzzetti, B. J., & Hynd, C. R. (Eds.). (1998). *Theoretical perspectives on conceptual change* (pp. 133–145). Mahwah, NJ: Lawrence Erlbaum Associates.

Lawson, A. E. (1988). A better way to teach biology. *American Biology Teacher, 50*(1), 266–278.

Richardson, V. (Ed.). (1994). *Staff development and teacher change in reading comprehension instruction: A new generation of programs.* New York: Teachers College Press.

4

Analyzing, Selecting, and Planning to Use Print Resources

Printed text in the classroom is common—indeed, print text resources are essential. Increasingly, digital text is also a mainstay of the classroom. This chapter discusses print text, and the next discusses digital texts. The purpose of this chapter is to provide guidance for analyzing, selecting, and planning to use printed resources in the content area classroom. The analysis and selection of concept-related print resources provides the foundation for planning instruction that makes reading assignments come alive and be accessible to your students. We begin by describing what we mean by print resources and then by discussing the politics and economics of print sources in the classroom. Next, we provide background about the nature of print resources and suggest analytical methods that reveal possible instructional options to help make print more accessible to your students. We are answering questions such as these: How do you know when a text is suitable for the concepts you are teaching? What makes a text friendly? How can you predict the appropriateness of texts for your students? What makes a text interesting? How do students use texts? Finally, we present instructional strategies, which can be incorporated into planning, that research suggests will help to make text more readable.

Print text includes textbooks, a mainstay of most classrooms, and trade books, commercial materials like historical fiction, biography, and magazine articles—any materials that are produced for the marketplace, but coincidentally relate to instructional concepts. We emphasize trade materials in this chapter for several reasons, but, for many content area teachers, the textbook is perceived as the cornerstone of curriculum and instruction in their content area.

Textbooks have achieved this status for several reasons. One reason is that they are written by those reputed to be authorities on the topic, although that is not always the case. Another reason is because they have passed muster through the rigors of publishing, and publishers' sales representatives visit teachers and administrators to encourage the adoption and purchase of textbooks and each content area teacher is usually provided with one. Further, schools, teachers, students, and communities have established norms and expectations for textbooks, which sometimes means that parents, teachers, and administrators are on textbook selection committees. The same book is typically used for approximately 5 years, when new books are once again considered for adoption. Students talk about the books among themselves, and the school grapevine links teachers and the textbooks connected with their classes. In other words, textbooks are well-ensconced artifacts within the culture of schooling.

TRADE MATERIALS

More and more, however, teachers are incorporating trade literature in their classrooms. How often have you curled up in bed at night with a good textbook? If you are like us, you are probably chuckling over that query. From our own experiences as students, we realize that textbooks do not make intriguing, humorous, or suspenseful reading. Trade materials offer several benefits.

For example, trade materials that are written in a variety of genres and difficulty can usually be found about a particular concept. This means that all students, whether they are proficient readers or not, can use some type of prose to negotiate the meanings of the content being studied. "One size fits all" instruction and materials often marginalize students, and, as a result, many teachers are experimenting with "differentiated instruction," which provides opportunities for a wide range of student interests, linguistic background, and educational experience (Holloway, 2000; Tomlinson, 1999). Trade materials are essential for differentiated instruction and inquiry-based approaches.

Further, trade materials are inherently interesting. The information is often presented within a narrative structure, which may be humorous or emotional, with beautiful illustrations and photographs. In fact, because of the high value placed on artwork in trade materials, there is an award for outstanding illustrations (the Caldecott Award). Likewise, there is an award for prose (the Newberry Award).

Teachers often read trade materials aloud to introduce a topic to be studied. Some secondary teachers are shy about reading aloud to students, but they shouldn't be. Everyone enjoys being read to, and well-written, interesting prose stimulates students' interests. Shared reading also provides common experiences for all class members and provides students with a model of good reading as the teacher shares meaningful language and ideas.

Barbara's personal experience bears this out. As an undergraduate in a "History of Western Civilization" class, she was required to select, read, and write a report on a work of historical biography. She chose to read *Alexander the Great and the Hellenistic World.* The author's view was biased against Alexander the Great, claiming that he really was not, in fact, great. The author credited Alexander's accomplishments to zeitgeist, that all things are determined by time and place, and concluded that anyone would have accomplished what Alexander did, given his background at that particular point in time. The author's view was so interesting to Barbara that 10 years later she watched a six-episode series on television about Alexander the Great to see if he would be portrayed in the same way. She realized that she would most likely never have become interested in this historical figure if she had merely read a textbook account of his accomplishments. Later, as a teacher, she regularly offered students content-related literature and found them to experience the same personal involvement.

Another reason to consider trade materials is that they provide background knowledge to compliment other prose, either in print, such as the textbook, or in digital form on a Web site. Teachers and students alike appreciate information that is presented in depth and is usually contextualized in ways that make the content more understandable. Authors of trade materials use a rhetorical style that brings the reader into a story or a context that is both appealing and interesting. This makes the material memorable and is more likely to provide elaboration on a reader's prior knowledge and evidence that confronts reader's limited or erroneous prior knowledge. For example, rather than the typical two or three paragraphs found in social studies textbooks about the Tea Act, an entire trade book may be devoted to the topic. Students may learn why the British passed the Tea Act, how the colonists reacted, and the results of those actions. Further, trade books are more likely to present both sides of an issue, which also assists in correcting misinformation students may harbor (like believing that there was no justification for the increased taxes on tea). As we suggested in the previous chapter, teachers must conscientiously attack student misconceptions; there are greater chances of finding refutational text structures in trade books than in textbooks.

Moreover, and this is very important, trade books are bound to be more relevant to students' lives and also be more current than textbooks. For example, if students are studying photosynthesis and cell division, a trade book might relate these processes to the student's experience of having to cut the grass more often in the summer. Literature is designed to help learners discover how concepts apply to their own experiences. This is particularly meaningful to students and teachers who value diverse opinions and experiences. Trade books are also likely to present unique backgrounds and feature people of color, religious minorities, elderly persons, women and men in counterstereotypical roles, and people of regional culture. Exposing students to viewpoints not represented in textbooks or personal experiences helps learners to gain empathy for and understanding of others' views and of themselves as world citizens.

Trade materials take an extra step because, in addition to analyzing the appropriateness of the material, they also have to be located. Fortunately, there are lots of resources to help locate trade materials. Your best bet is the librarian, who is waiting for you to ask for materials related to a topic you want to teach. We have never heard a teacher say that a librarian couldn't help, and we have never heard a librarian say that the number of requests he or she gets for help is overwhelming. Believe us—librarians want to help. In addition to actual materials, they also stock indexes by topic or theme. By perusing these indexes, ideas for materials within your conceptual unit will be found.

The next best source for trade materials is the professional association representing your content area. Each of these organizations publishes journals featuring annotated bibliographies of trade materials that relate to concepts typical of its content area. You should join the professional association of your choice, but most university libraries also carry their journals. Other professional organizations such as the International Reading Association and the National Council of Teachers of English also make recommendations and provide bibliographies for content area trade materials. Visit the Web sites of these professional organizations and you will be amazed at what you find. Another increasingly useful resource is the Internet. Type a key word from your concept map in a search engine and you will find more suggestions for print and digital resources.

Commercial magazines are also a rich resource of trade materials. Publications like *Science, Discover, The Smithsonian,* and *Sports Illustrated,* as well as literary and popular culture magazines, are all possibilities. Examples of magazines published for children and adolescents include *Ranger Rick, In Your Own Backyard* (a children's version of *National Geographic*), and *Consumer Reports for Kids* (reviews of consumer products adolescents purchase, like video games). Students may be encouraged to bring their personal subscription of these magazines (and relevant trade books) to school to share with others.

We hope this background is useful for helping to locate trade materials either in place of textbooks or as supplements to the traditional textbook. Some teachers may be hesitant to use trade materials because they fear that, without state or district approval, some materials might be controversial. The National Council of Teachers of English (www.ncte.org) has a strong policy statement regarding censorship, as well as recommended procedures and policies for teachers, administrators, and school districts. Following these guidelines should help to prevent any trouble that might arise from using materials that have not been approved by the State or the District. Despite the compelling reasons to use trade literature, the ubiquitous use of textbooks is a fact (DiGisi & Willett, 1995). Politics and economics play a major role in supporting the dominant use of textbooks.

POLITICS AND ECONOMICS OF THE TEXTBOOK INDUSTRY

Textbooks are political because public money is spent to buy them and because, in many states, the public is involved in selecting them. Not surprisingly, some politicians and other leaders see the textbook as an opportunity to shape the curriculum and instruction in taxpayer-supported schools. For example, several years ago, Patty served on a state social studies adoption committee. She was called to testify in a hearing at the Arizona State Department of Education to defend the adoption of one of the books recommended by the committee. Members of the Board of Education objected to the use of the term *radicals* in a seventh-grade social studies text. The authors of the textbook identified those who dumped tea into the Boston harbor during colonial days as radicals and also referred to those who objected to the Viet Nam war as radicals. Board of Education members thought that such language justified the actions of those who objected to the Viet Nam war by calling them the same name as those patriots who rebelled against England. Adoption of the book was threatened for political reasons. The board decided that the book could not be on the "main list," but could be on the "supplemental list." At that time, if local districts wanted state funds, they were required to spend a particular proportion of their materials money on the state-approved main list. Hence, the State Board of Education did not censure the social studies textbook outright, but they did "signal" that it was expected that the book should have limited use.

Textbooks are purported to be comprehensive; however, in an effort to be comprehensive, textbooks tend to gloss over some topics, especially if members of adoption committees might consider those topics controversial. For example, a review of seventh-grade American History texts might reveal that the suffrage movement, the Viet Nam war, and the civil rights movement (topics that may be considered by some to be controversial) are each presented in no more than one or two paragraphs. History teachers often believe that these topics, or perhaps others, deserve more in-depth treatment than that offered by the textbook. Limited inclusion of some topics could be due to the abstract nature of texts—there is so much to include in a comprehensive textbook that space allocations dictate only mentioning some topics. Even so, that does not explain the reason why certain topics are presented in an elaborate fashion and other topics are left out or only minimally discussed.

To understand why particular topics are chosen to receive more extensive presentation than other topics is difficult and fraught with political and economic realities. For example, some states, particularly those in the South and West of the United States, adopt texts for use by school districts throughout the state; hence, publishers want their texts adopted by an entire state, thereby increasing sales. To accomplish this economic goal, publishers sometimes write a book to be appealing to a particular state. For example, one edition of a fifth-grade social studies text (Hirsch & Bacon, 1988) was published using the community of Santa Rosa, California as its example of town government and another edition using the town of San Antonio, Texas. This publisher made the decision to appeal to the California committee in one edition and to the Texas committee in another edition. Those living in other states could buy either of the texts. Both towns are reasonable examples of town government, but that is not the point. The point is that the content of textbooks is influenced by politics and economics.

The adoption committees also add a political dimension of their own. The renowned Nobel Laureate for physics, Richard Feynman, was appointed to one such committee for the selection of mathematics textbooks in California. He describes at length his service on this committee in his book, *Surely, You Must Be Joking, Mr. Feynman!* (1985). We are not exaggerating when we say that Feynman was flabbergasted at the committee members' lack of mathematical expertise. He emphasized that the committee meant well, but that members simply did not have basic mathematical understandings. He also perceived that the publishers were heavy handed in their influence: Committee members were given gifts, treated to fine meals, and in a word, "sold" on certain texts. Studies of the textbook adoption process affirm that Feynman's experience was not unusual (Chall & Squire, 1991).

Other examples abound, including the pressures brought to bear on the authors and publishers of biology and literature texts. These pressures include demands that creationism be presented to parallel the presentation of evolution, and that certain kinds of literature not be included in an anthology. Individual teachers are relatively powerless to affect the politics and economics of textbook publication and adoption, but being aware of these influences contributes to making wise decisions about selecting and using textbooks and other reading materials for the classroom.

As a group, teachers can affect the politics of reading. Publishers respond to teachers' requests for certain kinds of materials. This was evident in the early seventies, when teachers asked for—and got—high interest, low-vocabulary books for students' recreational reading. Presently, publishers are providing bilingual materials because the demand has increased to a sufficient point that it is profitable for them to do so.

Politics and economics aside, students need high-quality and interesting print materials to negotiate content area concepts. In the next sections, we provide guidelines and analytical procedures that are designed to help you select print resources.

SELECTING PRINT TO ENGAGE CONCEPTS

Resources are chosen on the basis of the concepts you plan to teach and what you know about your students. We have emphasized the importance of both concepts and prior knowledge in the previous chapters, but, believe us, this is a radical notion! In most schools, teachers have a specific textbook and many assume that it should be used as the primary source of reading material. In the real world, however, that isn't how it works. Lots of times, the books are hardly used at all. We have walked into many classrooms and seen them neatly on the shelf with no evidence of wear in sight. In other cases (Hinchman & Zalewski, 1996), assignments are made, but students don't do the assignments! The bottom line is that teachers decide what and how print resources are used in the concept-driven curriculum. The information presented in this section provides ideas for analyzing print materials so that the most appropriate materials can be used for instruction.

The place to begin is with the conceptual map used as the beginning stages of unit development as discussed in the previous chapter. The conceptual map lays the foundation for text selection and for instructional decisions. The question you want to ask is this: Does this material relate to the concepts I wish to engage?

Conceptual Matches

An easy way to check the match between your conceptualization of a topic and that of an author is to compare your conceptual map with a *textual conceptual map* of the author's text. Using Klausmeier's theory of conceptual relationships, read the material you are considering to find the author's superordinate, or overarching, concept. Then, read to discern the author's presentation of the categorical, or coordinate concepts, and the details, or subordinate concepts, related to each of the coordinate concepts. When mapping the concepts, do not be fooled by an author's titles and subheadings. We have found that some subheadings are misleading: The subhead suggests that certain content is presented, but in reality very little information in the text is related to the title or the subheading. Sometimes the publisher inserted those headings to make the material more appealing to curriculum committees, who typically only skim the text. This is less likely to be a problem in trade materials, but reading the material for yourself will make your analysis more credible. Figure 3.1, in the previous chapter, provides an example of a concept map.

5 W and H. A second technique for ascertaining the ideas written about by an author is the *5 W and H analysis.* It is helpful because readers with expertise in a particular topic, like teachers, are likely to infer information in a text that might not actually be there. Patty consulted with a biology teacher who assigned students a list of vocabulary words each Monday, words that corresponded to the chapter they were studying in the textbook. He asked students to write a sentence defining each word, collected the students' work on Friday, and gave a quiz over the words. Patty put herself in the students' shoes: "How would a naïve learner figure out the meanings of these words?" She searched and searched the text and could not find one particular term. When she asked the teacher about the term, he said, "Why, it's right there," and turned the pages looking for the term. Much to his chagrin, the word was not there; he inferred it was there because his expert knowledge filled in a gap in the text.

To protect from these sorts of teacher-made inferences, the 5 W and H technique (Tierney, Mosenthal, & Kantor, 1984) is a good reality check. To do this analysis, put the central idea of the chapter in the middle of a page and draw a circle around it. Then, draw six lines from the circle and label each line as follows: One line is *Why*? the second is *When*? the third is *Who*? the fourth is *What*? the fifth is *Where*? and the sixth is *How*? Read the chapter and, as the text provides information that explicitly addresses a question on the wheel, write the answer, in a word or two in a circle at the end of the line. If it is a direct answer, draw a circle around it and diagram other related information by drawing lines from that circle and recording related information. If detailed, relevant information is provided, but a reader would have to infer the direct answer to one of the questions, draw a circle, leave it empty, and then diagram the related information under the empty circle. See Fig. 4.1 for an example of this technique used with this chapter.

Now examine the diagram and ask the following questions: Does the author include information that is important to my instructional goals? Does the author do this for my conceptual goals? Are there details and examples to adequately explain the answer to each question? Are my students likely to have the requisite prior knowledge to make the inferences where information is left out? Sometimes one question is answered very elaborately and other questions are answered sparsely—do the author's priorities for presenting information correspond to the concepts in your plans? Perhaps this print resource is good for the development of one coordinate concept but not others. In that case, this particular assignment may be of help for part of your unit, but not for other parts.

The purpose of this technique is to discover both the quality and quantity of content presented by the author. Conducting this technique provides a clue as to whether or not the author provides the content you are counting

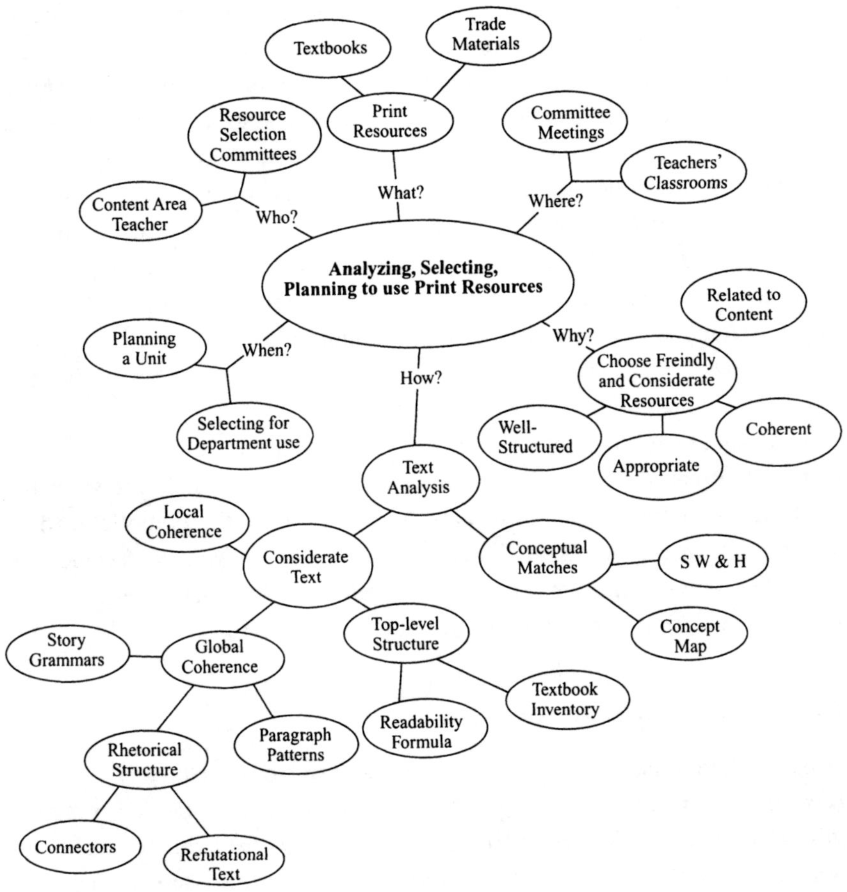

FIG. 4.1. 5 W and H analysis of chapter 4.

on when making the assignment. There is another consequence of doing this analytical exercise: Sometimes you learn from the author something you had not included in your original map. In that case, you would revise your conceptual map.

These two concept-related analytical tools, the conceptual map and the 5 W and H, each provide an opportunity to become better acquainted with the prose you might assign your students to read. They are appropriate analytical techniques for evaluating and selecting either textbooks or trade literature. The process of doing the analysis opens the door for the teacher and the author to get inside each other's heads and to find out the ideas each are emphasizing within a disciplinary domain.

What will you do if the author's conceptualization does not match yours? Throw away the material? No, not at all: When the author and you construct the ideas differently or emphasize different concepts, you use instructional strategies to bridge the two. Picking the instructional strategies that are most likely to provide a good bridge takes some decision making too, which we cover in the last section of this chapter and elaborate on in chapter 6. Suffice it to say that a single piece of print material is seldom a perfect match to your conceptualization, and that providing students with a choice among several materials is motivational as well as a more comprehensive approach to the development of any conceptualization. It might be true, however, that if you analyze several print resources, you will be able to select a few that you believe more closely match your conceptual goals.

Analyzing possible print sources for their conceptual content is only part of the information you will need to select reading materials for your students. Another part of the equation is the *coherence* of the potential reading assignment. In the next section we provide ways that you can predict the "friendliness" or "considerateness" of a possible reading assignment for your students by analyzing the coherence of the print material.

Predicting Considerate Text

Less able readers and those who are naïve about the topic being read are aided by well-written text. Armbruster (1984; also see Goldman & Rakestraw, 2000), whose studies are still referred to today, described "considerate" or "friendly" text as having ***structure, coherence***, and ***unity***. These terms are conceptually interdependent and imply analytical techniques that can be used to evaluate the appropriateness of a text for representing the concepts being engaged.

We begin with the task of selecting a potential reading assignment. Having found materials that are appropriate conceptually, we now turn to evaluating those potential reading assignments for coherence. Coherence is one critical aspect of well-written text. We have presented three tools that might be used to evaluate how well an author addresses the concepts you have in mind: a textual conceptual map, a concept-load analysis, and the 5 W and H method. But how coherent is the prose?

Local Coherence. Local coherence refers to "several kinds of cohesive ties—linguistic forms that help carry meaning across phrase, clause, and sentence boundaries" (Armbruster, 1984, p. 209). One example of a cohesive tie is the *conjunction*, words like *and, but*, and *because*. These conjunctions serve as the "linguistic mortar in the language" (Tierney & Mosenthal, 1980). A second type of cohesive tie is the *pronoun reference*. An example is "The teacher will be here in a minute. She is with another student right now." In this case, the pronoun *she* refers to the word *teacher* in the first sentence. A third type of cohesive tie is *substitution*: "My word processor is really out of date. I need a new one." Here, the word *one* is substituted for the words *word processor*. If these cohesive ties are missing from the text, the reader is left to infer the relationships between and among the ideas.

The following example provides an example of a locally incoherent text (Armbruster & Anderson,1981) written for sixth graders:

> In the evening, the light fades. Photosynthesis slows down. The amount of carbon dioxide in the air space builds up again. This buildup of carbon dioxide makes the guard cells relax. The openings are closed.

Armbruster and Anderson (1981) rewrote this paragraph to be more coherent by making the relationships more explicit:

> What happens to these processes in the evening? The fading light of evening causes photosynthesis to slow down. Respiration, however, does not depend on light and thus continues to produce carbon dioxide. The carbon dioxide in the air spaces builds up again, which makes the guard cells relax. The relaxing of the guard cells closes the leaf openings. Consequently, the leaf openings close in the evenings as photosynthesis slows down.

Notice the cohesive ties in the aforementioned paragraph: words like *however* and *thus*, the repetition and substitutions, and the word *consequently*. These ties demonstrate the author's perception of how particular ideas are connected. Check for cohesive ties in the text you might assign by reading the potential assignment aloud. Is the reading choppy? As you read, do you mentally insert cohesive ties? If so, you, as an expert reader in the topic, are making inferences about how the ideas are linked and your students, who are naïve, will need to make the same inferences. That is, the inferencing a reader is required to do for comprehension of a text with few cohesive ties is greater than for those texts with more cohesive ties.

Global Coherence. The notion of global coherence is how well the ideas cohere across the text. The seven rhetorical patterns given in the subsequent list are similar to those first listed by Aristotle (trans. 1960) and are models for representing information. Rhetoricians describe several structures; however, the rhetorical structures we find helpful for content area teachers to be able to identify are those that follow here.

1. Simple listing: This is a listing of items or ideas in which the order of presentation of the items is not significant.
2. Compare-contrast: This is a description of similarities and differences.
3. Temporal sequence: This is a sequential relationship between ideas or events considered in terms of the passage of time.
4. Cause-effect: This is an interaction between at least two ideas or events, one considered a cause or reason and the other an effect or result.
5. Problem-solution: This is similar to the cause-effect pattern in that two factors interact, one citing a problem and the other a solution to that problem.
6. Description: This elaborates on a concept or event, provides detail to fill in an image in the reader's mind, or develops an idea by explanation.
7. Definition-examples: This is common in mathematics books; a term is presented, which is followed by a brief explanation of the word's meaning and by an example of how to use the term.

One particular rhetorical structure may govern an entire text, with other rhetorical structures embedded within the text. This happens often in history text, where the overall structure is cause and effect but, within the text, a temporal rhetorical structure dominates. Likewise, in science texts, the overall structure is often problem-solution, but both temporal and cause-effect structures are embedded. This is not indicative of poorly written text because it is unlikely that any set of ideas would be related in only one way. Nevertheless, content teaching is improved by identifying the rhetorical patterns used by the author. Why? With this knowledge, the teacher can reflect on her or his own construction of the ideas. If the author's sense of the relationships between and among the ideas is concurrent with the teacher's perception, then the student's comprehension will be more closely aligned with the teacher's teaching. If, however, the teacher and the author construct the ideas differently, the teacher needs to choose instructional strategies that will help the student make inferences that correspond to the teacher's construction.

One analytical technique for discerning the author's rhetoric is the use of an analytical tool we label *connector listing;* that is, if we assume that

BOX 4.1. Connector Words That Signal Rhetorical Structures

Text Structure	Connector Words
1. Temporal sequence-process	then, and then, previously, before, prior, after, subsequently, next; precedes, follows, afterward, earlier, first, second, third, later, finally, dates
2. Explanation; if-then Cause-effect	causes, because, affects, enables, leads to, since, in order to, as a result (of), so that, consequently, produces, thus, hence, therefore, for this reason
3. Compare-contrast	is similar to, on the other hand, similarly, however, like, but, likewise, although, in the same way, instead, is different from, yet, on the one hand, while
4. Definition-examples	is a property of, is a feature of, is a characteristic of, is a part of, is defined as, means that, is named, is called, is labeled, is referred to as, that is, for example, for instance, type of kind of, example of, e.g., such as, includes, including
5. Problem-solution	the problem is . . . , the solution is . . . , How could we find out?

rhetorical structures are signaled by the connector words an author uses, then it is logical for us to analyze the use of those terms and better understand the signals being conveyed to the reader about how ideas are related. The idea is that if an author uses words associated with one rhetorical structure substantially more often than words associated with other types of rhetorical structures, readers will be cued to construct their understanding of the text in the dominant rhetorical structure.

To conduct this analysis, make a chart with the names of each rhetorical structure (i.e., cause-effect, temporal, descriptive, and compare-contrast) across the top. Then read the potential assignment. Every time the author uses a word associated with one rhetorical structure, list it in the column under that structure heading. Box 4.1 lists connector words that are associated with different rhetorical structures.

Our students have made an adaptation of this technique that may be of use. Instead of listing only words that the author uses explicitly, draw a line midway across the chart and list connector words that the author *infers*. What is sometimes found is that the author regularly cues one rhetorical structure but infers another rhetorical structure. This is very common in historical print resources. Often, a temporal rhetorical structure will dominate, but the author intends that a reader infer causal relationships. Likewise, in science print resources, an author might use a problem–solution rhetorical pattern but intends that the reader infer a cause–effect relationship.

An important point about this finding is that readers with much prior knowledge about the topic, such as the teacher, will be able to make those inferences. Other readers with less background knowledge, like students, are likely to find the text ambiguous and difficult to understand. After conducting this analysis, ask yourself the following questions: Do I organize this content in this rhetorical structure? What would be my purpose for assigning this material? Is the dominant rhetorical structure of this chapter congruent with my construction of relationships on my conceptual map? What instruction would students need to make the inferences I would expect? Reflecting on these questions will help to make a decision about the appropriateness of the material and about the instruction that may be needed to make the text more accessible.

Mathematical text presents another sort of challenge. In math textbooks, it is common for words that are used in nonmathematical prose as "connector" words to be used in ways that represent mathematical functions. For example, in nonmathematical prose the word *of* signals a prepositional phrase and contributes to the coherence of the text; in math, however, the word *of* often signals the multiplicative function. The math teacher should take note of and distinguish the connector words that signal rhetorical patterns and mathematical functions.

Rhetoric and Refutation. Science educators are particularly concerned about how text influences students' nonconventional concepts (Pfundt & Duit, 1991). Barbara and her colleagues (Guzzetti et al., 1993) conducted an analysis to learn what type of text best changes students' naïve conceptions. They found that most existing science textbooks were nonrefutational; that is, they used rhetorical structures to describe or explain (see Structure 6 in the aforementioned list), but they did not confront the alternative concepts typically held by students. They report that researchers rewrote published science texts to refute student readers' prior alternative conceptions and to explain the scientific conception. Overall, the refutational text was successful at challenging and changing students' preconceptions.

Some textbook publishers have paid attention to this research and the research identifying the commonality and tenacity of students' unconventional preconceptions. For example, an elementary science text teacher's manual

BOX 4.2. Text Refutation of Common Conceptions

The manual and text by Barman et al. (1989) show the following.

Teacher's Manual: Student Misconceptions. Popular fiction, including movies and television, frequently depicts encounters between dinosaurs and people. This lesson begins by informing students of the simple fact that "no person has ever seen a living dinosaur." You might begin this lesson by having students collect examples of stories and cartoons depicting people and dinosaurs as living during the same time. Follow through with a discussion on why they should trust the conclusion that no person has ever seen a living dinosaur.

Young people have little appreciation of historical time, let alone the vastness of geological time. One way for them to begin to appreciate this vastness is to recognize the sequence of changes that have occurred since a long-ago event happened. For example, many dinosaurs in museums came from quarries in the mountainous West. Students read that these animals lived in low, swampy, mild-climate lands, probably not far from the sea. Help them imagine all the changes since the animal lived to the present time in a place where scientists have found fossil bones. A focus on the extent, number, sequence, and kinds of changes will help students overcome egocentric notions of past time and make the claim that no person has ever seen a living dinosaur more believable. (p. 148)

Student's Text: Dinosaurs. Dinosaurs are land animals that lived millions of years ago. There were no people then. No person has ever seen a living dinosaur. But people have found dinosaur fossils. Fossils are traces of animals and plants that lived long ago. (p. 16)

(Barman et al., 1989) directs the teacher to refute common unconventional preconceptions. The publisher also provides refutational-type text for the students. The manual informs the teacher of typical student naïve conceptions and offers instructional strategies beyond the reading to refute the unconventional conceptions. An example from the teacher's manual and from the students' text that addresses naïve conceptions about prehistoric life is shown in Box 4.2.

Paragraph Patterns. Another aspect of coherence is the order of ideas within paragraphs or subheadings. Expository prose, prose that is designed to provide information, is organized in paragraphs that are grouped under

BOX 4.3. Paragraph Subheading Structures in Expository Text

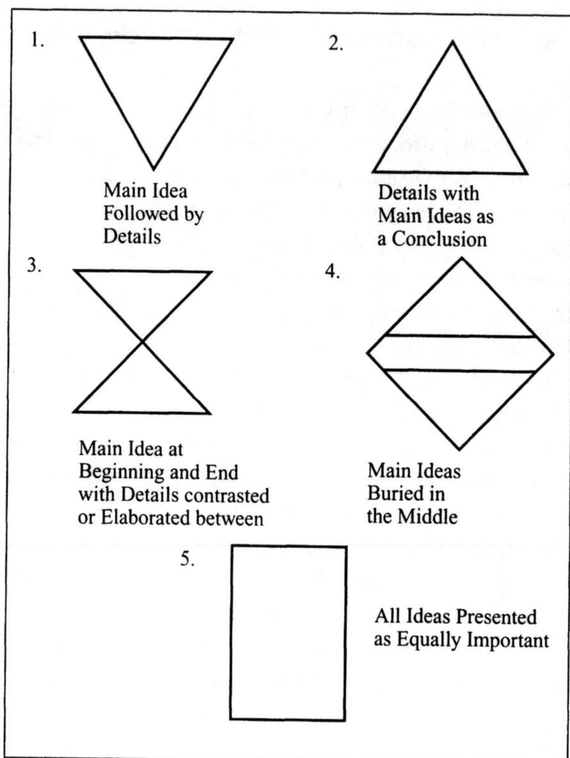

subheadings. The diagrams in Box 4.3 depict the five patterns that are most commonly found in expository text. We treat paragraphs and subheadings as the same because, in many texts, the prose set off by subheadings closely resembles the traditional definition of a paragraph.

The first pattern is the most common, stating the overall idea or gist of the paragraph in the first line or two with details following. The second pattern is the exact opposite: The paragraph or subheading begins with details and concludes with the main idea, or a statement that includes the details stated before. A third pattern is a combination of the previous two. The author provides an introductory statement at the beginning of the paragraph or subheading, provides details, and then concludes with a statement that restates the opening statement. Sometimes the details will be contrasting ideas, so the author might use terms like *on the other hand*, or *in contrast*. Other times, the author elaborates on the details by providing supporting documentation. These three paragraph patterns are very predictable to most readers. The fourth and fifth patterns are much less predictable and sometimes contribute to comprehension processing problems. The fourth type is difficult to understand because the author begins and ends the paragraph by providing details and puts the general main idea sentence in the middle of the paragraph. The final paragraph or subheading structure is usually found as an introduction or summary of a chapter. All the ideas appear to be of equal value; therefore, it is difficult to ascertain which ideas are the more important. Indeed, usually they are of equal value and the author is merely introducing or summarizing the main ideas of the chapter.

Studies support the efficacy of analyzing the structure of paragraphs and subheadings. For example, Meyer, Brandt, and Bluth (1980) rewrote ninth-grade science text by putting main ideas at the beginning of the subheading. Students' comprehension improved significantly when they read text written in this fashion. This analysis will help teachers to make instructional decisions about using the text. For example, Patty worked with home economics teachers who wanted to use a textbook chapter that explained the benefits of eating certain food for their nutritional value and the effects that such foods would have on how young people felt. The teachers complained, however, that their students seldom understood the cause and effect relationship between what was eaten and how they felt. We did the paragraph–subheading analysis and found that the one reference to a cause and effect relationship was made in the middle paragraph of the middle subheading in the middle of the chapter! The text that would inform students of the relationship the teachers wanted the students to find was placed in the most obscure place possible. The teachers then planned for an instructional activity—the pattern guide (described in chapter 6)—to help students read the chapter in a way that would foreground the causal relationship.

It is also possible that teachers' knowledge of the paragraph patterns is helpful for students for whom English is a second language. Kaplan (1966) and Montano-Harmon (1991) describe the unique linguistic and dialectic discourse patterns of American English, British English, Semitic, Oriental, Russian, romance languages, and Chicano English. Both American and British English discourse patterns resemble the first three paragraph patterns, but the other discourse patterns do not; hence, students who are not accustomed to those discourse patterns are likely to be less facile at comprehending them. Teachers, who point out these patterns and help students to see them, will facilitate the construction of meaning.

Top-Level Structure of Prose Materials

Children are most often taught how to read by using narrative materials, a top-level text structure that is framed as a story: There are characters who develop as they face a problem that is resolved within a setting. This structure is very predictable and readers are typically comfortable with it. They can use the elements of a story to predict what will happen, and the information is remembered partially because the framework of the story is so well embedded in their thinking that they only need to feed the information into those structured slots in their brain. The framework of a story is so pervasive that it is a cultural artifact. Preliterate people passed on their knowledge and cultural heritage in the form of stories. Christ and other great teachers used parables, stories, to convey their messages. So, it's not surprising that the story is familiar to children and that they are comfortable learning to read prose that is written in the narrative structure (Applebee, 1978).

In contrast, the expository structure is a highly organized abstraction of a body of knowledge. People who don't read as well as they would like often report that they first had trouble reading when they were expected to read highly structured, abstract, expository textbooks in about fourth grade. Expository text has an overall structure that is analogous to an elaborated outline. There is an overarching, all-inclusive topic, which is the title of the textbook. That topic is divided into units, chapters, and subtitles. The reader is called on to construct a story, by inference, from the information provided by the author. We suggest that one reason some students experience difficulty with reading in the content areas is because they are not prepared for the highly formalized structure of expository material. It is alien to their experience and presents barriers to the making of meaning.

For this reason, we recommended earlier in this chapter that content area reading materials include trade materials. Multiple genres of literature are useful in the content areas. For example, poetry that engages students in science and math concepts is recommended highly by Sharon Kane and Audrey Rule (2004; this includes a bibliography of poetry sources to use in content classrooms). They describe a project by Abisdris and Casuga (2001) using poems by Robert Frost to supplement a unit on atomic structure. After reading "Stopping by Woods on a Snowy Evening," they gave a short biography of Frost, emphasizing his particular interest in science. They helped students understand the intersection of literature and science: "We point out that symbolism, metaphor, and analogy are important parts of science, defining them and giving examples of each from science, literature, and everyday life" (p. 61). Similarly, Donaldson (2001) used Maya Angelou's poem "Africa" to teach about the continent's human and physical landscape and Dylan Thomas's "Poem in October" to help students understand, through descriptions of the natural environment, several principles relating to weather and spatial phenomena.

Children's picture books, which focus on concepts taught in the secondary school, are also valuable resources. World-class artists often illustrate picture books and the topics presented in depth and with accuracy. Appropriate picture books for any content area are easy to find. One person to ask is a children's librarian, and another source is to explore the Internet. Two cites that might be helpful include www.cobb.k12.ga.us and www.cynthialeitichsmith.com/authors-illustrators.

Researchers of prose have not neglected to describe story or narrative structure. Story grammars and story maps, systems of analyzing the structure of narration, map or list the components of a story such as setting, plot, characterization, event, and presentation of a problem and its solution. One concern regarding these grammars is that they do not fully describe a story. Brewer and Lichtenstein (1980) argue that a story is not a story unless a reader's response is also described. These authors use the role of suspense in a mystery as an example to demonstrate the limitation of story grammars and maps. Examples of story grammars and story maps are readily available (see, e.g., Tierney, Readence, & Dishner, 1995). These same criticisms are valid for the analytical techniques we have described in this chapter. We acknowledge these criticisms, but we believe that a teacher who does these analyses is better able to understand how to best meet students' instructional needs.

Generally speaking, then, the structure of prose falls into categories familiar to us all: narrative, biography, autobiography, poetry, plays, and exposition. Trade literature can be any of these structures; textbooks are likely to be mostly exposition, although some authors experiment with inserting the other structures. Textbooks receive a bad reputation for many of the reasons we have pointed out—poor coherence, too abstract, not relevant, and too superficial; nonetheless, a well-informed professional needs to be able to describe the strengths and weaknesses of a textbook. The following suggestions may be helpful—they have worked for us over many years.

Recommendations for Analyzing the Top Structure of Textbooks. Begin by looking at the book overall, evaluating the global structure. Box 4.4 provides a form you may want to use or adapt for your evaluation.

BOX 4.4 A Sample Textbook Inventory

This inventory should help organize your impressions of the material you examine. There are four options provided to choose between: Yes; No; Yes, but poorly done; and No, but not needed. Circle the one that best describes your evaluation of the item. There is also room to comment on each item.

1. The text contains a table of contents.
   Yes No Yes, but poorly done. No, but not needed.
   Comments:
2. The text contains a glossary.
   Yes No Yes, but poorly done. No, but not needed.
   Comments:
3. The text contains an index.
   Yes No Yes, but poorly done. No, but not needed.
4. Each chapter is divided into sections, as indicated by boldfaced or different colored ink.
   Yes No Yes, but poorly done. No, but not needed.
   Comments:
5. Each chapter has a "new-conceptual vocabulary" list (it is best if the list is presented at the beginning of the chapter).
   Yes No Yes, put poorly done. No, but not needed.
   Comments:
6. Each of the conceptual words is presented in italics or boldface print in the prose.
   Yes No Yes, but poorly done. No, but not needed.
   Comments:
7. The meaning of the conceptual words is presented within the context of the prose.
   Yes No Yes, but poorly done. No, but not needed.
   Comments:
8. Each chapter states a purpose for reading the prose at the beginning of the chapter.
   Yes No Yes, but poorly done. No, but not needed.
   Comments:

9. Each chapter has review questions.

   Yes No Yes, but poorly done. No, but not needed.

   Comments:

10. The review questions relate to the material in the chapter.

    Yes No Yes, but poorly done. No, but not needed.

    Comments:

11. The graphs and charts are presented on the same page they are discussed.

    Yes No Yes, but poorly done. No, but not needed.

    Comments:

12. The text has pictures, graphs, maps, and charts.

    Yes No Yes, but poorly done. No, but not needed.

    Comments:

13. New ideas are compared with experiences that the students are likely to have had.

    Yes No Yes, but poorly done. No, but not needed.

    Comments:

14. Each chapter has an introduction.

    Yes No Yes, but poorly done. No, but not needed.

    Comments:

15. Each chapter has a summary.

    Yes No Yes, but poorly done. No, but not needed.

    Comments:

What organizational features are there? Most texts include an author's statement to the teacher and the students, a table of contents, an index, and a glossary. Read the messages to the students and the teacher. Do you agree with the position put forth by the author? Does the author offer clues as to how to study the text? Next, examine the organizational features of the book. The table of contents is a good place to start. Ask the following questions: To what extent does the table of contents appear have a logical structure? Are the topics you would expect there? Next, examine the index. Are expected topics present? Another organizational aid present in many texts is a glossary. Read several entries in the glossary to see if the definitions are written in ways that you think students can understand. If the definitions are too abstract, the reader has to know what the word means to understand the definition. If that is the case, the glossary will not be helpful to naïve students. What other organizational features are in the text? Many content area texts contain appendices to provide detailed information such as a copy of the Constitution in a U.S. history text, the table of elements in a chemistry text, or answers to problems in a math text. Are the expected appendices there? Are they likely to be found and used by students?

Keep other questions in mind while conducting this general overview of the text. Is the text generally appealing? Is the arrangement of the pages likely to be attractive to students? Are the colors, pictures, and what publishers call "white space" attractive? Are the pictures and graphics accurate? Is the binding solid and does it appear that the book is likely to hold up when used by many students? If you are considering several textbooks and trying to choose one or two, this general overview will help you to narrow down the choices. Those books that rate poorly on the aforementioned characteristics are likely to be books that neither the teacher nor the students will find to be friendly or considerate.

After choosing a few books to examine more closely, proceed by picking out two or three topics about which you already know a lot, topics you look forward to teaching. Read the prose related to those topics and ask the following questions. What impresses you? What has the author left out? What would you add if you were writing this section of the text? What would you leave out? Is the information accurate? This analysis is subjective, but this initial reading will provide a sense of the style and tone of the book.

Read the sections again, this time putting yourself in your students' shoes. What will they think? Are there concrete examples provided to make abstract ideas come alive? Are the examples ones to which your students will be able to relate? Does the author seem to be aware of naïve conceptions students of this age group often have about the topic? Does the author address those conceptions explicitly? Does the text match well with pictures, diagrams, charts, tables, and other graphic aids? Do the subheadings cue the reader as to the content that follows? Are the subheadings parallel? Finally, use one of the analytical techniques for analyzing coherence. Are the sections you are focusing on coherent? Reading a topic about which you have particular expertise helps to narrow your selection of a textbook further. If the author handles topics you know and care about in a thorough and friendly way, chances are other topics that you know less about will be treated in a similarly thorough fashion. Similarly, if you and the author conceptualize, organize, and present the information in very different ways, it is likely that the text will be a disappointment to you and your students.

Most textbook publishers include adjunct aids in their texts to bridge students' reading and the author's writing. These aids include questions and notes to the reader in the margins, embedded questions in the text and at the end of the chapter, and guidelines for strategic reading of the text. Next, examine the adjunct aids provided in the text. Are the questions included in the text related to the concepts being discussed? Are additional resources recommended? Are there supplemental activities? Are there resources and worthwhile activities (rather than "busy work") that you can imagine your students using and doing to help accomplish their learning purposes?

The quality of the adjunct aids should also be considered. Judy Mitchell and Patty Anders (1979) analyzed the relationship between the questions asked in seventh-grade social studies textbooks—a typical adjunct aid—and the concepts the teacher's manual said were the purposes for reading the chapter and the quality of the prose related to those questions. Little relationship was found. In some cases, the teacher's manual claimed a text passage was designed to teach a particular concept, but little prose was related to that concept, although questions at the end of the chapter assumed deep understanding. In other cases, the prose related to a concept was elaborate, but no questions were asked that were related to that concept or information. The results of this study suggest that teachers are well advised to look for the connections between purposes for reading, quality of prose related to those purposes, and the questions supplied by the publisher to encourage students to think about the content. Sometimes, as shown in this study, the aids are not very well matched with the text.

Research suggests that these aids are helpful for some students, but they make little difference for other students (Stewart, 1989). There are at least two explanations why this might be true. First, some students find the adjunct aids intrusive. That is, students who are successfully processing the text find the adjunct aids redundant to their own thinking. Other students are not aware that the adjunct aids are to be of help and simply ignore them. Second, adjunct aids focus students on certain information, thus potentially limiting their attention. This tends to promote convergent and narrow thinking rather than divergent and creative or critical thinking (Duchastel, 1978; Spiro & Taylor, 1987).

Textbooks also typically include maps, tables, graphs, and diagrams to help make the author's presentation more understandable. Experts in science education believe visual representations are essential to scientific thought (Ferguson, 1977), and that expert and novice scientists alike must understand the graphics to successfully engage the concepts of science. Despite the importance of these graphic aids, naïve readers of science do not automatically find them helpful.

Reading text with graphics requires that students use strategies that are not usually called for when reading nongraphic text. For example, students need to coordinate the information in the graphics with the information provided in the text (Hegarty, Carpenter, & Just, 1991, p. 653). Text that is well designed (i.e., the text and corresponding graphic are on the same page) can provide readers with cues and signs to make that coordination easier for them; sometimes, however, school texts (perhaps as a result of production costs) are not so well designed.

An oft-overlooked virtue of textbooks is the additional resources publishers include. These resources are listed in either the teacher's manual or at the end of the chapter in the student's edition. They might include relevant films, videos, Web sites, and trade materials. Teachers who use multiple sources to both differentiate instruction and provide multiple perspectives on the concepts being engaged find these additional resources tremendously helpful. Unfortunately, some research suggests that teachers do not use these additional resources. Feathers and Smith (1987), for example, observed secondary classes and found them dominated by the textbook without reference to additional resources. This is likely to change as teachers become better acquainted with the shortcomings of using only one resource.

Readability Formulas. The last analytical tool for the surface structure of prose that we ask you to consider is the readability formula, which is a mathematical formula to predict the "reading level" of prose. We are not supportive of formulas for reasons we discuss in subsequent paragraphs, but we include a discussion of the formulas for two reasons. Publishers and educators commonly use them and we want you to be able to discuss them with your colleagues. Furthermore, computers have made calculations easy to do; as a result, this simplistic tool has gained resurgence in popularity.

Readability formulas are calculated by using two variables, a word variable and a sentence variable. The first, the word variable, is determined in one of two ways. One way is to estimate the "word frequency." That is, the creators of the formula select a standard by which to measure the frequency that a word appears in the English language. A common source of standardization is the *American Heritage Word Frequency Book* (Carroll, Davies, & Richman, 1972). Alternatively, some formulas call for counting the number of polysyllabic words (those with three or more syllables) in a sample passage.

Words are used as a measure because it is assumed that the greater number of infrequent or long words, the harder the text.

The second variable is "sentence length" or number of sentences per paragraph. That is, creators of readability formulas theorize that the longer the sentence (hence, fewer sentences per paragraph), the greater the demands on memory and, therefore, the more difficult the reading. Hence, it is common in directions for computing readability formulas to count the number of sentences per paragraph: The fewer the sentences in a sample text, the harder the reading. (See Box 4.5 for directions to compute the Fry Readability Formula.)

Research and common sense suggest that these two variables, sentence length and words, are unimportant and insignificant. For example, Beck, McCaslin, and McKeown (1980) found that, in some cases, the use of "difficult" words can actually improve comprehension. Anyone who has lived through a 5- or 6-year-old's affair with dinosaurs know that children (or anyone for that matter) can read a "big" word if motivated to do so.

Similar commonsense and research-based criticisms can be made about using the length of a sentence in a formula. Pearson (1974–1975) found, for the sake of low predicted readability, that publishers produce text with simple, short sentences. The result is that connecting words—words like *because, and, therefore,* and *since*—signaling the author's meaning and providing for coherence—were eliminated. For example, an author might write, "Paul's mother gave him a piece of cake because he cleaned his room." Shorter sentences would result in a lower readability, so the text might be rewritten: "Paul cleaned his room. His mother gave him a piece of cake." The reader is left to *infer* the ambiguous connection between Paul's cleaning his room and getting a piece of cake. Hence, the readability level is lowered, but the inference load is raised.

Content area teachers should keep certain aspects of the reading process in mind when either personally using a readability formula or working with a colleague who is using a formula. For example, prior knowledge has a significant effect on whether or not a text is understandable (Spillich, Vesonder, Chiesi, & Voss, 1979). Readability formulas ignore prior knowledge.

Readability formulas also do not take into account the interestingness of a text (Anderson, Shirey, Wilson, & Fielding, 1986). The extent to which readers are interested in the topic being read is far more important than how long the sentences are, or how unfamiliar the words. If they are interested, they are more motivated to read "harder" material. Third, the structure and

BOX 4.5. The Fry Readability Formula

Do the following to calculate a predicted reading level of a reading assignment or a book:

1. Randomly select three sample passages of 100 words, beginning at the first word of a sentence. Count proper nouns, initializations, and numerals as a word.
2. Count the number of sentences in the 100 words.
3. Count the total number of syllables in the 100-word passage. A syllable is a small unit of a word with a vowel sound; "shopped" is one syllable and "wanted" is two syllables; numerals like 2004 count as four syllables, and acronyms or abbreviations like the USA count as nine syllables.
4. Do the same counting for each 100-word passage.
5. Total and calculate an average of the syllables and the sentences.
6. Use these two averages to predict the grade level of the material according to the graph given here:

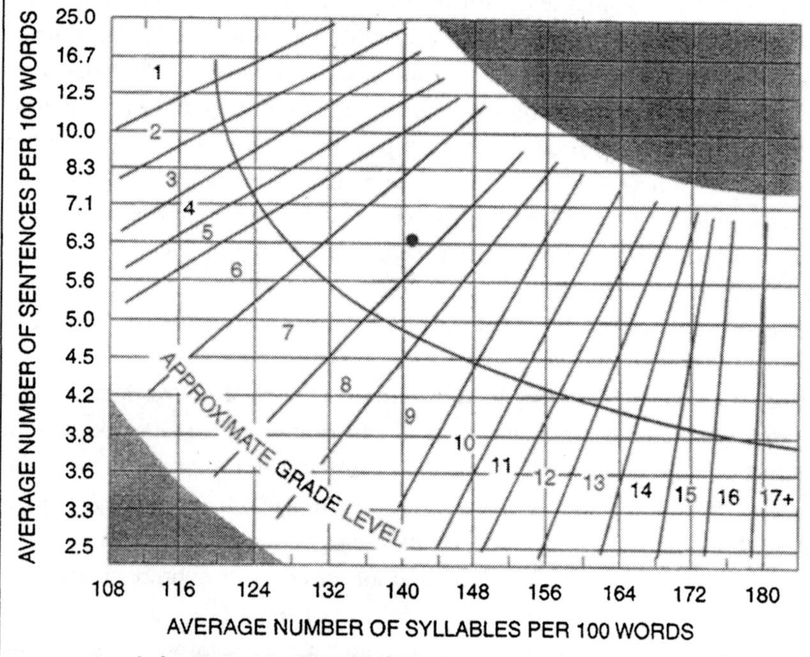

Graph for Estimating Readability—Extended (Fry, 1977).

coherence of prose, as discussed earlier in this chapter, are important aspects of comprehension (Kintsch & Vipond, 1979) and are not part of a readability formula. Fourth, many content area teachers want students to use and learn the language of the content. At times (again for the sake of a lower predicted reading level), publishers replace a technical content-related word with simple, less technical words. Examples include substituting *Mississippi* with a phrase like *the great river in the middle of the country*; or, for *photosynthesis*, the phrase *the way that plants make food*. To successfully use content area language, students need to hear it, read it, speak it, and write it. Instructional reading materials that do not present the language of the content area lessen the opportunities students have to learn the language.

Further, if the content words are not used in the text, educators may get the mistaken idea that students are unable to use the technical vocabulary. Students are put at a disadvantage if they do not encounter and use these terms. The terms are the labels for concepts that are needed for the development of schema and, if they are not taught and learned, students' schema development and long-term memory are shortchanged and further learning diminished.

All students need to learn the language of the content area, but acquaintance with content area words is particularly helpful for students for whom English is a second language (ESL). Often, content words in the first language are similar to words in English. These cognates can be helpful to students learning English and also content (Montano-Harmon, 1991). For example, consider the similarities between the following English and Spanish content words: photosynthesis–fotosinthesis; hypothesis–hipotesis; vertebra–vertebrado; perimeter–perimetro; dimeter–diametro; and congruent–congruente.

Finally, content area teachers find the readability formula troublesome because the results of the formula have no relationship to the conceptual load of the material being read. In fact, the formulas have nothing to do with the meaning of the text; rather, they deal only with surface features, that is, words and sentence length. Thus, the results can be misleading and may lead to ill-informed text selection decisions.

In addition to these criticisms and concerns, a content area teacher should know that readability formulas only predict or give a ball park estimate of reading level. In fact, if a formula predicts that a text is written at a certain grade level, an error of plus or minus 1 year is assumed (Fry, 1968). Hence, if a text is calculated to be a seventh-grade-level book, it should be considered as something close, in terms of sentence length and word difficulty, to being appropriate for a sixth, seventh, or eighth grader. It is not uncommon for publishers to argue wrongly that a book is predicted at a certain grade level and is appropriate only for that grade level. This is a myth that has to be dispelled at every opportunity—we hope readers of this book will help to do so.

In light of the commonsense and research-based criticisms of readability formulas, it is surprising that they are still used by teachers, reading specialists, administrators, and publishers. As educators become more aware of a social and constructivist view of teaching and learning and a holistic perspective of literacy, they are turning away from relying on readability formulas and are, instead, looking at structural qualities of text and characteristics of the reading process that research suggests make a text more usable. In the section that follows, we make suggestions for including students in the text-selection process.

Involving Students in the Analysis of Prose

Most teachers want student input when assessing potential reading assignments. This section provides two suggestions that involve students in the process. The first, the Content Literacy Inventory, is helpful to learn how well your students are likely to be able to handle a textbook; the second, the Cloze Procedure (Taylor, 1953), is designed to estimate who among your students is likely to be successful reading a particular prose passage.

The Content Literacy Inventory. This is an informal "test" of how well your students are able to use the parts of a textbook and how likely they are to be able to successfully read the textbook. It is a traditional question-and-answer task, which requires students to use their books to answer questions. To answer the questions, students need to use the various parts of the text (e.g., the table of contents, the glossary, the index, and appendices) and also read and answer questions from several passages in the text. The passages should require special reading skills like reading a map or graph along with the text. Some students will breeze through this task, and you can be relatively certain that they will be able to use the text with little instruction from you; other students, those scoring 65% or less, will need instruction on how to use the tools provided in the text.

The Cloze Procedure. This is a technique for predicting how appropriate a particular piece of reading material is for your students. The Cloze Procedure

BOX 4.6. Directions for Using the Cloze Procedure

- Choose a passage for students to read that is about 270 words long.
- Reproduce the passage as follows: Retype or word process the passage, using double spacing. Type the first sentence or two intact. In the following sentences, delete every fifth word and type a blank line of at least 15 spaces in place of the word. Continue deleting every fifth word and replacing it with a blank until 50 words have been deleted. Leave the last sentence or two intact.
- Make copies of the passage with the deletions for each student.
- Instruct students to fill in each of the blanks by using the word they believe the author would have used. Allow everyone enough time to attempt to complete the task.
- Score each student's passage. Award 2 points for each blank that is completed with the same word the author used.
- Multiply the correct number of responses by 2: Those students who score more than 60% on the task should be able to read the material easily; those students who score between 40% and 59% correct should be able to read the material with instructional support; and students who were able to correctly replace less than 39% of the words are likely to be very challenged by the material.
- Now, go back and examine the list of students who scored less than 39% correct. What is the nature of their errors? Some students may use words that are synonyms or more sophisticated than the author's words. If that is the case, those students are more likely to be able to read the passage than others who chose nonsense or ungrammatical words.

has been in use as an assessment measure for over 50 years and has stood the test of time and has a considerable research base (McKenna & Robinson, 1980). Like all methods of analyzing texts and assessing students, it is not perfect, but it does offer insights as to how well readers use lexical, syntactic, and semantic features of text. The directions for using the Cloze Procedure are given in Box 4.6.

One reason we recommend the Cloze Procedure is that it uses the three cuing systems—lexical, syntactic, and semantic—that are inherent to the reading process, and a reader's use of the cues influences his or her success of reading.

Reflections About the Analysis of Prose

The previous section has provided several techniques for becoming familiar with the prose that might be assigned to students. These techniques are helpful, but they are far from perfect. In some ways, each of the techniques is artificial, because for the most part they take into account only the author's representation of the meaning.

Rosenblatt (1938, 1978), a scholar of literature, makes the point that a reader's purpose, or stance toward a particular text, plays an instrumental role in the function of text—that is, whether a text is informative (efferent), aesthetic, or some combination of these two structures. For example, a mathematician might appreciate the qualities of a well written, aesthetically pleasing proof. Likewise, a student of literature might appreciate the information provided in a criticism of literature, or the structure of a story or poem. Readers and text transact in the process of reading to construct meaning. Even though we categorize expository text as separate from narrative for the purposes of discussing the structure of content area prose, we should be flexible in our evaluation. *The reader's stance dictates the expository or narrative function of text and the extent to which prose may be friendly to the reader.*

Selecting materials that are appropriate for students is tricky. It is not an absolute science, because readers vary according to their interest and prior knowledge about the topic being read, their purpose for reading, and the organization and conceptual load of the material. The reader and the author have a developing relationship, and, like all relationships, predictions about its quality are suspect.

MAKING TEXT ACCESSIBLE: INSTRUCTIONAL PRACTICES

We begin this section with the reminder that text is not, in and of itself, meaningful. There is no meaning until a reader engages the reading process by predicting, confirming, and integrating what is being read with his or her schema to construct a new understanding. The process is called *comprehending*; the outcome is *comprehension*. With that in mind, we offer recommendations about how content area teachers might facilitate the comprehending process to support students' comprehension. As with all recommended practices, most teachers will adapt and adopt the practice to suit particular contexts and content areas. For this reason, we provide some theoretical rationale for each strategy so that adaptations are made in theoretically consistent ways.

Students engage in comprehending when the prose they are reading is accessible to them. In the first part of this chapter, we recommend analytical strategies that help to analyze prose that students might be asked to read. The better a teacher understands the linguistic and structural aspects of the prose, the better she or he can choose instructional strategies to provide support for her or his students' reading of the assignment. In this section we discuss instructional strategies that help to make prose accessible to students.

At the risk of being overly redundant, let us once again emphasize that reading assignments, which are part of a coherent lesson or unit plan and related to the conceptual plan presented in chapter 2, are beneficial for helping students to engage the ideas being taught. The ideas we present in the subsequent paragraphs are appropriate for supporting students' reading of prose that is either trade or textbook. The idea is that instruction can make a difference in helping students construct meaning from what they read.

Text can be made accessible to students in two ways. First, some instructional practices, or strategies, help students become facile with using prose in your content area. Four instructional practices we are partial toward are text walks, connection questions, question–answer relationships, and the pattern guide. Second, other instructional interventions are designed to help support students' thinking and learning as they engage the processes of constructing meaning. The strategies we include in this section are book walks, extended anticipation guides, prewriting and postwriting, concept guides, dialectic and reflective journals, and think alouds.

Text Walk

Informational prose is seldom read in the same manner as narrative text. In narrative text, every word is important for conveying the elements of a story, but in expository text an author provides several cues that signal the reader as to where information is that the reader may be looking for. So, a reader's purpose is very important for the approach a reader uses to read exposition. When you are making a reading assignment, a text walk can be a good way to inform students about the different ways that a text can be read to accomplish the purposes for reading. It's a very easy instructional strategy to do and models the ways that good readers learn from text (see Box 4.7).

BOX 4.7. A Text Walk

At first, the teacher does the text walk with the students. As students become accustomed to the strategy, they can do it by themselves. This strategy helps students to get ready to read—it is designed to help students get a sense of the text organization, set purposes, become interested, and activate prior knowledge.

- The teacher pages through the reading to be assigned, noting features students should pay attention to while reading.
- The teacher selects features and chooses a method of sharing those features. If technology allows, the teacher shows the pages of the text as students look on their own copies and describes how that section or feature should be read.
- The teacher previews or surveys the entire reading assignment with students, pointing out and discussing parts that are particularly relevant to the concepts being engaged.

A text walk strategy also provides an opportunity to model how students can become good users of diagrams, maps, and graphs. During the text walk, model for students the thinking processes needed to "unlock the diagram." This involves putting the diagram on the overhead, reading the related text aloud, and helping students "see" the connection between the written language and the graphic representation. The text walk sets the stage for learning. It signals the brain that new information is being encountered; it helps to activate a reader's prior knowledge; and it helps to set purposes for reading. Interest in the reading may also be increased.

Connection Questions

Since Socrates, teachers have relied on questions to help students think in new and different ways. Muth (1987) suggests that teachers create two types of questions to help students see the connections between and among concepts and in content: (a) internal questions, those asked to draw students' attention to connections between and among ideas in the text; and (b) external questions, those that help students build bridges between their background knowledge and experiences and the text-based ideas. Box 4.8 provides examples of these questions. At regular intervals, when you are asking these

BOX 4.8. Connection Questions

Internal Questions	External Questions
1. How may textbooks be used as resources in a content area classroom? List and discuss several ways 2. What is a readability formula? How is it traditionally used to predict the difficulty of a textbook or trade book for students? What are the limitations of using this formula? 3. How can the 5 W and H technique help a teacher predict if a particular text meets the instructional and conceptual goals of a lesson?	1. What may be some of the limitations of using textbooks as resources? Compare and contrast textbooks as resources with other types of resource materials. 2. How are textbooks chosen and adopted in your school district? What are the criteria for selection? 3. What are some examples of books that use soft expository structure to teach content and area knowledge?

questions, point out to students that these sorts of questions are the examples of what they should be asking themselves while studying and that the thinking that results when they are answering these questions contributes to their constructing meaning.

Questions are powerful learning mechanisms; unfortunately, they are too often relegated to mere assessment exercises. Good students are continually asking questions about the content being engaged. Questions contribute to the processes of selecting, reviewing, and evaluating—all processes that are essential for learning.

Question–Answer Relationships

Those who analyze the quality of textbooks complain that questions supplied by the publisher are poor because they are not adequately related to the text, do not encourage students to think, and are seemingly designed to check whether or not students have done the assignment rather than whether or not they have understood the information. Despite these criticisms, a teacher may choose to assign textbook questions for students to answer. Raphael (1984) created the instructional practice of question-answer relationships (QAR) to explicitly teach students how to answer questions.

The thinking behind the practice is that some questions call for students to answer textbook questions by using the information supplied by the author. Raphael identifies these questions as being "right there." Other questions ask readers to take information from the text and reorganize it to answer the question; these questions are called "think and search." Other questions require the readers to think about what they already know and combine it with the information provided by the author; these are the "in my head" type. Finally, some questions rely primarily on the students' background knowledge to answer, and these are the "on my own" questions.

Raphael suggests that these question types be pointed out to students and that methods for answering the questions be modeled. Tierney et al. (1995) provide detailed steps for using the QAR practice instructionally.

One adaptation we have seen teachers make is to ask students to write their own questions reflecting the different types. Students then meet in cooperative study groups to discuss the question types and the possible answers. This adaptation would work well for trade materials as well as textbooks.

We like the QAR strategy because it has an extensive teacher research base and because it helps students to learn to ask good questions, both of others and of themselves. We particularly like the adaptation of the strategy because it contributes to students' metacognitive development—that is, students need to think about their thinking as they engage in discussing the quality of their questions in a group.

Pattern Guides

A pattern guide is used during reading to help students organize their thinking in a rhetorical pattern that is related to your construction of the ideas. (See Box 4.9 for directions to construct a pattern guide.) This guide is particularly helpful when the author uses a rhetorical pattern that is different from your own. For example, use a pattern guide if the purpose you have in mind is that your students will mentally relate ideas in a cause-and-effect rhetorical pattern, but the text is written in a temporal rhetorical pattern.

The pattern guide is used with expository materials and is most helpful to students who tend to read all prose as if it is narrative. The guide will help students to select what to pay attention to in the assignment and will help them to create a meaningful organization of the ideas.

Extended Anticipation Guides

This practice is an extension of the anticipation guide originally suggested by Readance, Bean, and Baldwin (1981). The anticipation guide provides

BOX 4.9. Directions for a Pattern Guide

1. Read the chapter, noting the overall dominant rhetorical structure. Conduct a connector-word analysis to ensure that the pattern you discern is the pattern actually used by the author.
2. Consider the conceptual goals you have for this reading assignment: What are the ideas you hope students will engage? What rhetorical pattern do you believe best organizes these ideas—that is, causation, temporal, problem-solution, compare-contrast, descriptive, or a combination of two or more of these patterns? Compare your considerations with the author's cues. Are they the same? Different?
3. Decide whether or not a pattern guide would help students construct a meaning that is consistent with the conceptual goals you have in mind. Appropriate considerations include the amount of prior knowledge your students have regarding this concept and the match between the author's rhetorical style and your teaching goals. If the students have little prior knowledge about the topic and if the author's rhetorical style is different from the rhetorical style of the lesson's conceptual goal, the use of a pattern guide is indicated. In addition, less able readers will benefit from a pattern guide even if the conceptual goals and author's rhetorical style match.
4. Construct a guide that directs students to pay attention to the appropriate rhetorical structure. The guide should require students to do very little writing, may be done cooperatively by groups of students, is not a graded activity (although students may receive points for attempting their guide), and leads to activities that will be done after the reading assignment and guide are completed. For example, a guide to help students think in a cause-and-effect pattern might be a list of causes on one side of the sheet and a list of possible results on the other side of the page. Students would match causes with effects. A timeline might be appropriate for a temporal rhetorical structure, and a chart asking students to make comparisons might be another type of pattern guide for promoting comparative type thinking.

BOX 4.10. Directions for the Extended Anticipation Guide

The first step to constructing the guide is to read the chapter and select statements that are important to the conceptual goal of the assignment. Restate some of these statements to be false. These statements are the first part of the guide. Use these statements as a prereading discussion guide or ask students to discuss the statements in small groups before doing the reading. Part 2 of the guide is an extension of Part 1 to encourage students to use text-based information to correct the statements in the first part of the guide. The intention of Part 2 is to involve students in confronting the naïve conceptions revealed in Part 1 of the guide.

students with a series of statements that are either true or false before they read an assignment. Students then predict whether or not the statement is true and then read to find out what the author says about the statement. The thinking behind this practice is that directing students to specific facts before reading focuses their attention on those facts and helps them to select the needed information. Many teachers reported a problem with the anticipation guide: Students treated the guide as a simple true–false exercise and did not become involved enough in thinking about the statements. The extended anticipation guide (Duffelmeyer, Baum, & Merkley, 1987) is a modification to increase students' involvement. A sample extended anticipation guide for the next chapter in this text is displayed in Box 4.10.

Prewriting and Postwriting

Compositions of students' understanding of a topic before reading about the topic and rewrites of those compositions after reading are likely to be productive aids for comprehending text. These compositions should not be graded for content, grammar, or spelling; rather, they should provide an opportunity for students to activate and record their prior knowledge and, following reading, an opportunity for students to reflect on the changes in their understanding. The process of reflection should enhance the processes of confirmation and integration necessary for comprehension. Teachers use these compositions as bases for small group discussion following the reading. The compositions can also be used to learn what students know before the topic is read and to determine what students selected to pay attention to during the reading.

Journals. Journals are very powerful strategies for teaching and learning. One of our favorites is what we call a *reflective dialogue journal*. When students reflect, they address such questions as these: What did I expect to learn in this reading assignment? Why did I read the assignment? What perspective or bias did the author present? Did what I read correspond to what I already knew? What was different about this information from what I thought I knew? What was hard about this assignment? How did I overcome the difficulties I had with this text? What do I want to know now? How can I find out? Many of these questions direct students to consider the process of their learning as well as the status of their current understanding. As with the prewriting and postwriting activities, the journal is not to be evaluated in terms of grammar or spelling; rather, the journal offers opportunities for students to "think on paper," that is, to get their ideas out of their heads and onto paper so that those ideas can be examined, thought about, and connected to previous knowledge. In addition, the process of writing a journal sometimes results in students' discovering future areas of study. The teacher should regularly read and respond to the student journal. This may seem like a burden, but it can be managed. For example, if you have 130 students, you should plan to read and respond to 10 journals per day, which results in your reading every student's journal every 2 weeks. When responding to the journal, use "I statements"—"I like how you reread that part of the text so that you could understand it really well," "I think you have really grown in your understanding here," "I wonder what else you could have done." The purpose for responding this way is to reinforce the constructive and social nature of negotiating meaning.

Another kind of a journal is the *double-entry notebook*. On the left side of the notebook page, students record the pages read and take notes from the text. Their notes should consist of important, interesting details from the text. On the right side of the page, students respond to the details from the left side of the page. They make connections with prior knowledge, with other texts, and with activities done in class. In addition to making connections, they might make predictions about what will be learned next or about how the information can be used. The point is that the double-entry notebook requires students to pause and think about what they are reading.

Think Alouds

Afflerbach and Pressley (1995) analyzed, summarized, and reported on studies that described the strategies that successful readers report using while reading. We have adapted this revealing study by creating a strategy for teachers to use to help students think while reading. The think-aloud instructional strategy begins with a teacher demonstration. The teacher projects challenging material and models the way he or she thinks while reading. The teacher describes the strategies he or she uses to transact with the text before, during, and after reading. The teacher then models prereading thoughts as he or she establishes purpose for the reading, makes predictions, activates prior knowledge, and makes a plan for how the material will be read. Next, while reading, the teacher models the connections he or she makes with other information, demonstrates the maps or other graphic organizers he or she draws to keep track of the information being read, and selects conceptual vocabulary that provides labels for key ideas. After reading, the teacher models how he or she summarizes the text, checks for whether or not the purpose for reading has been addressed, and thinks about what he or she will do with the information gained from the reading.

After the demonstration, ask students to complete a think-aloud worksheet. Divide a piece of paper into three parts: Before Reading, During Reading, and After Reading. Ask students to make notes as they do their reading, filling in what they are doing during each phase. After the reading, ask students in groups of three to discuss the employed strategies. After discussion, ask each group to report and record on the whiteboard the strategies used. Encourage students to try each other's strategies and make suggestions as to additional strategies they could use.

SUMMARY

In this chapter we reviewed and discussed features of expository prose that affect student's reading of that prose. We discussed the most common form of prose in the secondary school, the textbook, as well as trade materials. In this chapter we provided an overview of considerations related to the nature and selection of textbooks, including the political and economic considerations, additional resources provided by a textbook publisher, readability, and the structure of the textbook. In addition, we offered analytical techniques, which are designed to describe the coherence and structure of prose. We also suggested instructional activities, which are designed to help students access the textbook. An inference that a reader might draw from this chapter is that teachers need to critically analyze the value of the prose they invite their students to read.

Predicting the appropriateness of potential reading assignments is affected by the teacher's background knowledge, purposes, and expectations that are filters for understanding the text. As a result of the teacher's expertise, the meaning constructed will be different from the meaning constructed by less expert readers. This is an important distinction, because content area teachers want to select text that will be accessible to their students. The problem is that students vary widely in terms of prior knowledge, experience, and interest; hence, it is difficult for a content area teacher to be confident of his or her selection. At best, teachers can only make predictions about the usefulness and considerateness of text. Watching students as they negotiate the meaning of a text best validates these predictions. If students are observed resisting their assignments, teachers need to entertain the possibility that the text is inconsiderate.

We also shared sample strategies for helping to make prose accessible to students. Many such strategies are available from several sources. One of our favorite collections of strategies is by Buehl (2001), *Classroom Strategies for Interactive Learning*. This book is especially helpful because 45 strategies are described and linked to text rhetorical structures for which each strategy is the most useful.

Moreover, in this chapter we elaborated on a theme that we wish to promote: A teacher's perspective of education greatly influences how the text is used in the classroom. Two major perspectives anchor each end of a continuum: transmission or construction. A belief that education is the transmitting to students of the accumulated knowledge in a field suggests that the most authoritative text available should be selected, students should be required to read it, and they should be expected to recite the knowledge. Alternatively, a belief that knowledge is constructed results in a teacher's perceiving the textbook as but one source of information, providing multiple sources, and expecting students to construct their own meaning. Teachers reading this book are challenged to think deeply about their perspective of teaching and learning, because that perspective will affect the decisions they make regarding the selection and use of textbooks. In the future, as teachers come to better understand the strengths and weaknesses of textbooks and their own perspective on education, we predict teachers will use textbooks more flexibly and less rigidly. Textbooks might be regarded as a resource, recognized for the good content they provide on some topics and the superficial or minimal content they provide on other topics. Teachers will provide instruction that helps students deal with the textbook, but they will recognize that other reading materials provide a richness and diversity of opinion and facts that students who are critical readers need to access.

APPLICATION ACTIVITIES

1. Choose what might be a typical reading assignment in your content area. Conduct one or more of the analytical methods presented in this chapter. Compare your findings with those of your colleagues in similar and different content areas.
2. Investigate how texts are selected in a local school district. Do the procedures followed correspond with those discussed in this chapter? How are they the same and different?
3. Design a lesson to help students effectively and efficiently *use* their textbook. Try the lesson out with some students and evaluate the quality of the practice.
4. Design a lesson that includes some of the instructional strategies described in this chapter. Try the lesson out with some students and evaluate the quality of the practice and student engagement.

FROM OUR PROFESSIONAL LIBRARY

Afflerbach, P., & Pressley, M. (1995). *Verbal protocols of reading: The Nature of constructively responsive reading*. Hillsdale, NJ: Lawrence Erlbaum Associates.

Armbruster, B. B. (1984). The problem of "inconsiderate text." In G. G. Duffy, L. R. Roehler, & J. Mason (Eds.), *Comprehension instruction: Perspectives and suggestions* (pp. 202–217). New York: Longman.

Buehl, D. (2001). *Classroom strategies for interactive learning* (2nd ed.). Newark, DE: International Reading Association.

Chall, J. S., & Squire, J. R. (1991). The publishing industry and textbooks. In R. Barr, M. Kamil, P. Mosenthal, & P. D. Pearson (Eds.), *Handbook of reading research* (Vol. 2, pp. 120–146). White Plains, NY: Longman.

Feynman, R. (1985). *Surely, you must be joking Mr. Feynman*. New York: Norton.

Goodlad, J. I. (1976). *Facing the future: Issues in education and schooling*. New York: McGraw-Hill.

Meltzer, M. (1994). *Nonfiction for the classroom*. New York: Teachers College Press.

PROFESSIONAL ORGANIZATIONS FOR BIBLIOGRAPHIES OF TRADE BOOKS

American Library Association
50 E. Huron Street
Chicago, IL 60611

Children's Book Council
568 Broadway, Suite 404
New York, NY 10012

International Reading Association
800 Barksdale Road
P.O. Box 8139
Newark, DE 19714-8139

National Council for the Social Studies
23501 St., NW Washington, DC
20016-3167

National Council of Teachers
of English
1111 W. Kenyon Road
Urbana, IL 61801-1096

National Science Teachers Association
23501 Newark St., NW
Washington, DC 20016-3167

5

Digital Resources and Content Area Literacy

Print-based resources are pervasive in content area classrooms, but digital resources, which are rapidly becoming an integral part of content area teaching and learning, provide infinite opportunities for teachers and students.[1] Most students come to school with a wide array of experiences with digital resources. Those experiences have to be used by teachers to help students successfully negotiate conceptual learning in the content areas. The purpose of this chapter is to acquaint content area teachers with possibilities for incorporating digitized resources into content area curriculum and pedagogy.

What does the term *digital resources* mean? Any kind of information can be or may have been rendered as digital, or digitized. Images and text can be scanned, photographs taken, and music created or sampled, giving the user access to many sources of media in one or many virtual environments. The World Wide Web is also a digital resource. Digital resources are the content of the many electronic tools and devices that are now commonplace, such as phones, cameras, personal computers, and media players.

Understandings about digital resources and their related literacies emanate from several areas and fields of scholarship, such as information and communications technology, education, psychology, sociolinguistics, media, the arts, and entertainment. We refer to research and practice from these fields to discuss the history of computing in the classroom and also to address questions such as these: What is the history of technology in the school and what are its theoretical underpinnings? What "new literacies" are available for content

[1] J. David Betts, an assistant professor in literacy and technology contributed to this chapter.

area classroom use? How can digital resources be used to help students learn in the content areas? How can critical thinking be encouraged as students use digital literacies? How can teachers learn more about digital resources?

The themes of the previous chapters—young people's out-of-school experiences with multiple literacies, literacy as a social event, teachers' beliefs and knowledge, and the structure and coherence of text—provide relevant background for this chapter. Many adolescents come to school valuing digital text more than they do print-based texts; when the new literacies are not available or valued at school, students are likely to feel alienated and isolated (Gee, 2003). For example, *Pokéman* reached a vast audience of children and young adults (Tobin, 2004). Initially, it was a computer game for Japanese preteenage boys, but it was adapted for a wider audience, including girls, and became the most successful computer game in the world and also a top-grossing television series. Young people throughout the industrial and postindustrial world became aware of and were influenced by this phenomenon. Elizabeth Moje and her colleagues (Moje, Young, Readance, & Moore, 2000) recommend "reinventing adolescent literacy for 'new times'" (p. 400) by acknowledging, respecting, and integrating out-of-school experiences, such as those with games and media, with learning opportunities in the content area classroom. This is not a new recommendation; it has been a theme in education at least since the introduction of progressive education, but with the availability of digital resources, it may be a goal within reach.

Further, digital resources make transparent the social nature of literacy. The social landscape has changed as people instant message one another from coffee shops, and as they participate in "texting" or text messaging on their cell phones when oral conversation is inappropriate. Print and other symbol systems, whether on paper or digitized, are communicative systems that express social, learning, and aesthetic experiences. The digital world makes that more apparent than ever. *Situatedness* is an apt way to characterize how humans modify the many ways they use language to read and write in varying contexts. Individuals use multiple literacies appropriate to various situations (Alvermann, Moon, & Hagood, 1999; Gee, 2003; Kress, 2003).

Some teachers are less likely to be attuned to digital resources than are other teachers, and they will probably need to do some deep soul searching and update their pedagogical and digital knowledge to integrate digital resources into their teaching repertoire. Other teachers, however, are likely to be deeply in the midst of using digital literacies for their own purposes, and they only need to stretch their thinking to accommodate for classroom applications.

This chapter will help you to organize the available information and will give you ideas for using digital resources in the classroom.

A hypertext environment occurs when the reader is the navigator through the text, between nodes of information with multiple links. The concept of hypertext, or hypermedia, is easy to understand: Imagine that you are given a stack of cards with information on each card, a menu card on top that allows you to go instantly to the card of your choice, and on each card a way to return to the menu or elsewhere when you wished—that's a model of a hypertext environment. Create that stack in a virtual (computer-mediated) space where the navigation is instantaneous and the possibilities for linking are almost endless. Adding other kinds of information such as graphics, audio, or video makes it a hypermedia environment. The World Wide Web is a hypermedia space: innumerable pages with links that are available to be navigated.

An exciting realization about hypertext is that it mimics the ways sophisticated readers read nearly all print-based materials, with exceptions being novels and poetry. It is typical for readers to approach informational text in nonlinear ways, consulting dictionaries, appendices, and indexes, and skipping ahead and rereading. Hypertext makes such intertextual applications easier than in typical textual practices (Dwight & Garrison, 2003). The information about the structure and coherence of print-based resources in the previous chapter is a good background for thinking about using digital resources in the content area course.

Further, Elizabeth Schmar-Dobler (2003) maintains that print-based reading comprehension strategies transfer to digital text, creating a bridge to support students' literacy and learning (see Box 5.1). There is a toll to cross that bridge, however, as digital resources, such as the Internet, have an open, noncensored structure, requiring that students' possess sophisticated critical thinking and reading capacities. As Kathleen Hinchman and her colleagues (Hinchman, Alvermann, Boyd, Brozo, & Vacca, 2004) point out, "Internet searches on slavery will unearth web pages from the US Library of Congress as well as the Ku Klux Klan" (p. 307).

The reading process, as described in this volume, is employed by content area students who use digital resources in much the same way as print-based resources are used (Coiro, 2003). The substantial difference, however, is that critical thought processes are foregrounded with the use of digital resources. We devote a section of this chapter to critical thought, and we suggest that this topic is likely to become one of the most important that content area teachers need to deal with when using digital resources.

BOX 5.1. Comparison of Reading Strategies

Strategies	Book	Internet
Activate prior knowledge	Reader recalls experiences and information relating to the topic.	Similar strategies are used.
Monitor and repair comprehension	Reader adjusts reading rate,depending on the purpose for reading.	Skimming and scanning becomes crucial for reading the sheer volume of text.
Determine important ideas	Reader analyzes text to determine those parts important for developing an understanding of the text.	Similar strategies are used.
Synthesize	Reader sifts important from unimportant details to determine the kernel of an idea.	Similar strategies are used.
Draw inferences	Reader reads between the lines, using background knowledge and text to help fill in the gaps.	Similar strategies are used.
Ask questions	Questions give purpose to reading and are motivating.	Guiding questions must be in the forefront of the reader's mind or getting lost or sidetracked is likely.
Navigate	Reader uses the features of print text to search for information (e.g.,table of contents, glossary, headings, rhetorical structure of text).	Reader uses features of the Internet to search for information (e.g., pop-up ads, downloading, links, search engines).

DIGITAL RESOURCES: HISTORY AND THEORETICAL FOUNDATIONS

David Jonassen (1996) describes the history of digital advances in education in three stages. Initially, learners were told *about* computers—how they operated, what the parts were, how to use the keyboard, and how to program. When desktop computers first came to K-12 education, they were a novelty. The new languages and processes that the machines required were as interesting as the limited things that they could actually do to support curriculum. The potential was recognized however, by researchers such as Seymour

Papert (1980), who, in his book *Mindstorms*, predicted dynamic ways that computers would impact learning.

In the last part of the 20th century, as more powerful desktop computers with greater storage became available in the classroom, the relationship between the learner and the technology changed. Students began to learn *from* computers. An incredible amount of information was stored and accessed through the personal computer, or PC. At first, the lessons stored on the computer were mundane. For example, information from textbooks and exercises from workbooks were replicated in digital form on the computer, thereby digitizing certain types of learning routines. Students interacted with scripted programs and databases as they worked through a subject. The computer became an accepted and expected part of the classroom.

At present, the most useful paradigm is one of learning *with* a computer, using the computer to access, organize, and use information. This distinction has important implications for the classroom and the roles of students and teachers. With the computer in the classroom, opportunities for engaging content-related resources are expanded to an infinite capacity. By acknowledging the memory capacity, computational speed, and connectivity of the PC, the teacher becomes a facilitator or guide for students' exploration and discovery.

A compelling theoretical base for supporting these different modes of communication is *social constructivism* (Bruner, 1986). Jerome Bruner theorized that a child develops *into* the intellectual discourse community in which he or she resides. This notion is similar to Gee's (2003) suggestion that people belong to affinity groups—groups that share a common language and interests. Bruner (1990) suggested that successful learning environments (e.g., content area classrooms) provide learners with the following:

- *Agency,* as students engage in activities that provide for some measure of choice and control;
- *Opportunities for reflection*, as students write, talk, or think about ideas and experiences;
- *Collaboration*, as students work with others to construct understandings; and lastly,
- *Opportunities for cultural expression*, as students engage in activities that value the history and situatedness of each learner.

In a constructivist classroom, a learner conducts inquiries and research, reorganizing and re-presenting his or her newly constructed knowledge by using multiple literacies.

Lev Vygotsky (1978), whose theories are similar to those of Jerome Bruner, promoted learning and development as the construction of knowledge with tools available in the social environment (Wertsch, 1985). Key elements of Vygotsky's ideas about development are how an individual uses *activity* in a social environment to internalize and construct knowledge. Activity, which involves learners' constructing and re-presenting knowledge by using a variety of tools, including the computer, results in learning.

Reading is a transactional activity; that is, meaning is constructed as a reader negotiates and constructs a text's meaning in a social context (Goodman, 1994). Reading digitized resources make this relationship transparent. Reading from the computer involves transaction with many forms of text in both virtual and actual contexts, which has the potential for increasing learners' engagement and therefore their learning.

The PC is a powerful tool for discovering and constructing multimodal information. As Bertram Bruce (2003) states, "The computer not only makes it easier to transmit text and mix different media, but it also requires us to be able to read and write hypertext and multimedia documents" (p. 168). Computer-mediated, multimodal discourse communities support classroom environments where learners construct knowledge through engagement, inquiry, and problem solving. Language mediates this process as information is constructed, exchanged, and stored.

Most of us are just users of the computer and know only generally how the machine works. It is just language in, language out. So our discussion here is not about the computer but about learners using resources that are engaging and provide them with learning opportunities. Literacy and learning exist within a context, a particular situation (Barton, Hamilton, & Ivanic, 2000; Gee, 2000), which affects the quality and quantity of their use. In the content area classroom, this is a very important point. The *ways* that digital resources are used in the content area classroom affects the learning that occurs.

In light of this theoretical foundation, the PC and similar tools provide resources, which expand instructional and learning possibilities. The teacher's choices and decisions about using digital resources shape those possibilities. The following points encapsulate why we think digital resources are of such great value for content area teachers.

1. The PC is a tool for constructing knowledge. Using the computer, a learner takes advantage of the many potential uses it affords and that are part of the software. The difference between what a learner can accomplish

alone and what he or she can do with the help of a more capable peer is called the *zone of proximal development*, or ZPD (Vygotsky, 1978). The computer has the potential of serving the role of a more capable peer in a ZPD (Salomon, Globerman, & Guterman, 1989). In this model the learner's experience is scaffolded, or supported by the computer. As the learner's competence increases, the zone moves, the scaffolding shifts, the learner moves into a new ZPD, new scaffolds are provided, and so on, moving the learner toward independent learning.

2. The PC provides an environment with a cognitive support system that is well matched to human capabilities. It has unlimited storage and retrieval capacity and high computational speeds that complement human skills. The PC can provide scaffolding for the learner, a structure for searching, organizing, and re-presenting knowledge.

3. The PC utilizes many symbol systems. Text, photographs, video, and music are brought together in the computer-mediated environment. The term *multimedia* refers to this multimodal communication. It has a loose meaning that encompasses all the various forms of information that can be used to make narrative. A PowerPoint presentation with an audio clip from a student, photographs of a project, and prose is a multimedia presentation. So is an off-the-shelf CD-ROM computer program that has images from a museum, text, and spoken explanations of featured exhibits. Language takes many forms across multimedia, just as it does in day-to-day life. The capacity to make that language a digital resource is a boon for teachers and students.

4. Users of digital resources are able to access, use, and create products that are multimodal—music, art, graphics, words, and photographs are all combined in ways that are used to create and construct meaning(s) in new and unique ways. This should encourage the integration of learners' feelings, emotions, and aesthetic senses with their cognitive and information-construction thoughts, thereby providing for engaging experiences that have long-term learning and developmental effects (Coles, 1998).

WHAT DIGITIZED NEW LITERACIES ARE AVAILABLE?

Digital information comes in many forms and packages. The ways that digital information is packaged change as computer power, storage space, and file compression steadily improve. Access is often through a disk, most likely a

CD-ROM, or DVD, that either runs on the workstation or is installed in its hard drive. Digital resources can also be accessed through a network or the Internet.

A CD-ROM or DVD accompanies many content area textbooks, which can be installed on a PC. The content can be of many types such as information banks or databases, like encyclopedias, dictionaries, maps, or art museum collections. Gone are the hours required for teachers to locate suggested or supplementary resources. It's all at the click of a mouse. Storage requirements can be massive for these sorts of supplemental materials, but disks of various types hold increasing amounts of data, from a floppy with 1.4 MB, to a CD-ROM at 640 MB, to a DVD with more than 5 GB of storage. Keychain hard drives and online storage make it possible to easily transport large application or data files. This capacity will continue to increase as processing speed and miniaturization accommodate more and more complex information.

Information Banks and Databases

Discussed in the paragraphs that follow are information banks and databases available to the content area teachers and students. These provide heretofore unavailable or difficult-to-find resources for students to find facts and information for content area learning.

Indexed Resources. The first CD-ROMs for educational purposes were products such as dictionaries and encyclopedias, which are relatively easy to assemble in digital form. Users find it faster to look something up electronically than manually, and the beautiful illustrations that accompany the texts make learning experiences richer. Computers sold to the educational market usually have several built-in resources such as these, including virtual tours of major art museums, such as the Louvre, with indexed collections, pictures, and commentary.

Electronic Books. Anderson-Inman and Horney (1997) discuss the advantages and disadvantages of e-books. The disadvantages include the need for sophisticated hardware and software, and the fact that it is difficult to cuddle up with an e-book or carry it on a backpacking trip. Nonetheless, e-books are growing in popularity. Their accessibility means that some classroom resources can be made available that otherwise would be difficult to obtain. These digital resources, which include fiction, manuals, and reference materials, provide three advantages over print resources: (a) they are searchable, that is, a reader can do word searches to locate related occurrences; (b) they are modifiable, making it easy for the reader to select a comfortable font style or size, or, in some cases, to select a language; and (c) they are enhanceable, in that meaning-making resources can be added to the reading experience, such as illustrations, word definitions and study guides. It is possible to read western literature online; see Project Guttenberg at http://www.promo. net/pg/ for books in English and http://www.csusm.edu/csb/ for books in Spanish.

Simulations and Games. Other disk-based content types include games and simulations on CD-ROM or DVD. Simulations are interactive games in which the outcome depends on skill and decision making. These programs are based on what are known as "expert systems," which use the PC's memory to store facts about a given phenomenon and its processing speed to react to the user's decisions in real time and in a real-world manner. James Gee's (2003) studied people playing video games and observed 36 principles of learning being used—suggesting that, for some learners, video games provide students with learning experiences that teachers may be able to tap into and build upon in the classroom. Theoretically, simulations are a good way to take advantage of students' out-of-school experience with games. Clark Aldrich (2003) concurs and explains that simulations are successful learning tools because they provide authentic and relevant scenarios, they tap user's emotions and force problem solving, they provide a sense of choice, and the games can be replayed. In the classroom, many simulations can be played collaboratively with students on teams, gathering information and making decisions. Well-chosen simulations provide a meaningful context for problem solving, inquiry, and group decision making, which is a good setting for acquiring information and developing critical thinking.

A visit to the Web, local bookstore, or publisher's catalogue provides ample simulations from which a teacher may choose. One simulation, *SimCity* by Maxis, provides interactive urban scenarios appropriate for social studies content, especially geography and world cultures, allowing students to experience and attempt to solve real-world problems of population and resources (see http://www.dosgamesarchive.com/download/game/77 for a playable demonstration of an early version of the game.) Maxis publishes another program that has potential for the science classroom, *SimAnt*, which puts students in the place of a homeowner in a contest with an ant colony in a suburban yard. There are many other scenario-based games that provide students with resources and problems to solve (see Tycoon LemonadeStand for economic and business games, and http://www.cascoly.com for science examples).

Anchored Instruction. Anchored or case-based instruction is designed to link media to curriculum, which helps students to make connections and visualize concepts. One example is the curriculum based on the *Adventures of Jasper Woodbury* series developed at Vanderbilt University. Presented on videodisc, a series of short vignettes illustrate real-life situations that require students to mine the media resource for data to solve mathematical problems.

Technology-supported case-based learning becomes a central core around which curriculum can be based (Leu & Kinzer, 2000). Educational researchers at the University of Connecticut are experimenting with multiple literacies, teacher education and student learning and literacy. One of their projects links a social studies unit on 19th-century London to the movie *Young Sherlock Holmes*. For a more complete description of case-based literacy projects, see the www.literacy.uconn.edu/ctell.htm Web site.

Application Program–Productivity Tools

Disk-based digital resources include application programs of many types, from word-processing programs to database and spreadsheet programs, allowing the user to create a unique product. These cognitive support tools (Salomon, 1994) amplify and extend the learner's capabilities as they serve to mediate the processes of research, reorganization, and re-presentation of knowledge.

Word Processing. Most likely, word processing is the most widely used computer tool in the classroom. Some teachers are concerned that students' lack of keyboarding skills interferes with effective word processing. Research is not conclusive on this issue (Waner, Behymer, & McCrary, 1992), but it suggests that keyboarding can be taught in third or fourth grade (Wronkovich, 1998) and that most children and young people rapidly learn to use the keyboard when presented with meaningful communicative reasons to do so. Elementary school students use a graphics program like KidPix and middle-school students use presentation software like PowerPoint or a multimedia production tool like HyperStudio to create authentic products.

Spreadsheets and Databases. Spreadsheets and databases, examples of David Jonassen's (1996) *Mindtools*, can be used to organize information from any knowledge domain. These are computer applications that are ubiquitous and inexpensive, are commonly found as part of the computer office utility packages like MS Office or Applewords, and are powerful, but often overlooked, tools for learning.

Teachers in all content areas can integrate these tools by introducing the simple matrix of rows and columns to organize information. For example, a teacher might begin by lebeling the columns for days of the week and the rows for hours of the day, and then ask students to fill in and predict their daily schedules. Using the formula functions of spreadsheet programs, the students could enter their reading amount by pages each day and find the daily sums and weekly averages. The recording and manipulation of data in a spreadsheet, with magical ripple effects for changing values of observed data, show how equations work in the real world by relating outcomes and consequences which helps students to move from the concrete to the abstract. Spreadsheets are useful with both numeric and nonnumeric data. Determining what the rows and columns will represent can be a collaborative process to begin an inquiry.

Once students are comfortable using the tools, they can search their tables for words and phrases, tally references, and ultimately construct a database. A database, a digital resource, is any system that organizes information and permits sorting and searching. The World Wide Web is a database, albeit a very large one. Information that was once stored on index cards and sorted by hand can be organized and stored electronically. Databases can be very complex multidimensional relational structures. The phonebook is an example of a database. For example, students can sort a digitized phonebook by last name, street number, zip code, or even first initial. Showing the class an example with a few fields and having the students complete the process of categorization and sorting of information provides a model for understanding the construction of databases and how to sort and search a database. Database construction, creating a digital resource by setting up fields and manipulating data, is an activity that promotes critical thinking, problem solving, and learning.

Semantic Networking Tools. Inspiration, a very popular, flexible, and useful semantic networking tool, helps teachers and students to organize information and to show relationships among ideas by facilitating the creation of semantic webs, concept maps, and other graphic organizers. Digital resources like graphic organizers created with a program like Inspiration are much more nimble and facile than are those created on paper, a transparency, or the chalkboard or whiteboard. Students and teachers who use Inspiration are able to identify important aspects of the knowledge domain, define categories, establish relationships, and input data. These tools can be used in any content area; students can analyze poetry, portray weather patterns, and represent chemical reactions.

Multimedia Production Tools

Macromedia Director, HyperStudio, and other authoring tools allow learners to create interactive environments. These programs make it possible to blend several information streams and modalities into one cohesive message. There are programs for print and graphics, music sampling and synthesizers, animation, video production, and Web design tools that go way beyond what is otherwise available to classroom artists and musicians (Lockhard & Abrams 2004). These tools and resources provide students with opportunities to learn through design, which is enhanced by the collaborative and communicative nature of the projects. Gee (2003) emphasizes that collaborative ways of learning are enhanced through connections with others in affinity (those who share common interests) groups.

The PC also supports arts activities that can be used across the curriculum. There are programs for drawing, painting, composing music, creating video, or making combinations of several art forms. Encouraging students to use the computer to create graphics, animation, video, or other media engages both aesthetic and cognitive responses, which affects motivation, or willingness to engage, in learning (D'Amasio, 1999). Educators are concerned about ways to engage students (Baker, Afflerbach, & Reinking, 1995; Shneiderman, 1998), as surveys regularly report the low engagement of many students in school (Shernoff, 2001). David, Betts, our collaborator on this chapter, conducted an investigation of an after-school program in arts technology for underserved minority middle-school-aged youth in downtown Tucson (Betts, 2000, 2003). He found that, when a learner began to care about the activity in which he or she was involved, engagement soon followed. The initial learner investment might be as little as caring what color was selected for a part of the art project. The following types of multimedia arts software provide tools and resources for bringing these engaging possibilities to the content area classroom.

Desktop publishing: Students produce a volume of their own by using a computer with word processing (or other publishing software) and a printer.

They create or acquire and organize the content. They choose the font, paper, layout, and content, and, from planning to production, they care about what it's going to be. This computer-mediated activity makes literacy an authentic task and introduces design concepts as well. Students can write poetry, and they can practice journalistic skills, research, and design layouts. They also get to work collaboratively on the publication of their own work.

Computer graphics: There are many software tools that allow for artistic expression in many media and make the artist's job easier. For example, in addition to the "eraser" function, many programs include an "undo" function. So, should a mistake be made or a mind changed, it is easy to go back and repair the product. Can't draw a straight line? The curve tool's function draws lines, circles, cubes, and graceful arcs and figures. An image from a magazine or the web can be captured and imported. Students who have the opportunity to design fonts, logos, business cards, or t-shirts are involved in making aesthetic decisions as well as taking measurements, scaling patterns, or transferring designs. A middle-school-age girl used a photograph and special fonts to create

FIG. 5.1. Image 1 by a middle-school-age girl.

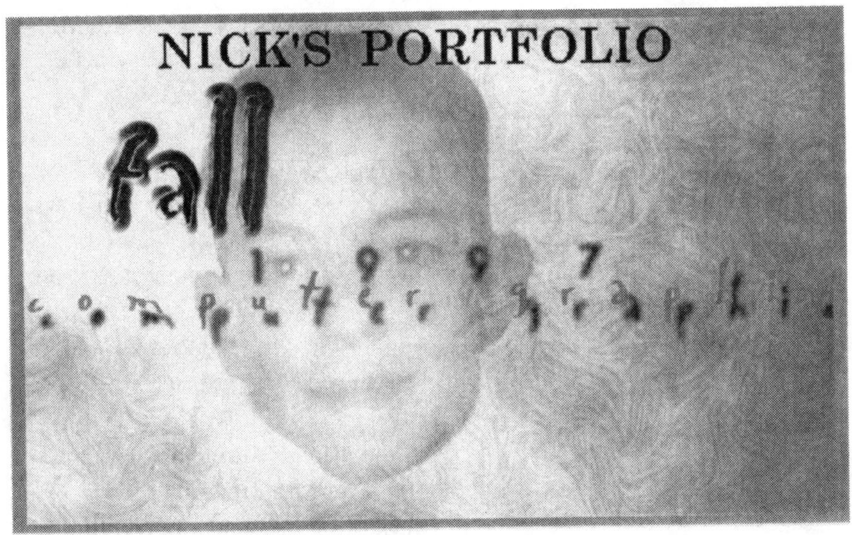

FIG. 5.2. Image 2 by a middle-school-age boy.

Image 1 (see Fig. 5.1) on a computer. A middle-school-age boy used a three-dimensional modeling program and created Image 2 (see Fig. 5.2).

Animation and presentation: Planning and organizing are keys to these related activities. Presentation tools like PowerPoint assemble data and images to deliver a message. Animation programs create virtual moving pictures from graphics. These tools overlap. Simply put, by changing PowerPoint slides fast enough on the screen, it looks like animation (see a simple and free animation program online at http://www.anim8or.com/; The National Institute of Health also has a free program that is very versatile at http://rsb.info.nih.gov/nih-image/). Creating an animation requires planning by creating storyboards, which is also a good prewriting exercise, to develop narrative or expository structure and move objects around over time.

Video production: Planning, recording, and editing videotape is a literacy process that involves real-world problem solving and creative thinking, often in a collaborative setting. Again, the storyboard is a basic tool in video production for laying out script ideas. Digital cameras and computers with built-in software make it possible to produce videos in the classroom. See Box 5.2 for methods used by Sara Kajder (2004) to help struggling readers tell their personal narratives through video production.

Web design: The language, or computer code, that makes the World Wide Web work is called HTML (hypertext markup language). It is a tag language

BOX 5.2. Personal Narrative and Digital Storytelling

These are some of the methods used by Kajder (2004, pp. 64-68):

1. Begin by discussing a definition of literacy and the concept of story with students. Help students find a story "worth telling." Sara asked her students to draw and orally describe a detailed map of the neighborhood where they grew up. She also asked each student to write about a favorite coat and to describe what was in the pockets.
2. Ask students to choose artifacts—photographs of important places and people and images from magazines—that represent the story being told.
3. Make a storyboard that has two dimensions: chronology and interaction, which is how the audio interacts with the images.
4. Revise by asking students to mark up their scripts, highlighting all the action in green and all the reflection in pink. If their scripts are marked with too much pink, it suggests too much preaching and not enough showing; too much green indicates action without enough rich description or context. Rearrange the order of events, making them either more or less chronological. Choose sentences to either "explode"—make them bigger by providing more elaboration—or pinpoint an idea and describe it more deeply.
5. Construct the video by importing or digitizing the photos, adding transitions and special effects, record narration, add sound tracking, and burn the finished CD.
6. Have a screening, complete with popcorn and student-written responses to each video.

(<*tag*>), with about 200 basic tags, which are short commands that are bracketed with fences (<and>). A Web page can be created with less than a dozen tags. Creating and maintaining a Web page in any knowledge domain or field brings learners into new literacies in an active way.

The Internet as a Communication Tool

The Internet represents important communications potential. School administrators and teachers may use e-mail to communicate with students and parents. Teachers may provide students opportunities to make Web pals by sharing research projects and learning experiences with distant peers.

Web Sites. Teachers create Web sites to serve their teaching practice by coordinating lessons and curriculum with students, parents, and other professionals. David, our contributor to this capter, uses his Web site as a tool for the classes he teaches, and he finds it useful to link the various assignments, class schedules, syllabi, blogs (described in subsequent paragraphs) and other resources in one online presence. As a result, students in his classes, who are future teachers, experience a model of how to create Web sites for the classes they will teach one day.

Electronic Communications Links. The most commonly used communication links include e-mail, chat rooms, listservs, and blogs. Students are likely to be familiar with e-mail and chat rooms. Catherine Doherty and Diane Mayer (2003) suggest persuasively that e-mail can be a "contact zone" for teachers and students. They report on the Plus Project, an ongoing collaboration between the schools, parents, and the University of Queensland in Australia. This project links teachers with indigenous youth, those of Aboriginal and Torres Strait Islander backgrounds. An analysis of the project revealed that e-mail communication between "teacher and student provides a new space—new in scope, location, time, mode, and interactional protocol—in which to explore and build" (p. 593) a core relationship between students and their teacher. They point out that a good relationship between a teacher and students is crucial to maintaining students' commitment to learning in middle school and the upper grades (National Middle School Association, 2001). In their study, they found both teachers and students engaged in authentic conversations as they communicated online, which positively affected classroom learning.

Patty uses e-mail for dialogue journals in her university classes. Each student is asked to write his or her reflective responses to the readings and class discussions after each class meeting. Students are encouraged to make connections between their real-life experiences, content from other classes, and Patty's class. Patty responds in a conversational manner to each message, sharing her own understandings and answering and asking questions. Sometimes, the entries become text for the whole class to think about—the e-mail exchange is shared with the class listserv or is read aloud in class (of course, the student agrees to have the entry made public). The e-mail messages in one class, "Essentials of Reading and Writing," a beginning graduate course, were analyzed (Zhang, 2003) along with students' reports of their perceived value. This analysis revealed three findings: (a) students made intertextual connections as they linked a class reading with another experience,

(b) students' thinking was "pushed" by these interactions, and (c) students appreciated the immediacy of the communication.

E-mail communication is asynchronous; that is, the message is posted and can be read at the recipient's leisure. Chat rooms, in contrast, are synchronous in that those who are participating in the communication are online at the same time. Identity and privacy are issues in both types of communication, a matter to be discussed with students.

Web logs, or blogs, are becoming more and more common; a growing number of K–12 and college teachers are using them, citing their simplicity and ease of publishing. They add cross-referencing capability and information-gathering functions to other student- or teacher-produced communications. Blogs permit individuals to participate by reading, writing, and collecting information on specific topics online without having to learn any computer code. Here are some examples of blogs: *Mathmagenic* is a site for discussions about blogging and learning mathematical concepts. See http://blog.mathemagenic.com/ (see screen shot 1).

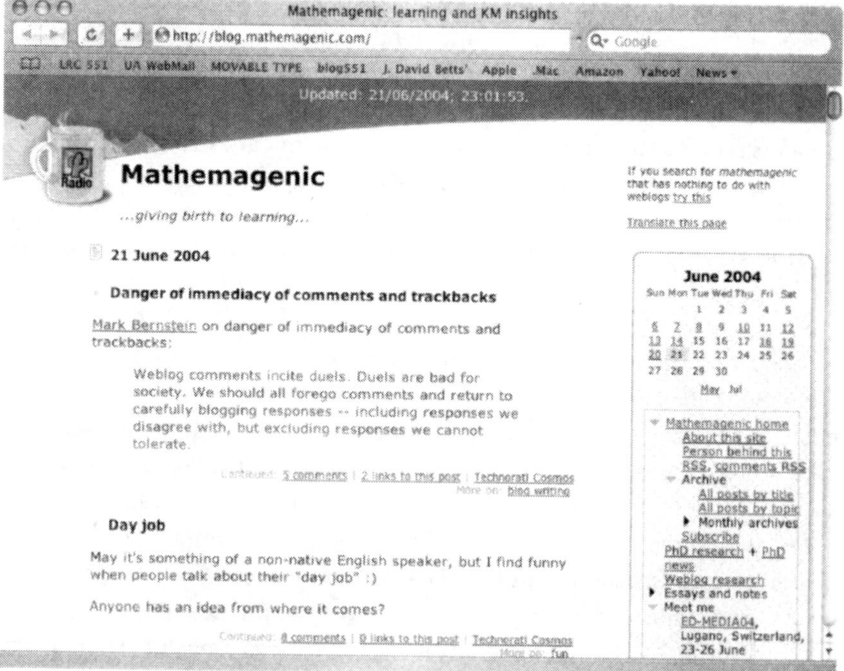

Screen shot 1.

Screen shot 2.

Teachers and librarians can learn about blogging from *A Teacher's Personal Blog* at http://www.beaconschool.org/~clehmann/MT/ or *Liblog*, at http://www.rcpl.info/services/liblog.html. The Brooklyn International High School blog site (<http://www.brooklyninternational.or/jluft/>) is an example of blogs being used in the classroom. It features weblogs for students from several classes allowing students to respond and reflect on class discussions and readings (see screen shot 2).

These resources provide opportunities for multimodal literacy and give learners tools that can be used across their studies.

TEACHING AND LEARNING WITH DIGITAL RESOURCES IN THE CONTENT AREAS

Researchers writing about new literacies (Gee, 2000; Leu, 2002; New London Group, 2000) are helping educators to change from print-constrained teaching and learning activities to an approach that is more in line with the reality of multiple literacies in today's society. Cope and Kalantzis (2000) argue that all meaning making is multimodal, and information communication technologies (ICT) and media (e.g., the Internet, cable, hypermedia, and DVD) make attractive new tools for accessing digital resources and participating in new kinds of literacy and learning engagements (Alvermann, 2004; Zhang, 2003). These engagements are particularly important "in the context of our culturally and linguistically diverse and increasingly globalized societies; to account for the multifarious cultures that interrelate and the plurality of texts that circulate and for the variety of text forms associated with information and multimedia technologies" (The New London Group, 2000, p. 9).

Bertram Bruce and James Levin (1997) surveyed the literature and created a taxonomy of educational technologies based on a curriculum classification system recommended originally by John Dewey (1943): inquiry, communication, construction, and expression. They tested the utility of the taxonomy by classifying "advanced applications" of educational technologies (See Box 5.3). Their taxonomy is helpful because it reveals many possibilities for using educational technology to constructively engage students in concepts.

The National Science Foundation's program in Applications of Advanced Technologies provides funds for projects designed to investigate educational technologies. The short descriptions of these projects are available at http://www.ehr.nsf.gov/RED/AAT/AATABS06.htm. One or more of the projects described at that Web site relate to nearly all aspects of the taxonomy, which confirms our hope that new literacies and their related technologies provide opportunities for progressive and constructivist ways of teaching (Bruce & Levin, 1997). Presented in what follows are several digital resources from the taxonomy that are useful for supporting content area study. They are each examples of what is being researched in the National Science Foundation study, are grounded theoretically, and are appropriate for all students.

WebQuests

A WebQuest is a scaffolded learning structure that uses links to essential resources on the World Wide Web. There are several advantages to using WebQuests. For example, students perceive the WebQuest as being an authentic task, which contributes to their being motivated to participate. Students can work individually to investigate a central, open-ended question and can also work with others to create a more sophisticated understanding of the topic being explored (Marsh, 2004; <http://www.bestWebQuests.com/>).

BOX 5.3 The Technology Taxonomy for Educators

This is the taxonomy according to Bruce and Levin (1997, pp. 86–87):

A. Media for Inquiry

1. Theory building—technology as media for thinking

    Model exploration and simulation toolkits
    Visualization software
    Virtual reality environments
    Data modeling—defining categories, relations, and representations
    Procedural models
    Mathematical models
    Knowledge representation: semantic networks, outline tools, and so on.
    Knowledge integration

2. Data access—connecting to the world of texts, video, and data

    Hypertext and hypermedia environments
    Library access and ordering
    Digital libraries
    Databases
    Music, voice, images, graphics, video, data tables, graphs, and text

3. Data collection—using technology to extend the senses

    Remote scientific instruments accessible via networks
    Microcomputer-based laboratories with sensors for temperature, motion, heart rate, and so on
    Survey makers for student-run surveys and interviews
    Video and sound recording

4. Data analysis

    Exploratory data analysis
    Statistical analysis
    Environments for inquiry
    Image processing
    Spreadsheets

Programs to make tables and graphs
Problem-solving programs

B. Media for Communication

1. Document preparation

   Word processing
   Outlining
   Graphics
   Spelling, grammar, usage, and style aids
   Symbolic expressions
   Desktop publishing
   Presentation graphics

2. Communication—with other students, teachers, experts in various fields, and people around the world

   Electronic mail
   Asynchronous computer conferencing
   Synchronous computer conferencing (text, audio, video, etc.)
   Distributed information servers like the World Wide Web
   Student-created hypertext environments

3. Collaborative Media

   Collaborative data environments
   Group decision support systems
   Shared document preparation
   Social spreadsheets

4. Teaching Media

   Tutoring systems
   Instructional simulations
   Drill and practice systems
   Telementoring

C. Media for Construction

Control systems—using technology to affect the physical world
Robotics
Control of equipment
Computer-aided design
Construction of graphs and charts

D. Media for Expression

Drawing and painting programs
Music making and accompaniment
Music composing and editing
Interactive video and hypermedia
Animation software
Multimedia composition

The WebQuest is an instructional strategy to counter a tendency to aimlessly search the Web; as one teacher told David, "students find information, write it down, and then go off looking to see what else is interesting, and that is a limitless journey." To help prepare students for a WebQuest, teachers and students organize initial online searches by using simple online scavenger hunts for specific information from specific Web sites. An excellent example of a starter activity is Michael McVey's Internet Tour and Scavenger Hunt at <http://www.ed.arizona.edu/onlinetour/>. The computer and the Internet scaffold the research. Teachers find this activity an excellent introductory activity, especially if the student is also asked to classify, reorganize, and represent the information found in the scavenger hunt.

There are also WebQuest opportunities for learners to participate in real-life adventures and scientific expeditions. Using wireless communications and portable computers, scientists and explorers include others from distant places in the adventure and the science. NASA maintains Web sites where the public can get real-time information about the status of a space launch or extraterrestrial activity (see http://quest.arc.nasa.gov/; a complete listing of links to other WebQuest resources can be found at http://webquest.org/).

Research Projects

Perhaps the most important use of the Internet is to do student-initiated research. Finding new information on the Internet can be daunting, because the Internet is vast and the many connectivity possibilities are often very inviting, which may distract students far from their original quests. The Internet also provides many more examples of information genres than is readily available to many young people (Williams, 2003). "Surfing" on the World Wide Web is a little like wandering through the stacks in a library, but it is much quicker. The Internet is so well designed for surfing that we can be sure it will be used that way, and, depending on the instruction teachers provide, it can be made more efficient.

Finding out how information is organized in a particular knowledge domain and what key words to use in a search are the first issues confronting students. Several instructional strategies will help to overcome these problems. For example, providing students with a list of possible key words or phrases from the unit's conceptual map and asking them to brainstorm other related terms is a good starting point for doing a search. The list might be divided up among students and, after they conduct Web searches, sites that students believe to be relevant could be downloaded and shared with the rest of the group. Different students could use different search engines so that different sources will be found. Small group activities might include comparing and prioritizing source material with special attention to its reliability. Students can be helped to organize the material found by creating a conceptual map or other type of graphic organizer such as Inspiration to identify and label the relationship between resources and concepts found.

The second challenge is helping students to organize the information gathered in ways that are suitable for interpretation and presentation. Spreadsheets can be used to arrange data for interpretation. Surfing the Internet, a reader needs to compose a text, at least in his or her mind, from what is selected from the Web. To compose, a student needs to produce coherent and well-structured text. Hence, we can imagine that the qualities a teacher would look for in print-based text chosen for the classroom (chapter 4, this volume) would be the same qualities, well structured and coherent text, that students need to know about to compose from the Internet. We suggest, then, that text-analysis strategies such as concept mapping, connector word analysis, paragraph analysis, and the 5 W and H, be taught to students to use as they compose from multiple digital resources. These strategies can also provide students with tools for helping them to evaluate their own compositions.

Collaborative Projects

Collaboration can be enhanced via the Internet and e-mail, and publication can also be mediated by technology. As with Web quests, many computer-mediated activities lend themselves well to collaborative work patterns. "I'm the thinkist and you're the typist," is part of the title of an early paper describing kindergarteners at the computer (Sheingold, Hawkins, & Char, 1984). These young learners negotiated the division of labor at their computer activity center. Group projects can be organized at any level so that the need for someone at the keyboard is balanced by the need for note taking and finding and using other resources. A multimedia project as an ensemble effort provides opportunities for participation by individuals with a variety of skills and interests. Software programs and Web sites that support collaboration are also available. Programs such as Microsoft Word, for example, include many helpful shortcuts for co-writing such as "version tracking" and network access.

Online Self-Publishing

Online self-publishing and journaling, now very possible through zines and blogs, allow learners to have their own personal virtual place to gather resources and share thoughts and ideas. Zines, as discussed in chapter 1, are personal projects that take advantage of desktop publishing. No one is suggesting that zines become part of the content area curriculum, but these creative publications are good reminders of the talent young people are capable of displaying. Blogs are interconnected online writing spaces that take little computer know-how, are largely public, and are appropriate for use in a classroom application, inviting authentic publication and peer review.

Another possibility is a *wikki*. A wikki is a Web page that anyone can add to or edit. Some are moderated, such as a dictionary project that accepts and saves every entry or correction and sorts the results for consensus. A wikki can also be a stand-alone free-for-all virtual graffiti wall. Any of these may be used to support a long-distance collaboration on a science project, share anime resources (animes are animated movies made in Japan), or supplement class discussions.

These digital resources provide multiple new ways to engage students in exciting content area concepts. The nature of these resources requires that students, more than ever before, develop their capacities to be critical and thoughtful learners. In the next section we provide a framework for developing these capacities.

Critical Thinking, Critical Reading, and Critical Literacy

The Internet makes transparent the need for students to think critically and to engage in critical literacy. Critical thinking and critical reading, very similar concepts, are not the same as critical literacy. One of our purposes in this section is to distinguish between critical thinking and critical reading on the one hand and critical literacy on the other hand. We deal with both concepts in this section because, although distinctive, they each represent aspects of thinking that have to be promoted across the curriculum. We discuss critical thinking and critical reading first, because we predict that most readers' have prior knowledge about them.

Critical reading is the act of incorporating principles of critical thinking with the act of reading. Critical reading is necessary for engaging literacy in any mode, either print or digital. To a certain extent, school officials are responsible for ensuring that the print-based resources supplied to students are appropriate; such censorship, however, is not possible when students have access to the Internet. This means that the ante has been raised: Students need to develop their abilities to think critically. There are few gatekeepers or librarians to monitor the overwhelming amount of questionable material on the Internet; students, therefore, need strategies for sorting material according to its voracity and credibility.

David colleague shared a story about one of his high school freshmen, who came to him with information from a Web site asserting that the Holocaust had not occurred. The young man was struggling with the contradiction between what he had been told and believed and this new contradictory information. The teacher coached him to go to the sources that were cited, and there the student discovered a circular pattern among a group of authors who cited each other and who belonged to the same political group. This freshman learned a lot about the nature of the Internet and how to be a critical evaluator of sources of information. Students need to be aware of any unstated texts or agendas and note what information is not being offered. These covert messages and silences can signal the site's political intentions.

Critical thinking and reading involves the reader's asking several questions about the voracity and quality of the material being read. Critical reading is rooted in the liberal-humanist philosophical view of what it means to know and understand the world. It is a belief that thinking is "eminently rational in origin: it is deliberate, orderly, critical, and purposeful" (Cervetti, Pardales, & Damico, 2004). Critical reading has a long tradition in the reading field, emanating from early in the 20th century. Bond and Wagner (1966, p. 283, cited by Cervetti et al., 2004) state this:

> [Reading specialists and researchers have promoted] the process of evaluating the authenticity and validity of material and of formulating an opinion about it. It is essential for anyone dealing with controversial issues to be able to read

> critically.... [The reader] must understand the meanings implied as well as stated. He must evaluate the source from which he is reading. He must differentiate the important from the unimportant facts.... He must be able to detect treatments warped by prejudice. He must keep in mind the authors' precepts and intentions and judge whether in drawing his conclusions the author considered all the facts presented.

A contemporary proponent of critical reading and thinking is Arthur Costa (2000), who promotes the teaching of strategies for these reasons:

- to help students think rationally, separate facts, inferences, and judgments;
- to help students refer to the authority of the text to justify reasoning; and
- to detect author's intentions and develop "higher" level thinking skills.

He argues that many of the strategies—such as concept mapping, reflective writing, and discussion—recommended in this volume are helpful to develop critical reading on the part of students. We agree.

In contrast, critical literacy, as we discussed in chapter 2 of this volume, is a stance taken by the reader toward the text that is different from the critical reading or thinking stance. A student with a critical literacy stance realizes that "textual meaning is understood in the context of social, historic, and power relations, not solely as the product or intention of an author. Further, reading is an act of coming to know the world (as well as the word) and a means to social transformation" (Cervetti et al., 2004). This understanding of critical literacy emanates from two poststructuralist influences: that of critical social theory and critical theorists from the Frankfurt school. The first theory attempts to explain the social and political problems of the world and seeks to suggest alternatives to oppression and inequalities. The second maintains that language and literacy are basic tools for learners to engage in dialogue to better understand themselves in a socially unjust context. Teachers who engage students in a critical literacy stance help them to question the authority of the text through dialogue, asking how meanings are assigned to a certain figure or events in a text, how the text attempts to get readers to accept its constructs, what the purpose is of the text, whose interests are served by this text, what view of the world is put forth by the ideas of the text, and what alternatives there might be to the apparent meaning of the text (Cervetti et al., 2004).

BOX 5.4. Distinctions Between Critical Reading and Critical Literacy

Area	Critical Reading	Critical Literacy
Knowledge (Epistemology)	Knowledge is gained through sensory experience in the world or through rational thought; a separation between facts, inferences, and reader judgments is assumed.	What counts as knowledge is not natural or neutral; knowledge is always based on the discursive rules of a particular community and is thus ideological.
Reality (Ontology)	Reality is directly knowable and can, therefore, serve as a referent for interpretation.	Reality cannot be known definitively, and it cannot be captured by language; decisions about truth, therefore, cannot be based on a theory of correspondence with reality but must instead be made locally.
Authorship	Detecting the author's intentions is the basis for higher levels of textual interpretation.	Textual meaning is always multiple, contested, culturally and historically situated, and constructed within differential relations of power.
Instructional goals	Development of higher-level skills of comprehension and interpretation.	Development of critical consciousness.

Box 5.4, which uses information from Cervetti et al. (2004), helps to distinguish between the two stances, that of being a critical reader or thinker and that of being engaged in critical literacy.

It is likely that the instructional strategies promoted in this volume are helpful for developing critical literacy; the important distinction is the purpose the teacher and students share for engaging the text. Socially conscientious teachers are likely to adapt a stance that encourages their students to ask critical literacy questions when engaging content area concepts.

A good place to begin thinking about helping to develop students' capacities to be critical, adapting either a critical thinking or a critical literacy stance, is to examine and take advantage of students' experiences with the media and popular culture. "Popular culture is popular for a reason. It plays an important role in the daily lives of students and definitely deserves a place" (Evans, 2004, p. 38) in the secondary curriculum. In the next section we consider popular culture and students' experiences that can be built on to help them learn to be critical in the content areas.

Popular Culture and the Classroom. Williams (2003) reports, "if we listen carefully to what students say when they talk about watching television we find that, when they engage in discrete use, they employ interpretive and critical skills that should not be discounted" (p. 550). Kevin Mannes (2004) agrees; after describing research related to the ways young people use the media, he makes this claim:

> There are two important insights that can be gained from understanding the purposes for which young people use the media. First, adolescents' uses of media are as wide-ranging and complex as adults' uses of media. Second, young people use media to achieve goals that are intimately connected with their identity and their social interaction. These media uses are neither good nor bad, healthy nor unhealthy. These uses are significant in the lives of young people. (p. 47)

Listening to students' experiences with popular culture and the many digital technologies that support it is the first step to critically incorporating digital resources in the curriculum. Nearly all students have had some digital experience; by carefully listening to and observing their students, teachers know which experiences can be built on in the classroom.

This may seem obvious, but some teachers are reluctant to recognize and acknowledge students' prior experience with out-of-school media. There is evidence (Williams, 2003), in fact, that middle-school students are taught to *not* bring their experiences with popular culture into the classroom. It seems that there is a hierarchy in many teachers' minds that marginalizes and diminishes popular culture, deeming it as inappropriate for the classroom. As a result, students know that it is better to not let the teacher know about their experiences.

Educators who ignore or do not acknowledge or permit students' out-of-school literacies in the school or classroom send those students and their literacies underground (McArthur, Penland, Spencer, & Anders, in press), pushing youth who may already be alienated or marginalized further away from school. We are of the mind that the better we understand the literacies in which students are engaged, the more likely it is that we can find ways to connect out-of-school literacies with in-school literacies. We need all our young people to be learning in school, and one way to do that is to provide a place for students to connect their in- and out-of-school literacies.

Bridging Popular Culture and Content Learning. With some knowledge of students' experiences in mind, our next step is to invite students to use those experiences to thoughtfully and critically engage content-related digital resources. This chapter provides possible tools and resources; the trick for the teacher is to operationalize these resources—the Internet, spreadsheets, databases, videos, WebQuests, Weblogs, research projects, and so forth—in ways that help students to advance their learning. The new literacies involve more than just collecting information and producing products, though. They also involve providing space and time for students to reflect on how well the multimedia tools helped them to accomplish their learning. The beauty of this for educators is that digital resources make learning and critical thought not only necessary but also an authentic school activity.

Incorporating space and time for reflexivity about the benefits of tools and learning goes a long way toward developing sophisticated learners with critical abilities. Too often, units of study end without granting students and teachers the opportunity to pause and reflect on the quality of both the processes of the learning experience and the meaningfulness of what is learned. Teaching students to become self-critical through reflection contributes greatly to their becoming independent learners.

Students increase their repertoire of critical thinking skills and critical literacy sensitivities when they participate in creating and doing media production. Media literacy is at the heart of critical literacy (Goodman, 2003) where the culture, to a great extent, is conveyed via the media. Patty recalls when her son, Paul, took a video-production class in middle school; watching television suddenly became a more critical experience as he explained what went into making a commercial and the subtle embedded messages. In effect, Paul was able to explain the semiotics—the meanings of the different symbols in the message—that affected the interpretation and impact of the commercial.

Students' experiences viewing media may provide prior knowledge for their understanding of a story and therefore contribute to the writing of stories. David worked with fifth graders as they learned to produce a televised daily news program. In the process of producing the program, the students learned that a variety of tools—photographs, graphics, music, scripts, interviews, and video clips—could be used to tell a story; they also learned that the tools selected made a difference in the message conveyed. Video-production tools and techniques used by students as a medium to re-present knowledge they have constructed in a physics class, for example, are basically the same as might be used in a history class.

In addition to acknowledging and building on students' experiences with popular culture and involving students in the creation of media, critical literacy is developed when teachers focus on the ways that issues of power, privilege, and social justice permeate the texts in students' lives. Margaret Finders (1997) reports being appalled when she found that the girls in her study easily confused the difference between advertisements and the editorial content of magazines. We have probably all experienced surprise when an interesting television program turns out to be a paid advertisement.

Laraine Wallowitz (2004) describes a teaching unit designed to help students discover the gendered messages in literature and the media. She wanted students to understand the ways that "notions of femininity and masculinity are socially and culturally constructed by the music we listen to, the books we read, the television we watch, and the stories we heard growing up" (p. 27). Through several activities and the analysis of several sources, both print and media, she helped the students to see the continued—and misdirected—social expectations regarding perfection in both men and women. This example suggests similar "critical" lessons that could be incorporated in any content area. Gender, race, and social class are powerful variables that affect every content area from the arts to zoology. We educators need to support students as they live and strive to understand themselves in an increasingly pluralistic and complex society.

The Digital Divide. Naturally, some teachers worry that their less sophisticated students will be left even further behind the more sophisticated learners when new literacies are incorporated into the classroom. One reason students are left behind is identified as the digital divide. Those students who come to school already familiar with the latest technology, who have money to spend on hardware, software, and movies, and who have access to cable or satellite television are privileged over those with less wealth (Feirro & Teberosky, 1982; Gee, 2003). Consider the data provided by U.S. Census and summarized by Ann Peterson Bishop (2003, p. 324), which we paraphrase here:

- Households with incomes of $75,000 and higher are more than *twenty times* more likely to have access to the Internet than those at the lowest income levels, and more than *nine times* as likely to have a computer at home.

- Black and Hispanic households are approximately *one third* as likely to have home Internet access as households of Asian–Pacific Islander descent, and roughly *two fifths* as likely as White households.
- The gaps between White and Hispanic households, and between White and Black households, are now more than 6 percentage points larger than they were in 1994.
- The digital divides based on education and income level have also increased in the past year alone. Between 1997 and 1998, the divide between those at the highest and lowest education levels increased 25%, and the divide between those at the highest and lowest income levels grew 29%.

The good news is that teachers can locate good hardware and software for their classroom through local technology grants and connections with the business community. In addition, the U. S. Department of Commerce and the U.S. Department of Education provide resource directories. David (Betts, 2002), in a project with a Native American village, documented how access to computers and the Internet substantially increased literacy practices in the community. Access to the technology gave community members a new sense of community and encouragement, especially as they saw the advances their children made when using the technology.

After-school programs and community computing centers are two other ways to address the digital divide. One after-school program, the Fifth Dimension (Blanton, Greene, & Cole, 2003), is a distributed literacy consortium of specially designed after-school enrichment programs involving cooperation between local community organizations, such as school-based recreation centers, Boys' and Girls' Clubs, and YMCAs and YWCAs, and colleges and universities in their communities. Fifth Dimension programs demonstrate that students, including special education students, are able to acquire proficiency in using technological tools, attain personal learning goals, take advantage of opportunities to extend and increase their understanding of school subjects, expand their abilities to navigate social complexities, and increase their perceptions of self-worth.

Community networks (Bishop, 2003) make up a movement dedicated to narrowing the digital divide. Typically, community network centers provide ways for community members to be informed about local events and to acquire public access to computing sites and Internet accounts. These community centers can also provide computer training and technical support. The Community Connector at http://www.si.umichi.edu/Community is a comprehensive online repository of information related to community networking. True to its mission, public libraries provide computer and Internet access. Some community networks are housed at libraries. A survey (Bertot & McClure, 2000) reports that 98% of all libraries are connected to the Internet, which is a marked increase (from 78% in some communities to 88% in other communities) since 1998.

As socially conscious educators, we can do a lot to support these and similar efforts, realizing that doing so help to provide students with a more equal learning field. Teaching in a community that suffers from the digital divide is challenging. Teachers need to take special strategic steps both to get needed digital tools and resources and to help students become acquainted with their use. Students are likely to be interested in using digital resources, and that fact along with opportunity and good teaching will go a long way toward propelling many students past economic limitations.

HOW CAN TEACHERS LEARN MORE ABOUT DIGITAL RESOURCES?

There are several sources to which teachers might turn for ideas to use digital resources in their instruction. Among these are the professional organizations to which most teachers belong. These professional organizations, such as the International Reading Association, the National Council of Teachers of Mathematics, the National Council of Teachers of English, and so forth, publish print-based and online journals and maintain Web sites that strive to help teachers stay abreast of technological advances.

Many teachers with years of experience using Web-based resources share their experiences online. Among their many contributions, they identify important traits of successful software and provide teacher-created rubrics for evaluation. For example, Schrock (2004) offers a collection of rubrics for evaluating a wide variety of multimodal student projects, teacher projects, and Web sites (see http://school.discovery.com/schrockguide/assess.html).

Hundreds of teacher Web sites share lesson plans, activities, and reviews of educational materials. Teachers in David's classes often make these a part of their first personal Web pages, finding and posting links to online resources. Several nonprofit or governmental education organizations maintain Web sites to do this. Many are nonprofit or individuals' labors of love. Most are commercial sites, however, and like anything, you've got to be careful what you buy online.

Here are a few examples:

- http://www.sitesforteachers.com/ is a database of education-related links that invites submissions.
- http://abcteach.com/ is a membership site with many shared resources for teachers.
- http://www.teachersfirst.com/ is a free site with many digital resources such as tutorials, WebQuests, and student-produced videos about copyright.
- http://www.edu-cyberpg.com is a free site for teachers sponsored by Comcast, a cable television company (see screen shot 3).
- *Tapped In*, http://ti2.sri.com/tappedin/, is the online workplace of an international community of education professionals. SRI International, a nonprofit research institute, sponsors Tapped In. David uses this site for some of the classes he teaches at the university and maintains a virtual office there. There are many opportunities present online for interacting with other teachers in your specialty or interest area (see screen shots 4 and 5).
- The Public Broadcasting Service (PBS) provides a Web site with more in-depth information and original sources (see www.pbs.org) to accompany their broadcasts. In addition, many local TV stations maintain a Web site for news, information, and resources.

This brief summary of resources suggests that plenty of information about using digital resources is available. Most likely, however, many teachers need the support and encouragement of their colleagues to leap into the virtual world of digitized literacies. As suggested in chapters 7 and 8, collaboration among peers and mutual support is likely to make the leap much easier.

SUMMARY AND REFLECTION

Digital resources are likely to become the resource of choice of teachers and learners in the very near future. The computer keyboard has become an icon, a ubiquitous interface for finding new knowledge, collaborating with learners and experts around the world, reorganizing knowledge, and for re-presenting it as new understanding. Teachers are including information and communications technology in their instruction with new understandings of multiple literacies and the roles of technology.

In this chapter we suggest that advances in digital resources and their uses have found a place in teachers' and learners' backpacks. For many, the

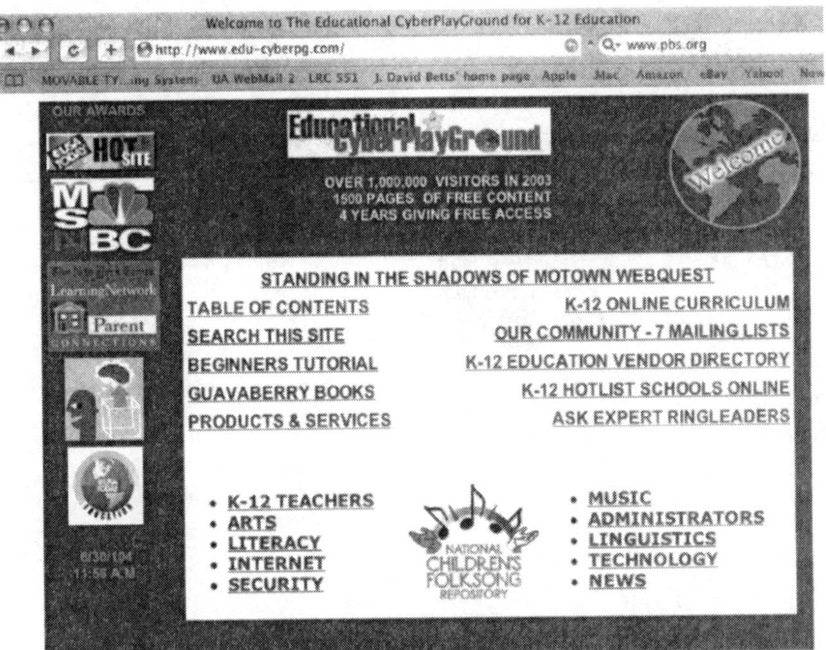

Screen shot 3.

computer is as integral to our lives as a book is, and further miniaturization and increased portability are likely to make digital tools and the resources they provide even more important in the immediate future. Students bring to school increased technological capabilities and experience, and so do many teachers. If a teacher is not particularly facile, he or she is likely to be more and more marginalized.

For those reasons, we provided in this chapter a compendium of digital tools and resources that are available for content area teaching and learning. These include information banks, databases, application programs and productivity tools, multimedia production tools, and the Internet. We then linked these tools to activities that can be used in the content area classroom, such as creating spreadsheets, using WebQuests, conducting research projects, creating collaborative projects, and publishing online.

Paramount in our discussion is the role of critical thinking and critical literacy. Critical thinking requires that users assess the credibility and accuracy of a source. Critical literacy challenges students and teachers to confront

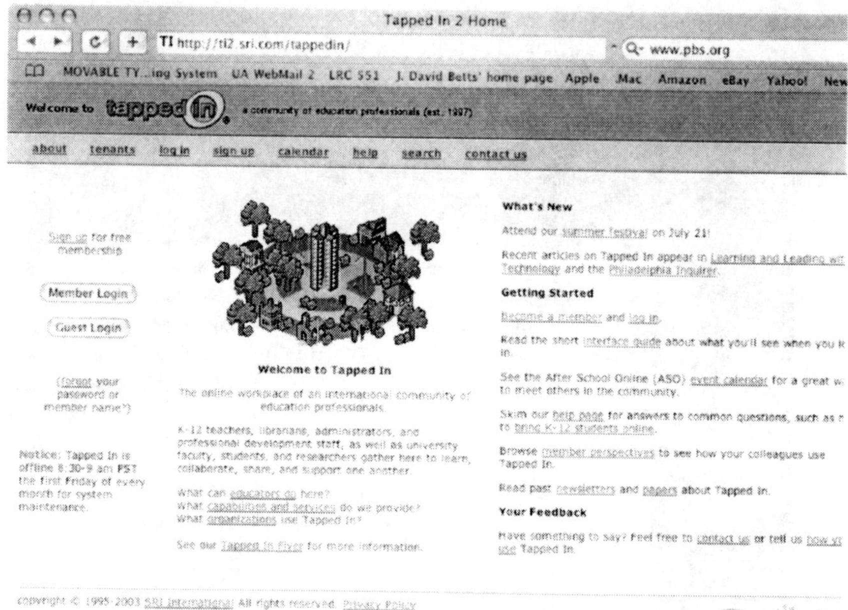

Screen shot 4.

issues of social justice and questions of power relations within any given knowledge domain. We encourage teachers to incorporate critical literacy in their instruction by beginning where students are, which means building on students' experiences with popular culture.

We also maintain that effective teaching to promote critical thought and critical literacy of digital resources contributes to the capacities of all learners. Navigating digital resources and printed resources are similar processes. Providing support and instructions for the most disenfranchised learners in our classrooms improves all students' literacy capacities.

Many online and in-print resources are available to teachers who are looking to advance their use of digital resources. Professional organizations and the Internet provide seemingly limitless ideas for resources, teaching practices, and evaluative rubrics.

Teachers who model a willingness to explore with new technology demonstrate that risk taking is an important part of learning. Learning how to learn

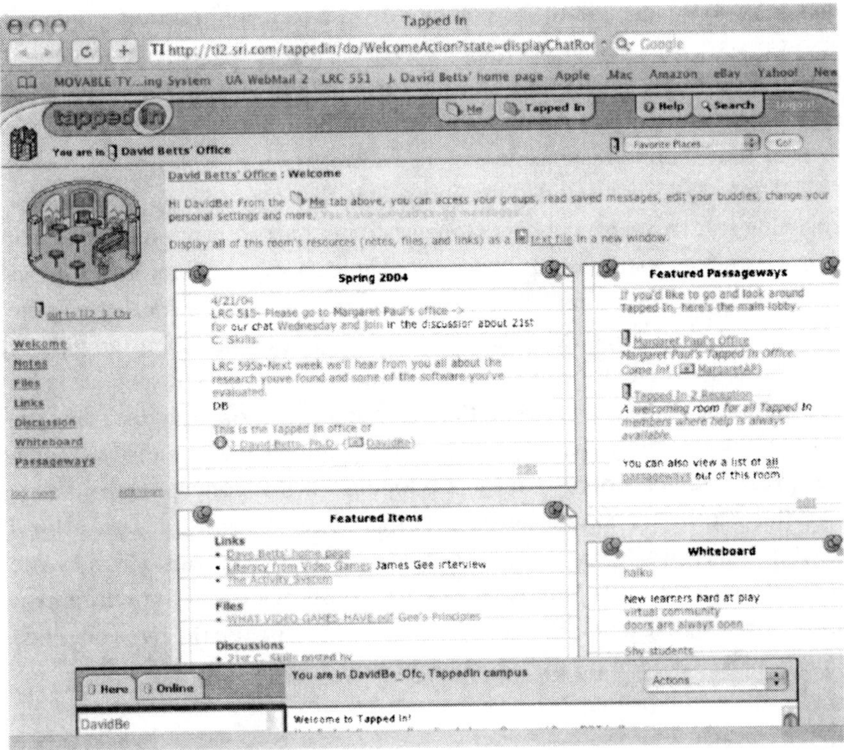

Screen shot 5.

is the essence of new literacies (Leu, 2002). The key to the treasure *is* the treasure, as John Barth (1972) tells us in his novel *Chimera*:

> It's in words that the magic is—Abracadabra, Open Sesame, and the rest—but the magic words in one story aren't magical in the next. The real magic is to understand which words work, and when, and for what; the trick is to learn the trick.... And those words are made from the letters of our alphabet: a couple-dozen squiggles we can draw with the pen. This is the key! And the treasure, too, if we can only get our hands on it! It's as if—as if the key to the treasure is the treasure! (p. 11)

APPLICATION ACTIVITIES

1. A concern shared by many educators is the "digital divide"—that is, students who have ready access to digital tools versus those who have very

little access. Do an audit of the community in which you teach. What digital resources are available in the public domain? How do students with limited resources at home access those resources? What can you and/or your school do to make those digital resources more available to students? What can you or your school do to make access more available?

2. Do a search for simulations and games that might be appropriate for engaging students with concepts in your content area. Search for reviews of these resources, especially at web sites related to your content area such as professional organizations. What do the writers of the reviews perceive as the strengths and weaknesses of the materials? Begin to think about how these digital resources might be integrated into instruction.

3. Become familiar with using the program Inspiration. Practice using the program by analyzing a reading assignment (planning and text analysis strategies presented in chapter 4) or by developing a digital concept map.

4. Revisit the section in this chapter that compares and contrasts critical reading and critical literacy. Using your own content area, consider and write about the two concepts. How do the two concepts relate to your own content area? How might teachers in your content area incorporate the two concepts? Does it make sense to do so? Why or why not?

FROM OUR PROFESSIONAL LIBRARY

Alvermann, D. E. (Ed.). (2004). *Adolescents and literacies in a digital world*. New York: Peter Lang.

Bruce, B. C. (Ed.). (2003). *Literacy in the information age: Inquiries into meaning making with new technologies.* Newark, DE: International Reading Association.

Finders, M. (1997). *Just girls: Hidden literacies and life in junior high*. New York: Teachers College Press.

Flood, J., Heath, S. B., & Lapp, D. (1997). *Handbook of research on teaching literacy through the communicative and visual arts.* New York: Macmillan.

Gallego, M. A., & Hollingsworth, S. (Eds.). (2000). *What counts as literacy: Challenging the school standard.* New York: Teachers College Press.

Hancock, J. (Ed.). (1999). *Teaching literacy using information technology: A collection of articles from the Australian Literacy Educator's Association*. Newark, DE: International Reading Association.

Kajder, S. B. (2003). *The tech-savvy English classroom*. Portland, ME: Stenhouse.

Kress, G. (2003). *Literacy in the new media age*. New York: Routledge.

Reinking, D., McKenna, M. S., Labbo, L. D., & Kieffer, R. D. (Eds.). (1998). *Handbook of literacy and technology: Transformations in a post-typographic world.* Mahwah, NJ: Lawrence Erlbaum Associates.

Wepner, S. B., Valmont, W. J., & Thurlow, R. (Eds.). (2000). *Linking literacy and technology: A guide for K–8 classrooms*. Newark, DE: International Reading Association.

6

Possibilities for Literacy Instruction in the Content Areas

As we begin to write this chapter, the popular poster of the teacher leaning back in her chair, hand on her head, and a bedraggled look in her eyes comes to mind. The caption on the poster is "No one ever said it was going to be easy!" Putting ourselves in the shoes of a content area teacher, we recognize that supporting students' efforts to use multiple literacies to construct understandings in the content area is challenging. The previous chapters have laid the groundwork for addressing issues of planning, preparation, and instruction.

Content area literacy has a long history that reflects priorities and theories of schooling since the early 1900s. Theories have waxed and waned, but requirements for students to use literacy to learn are a theme throughout. We suggest that Fig. 6.1 is a representation of the currently understood dimensions of content area literacy.

Our intentions thus far are to have elaborated on the nature of students, the literacy processes, conceptual objectives, and characteristics of prose and digital media. Throughout we have alluded to teachers' beliefs, provided some nuggets of pedagogical knowledge, and emphasized that literacy is a social practice that takes place in contexts. Society at large is part of that context. The recent emphasis on accountability has created a "culture of testing" (Anders & Richardson, 1992) that permeates school walls and affects what is done in school. Similarly, there are local community attitudes, beliefs, and pressures that affect what happens in a particular district or school. Every classroom exists within a school, and schools have their own personalities—cultures,

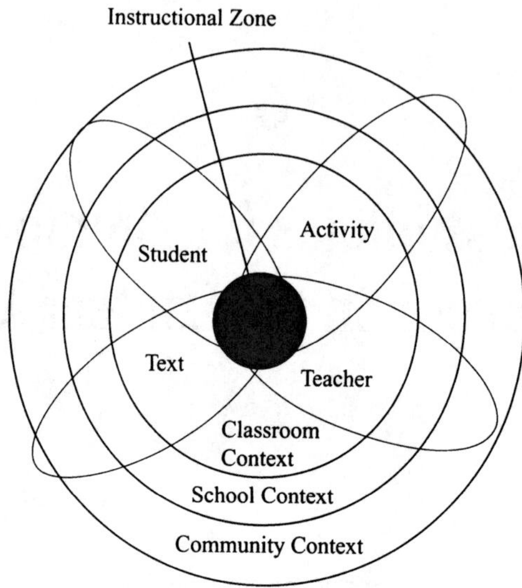

FIG. 6.1. Dimensions of content area literacy instruction.

so to speak, that also affect the classroom. And, of course, each classroom is a culture onto itself. A teacher is the leader in the classroom and contributes greatly to establishing the culture and climate in the classroom, but it is naïve to assume that an individual teacher isn't also affected by the cultural contexts around the classroom. Decisions that teachers make about instruction affect the culture and climate of the classroom. This theme is carried through this chapter and is expanded in chapter 7.

Inside the classroom, the students, teacher, curriculum, and related resources are the components that intersect and create the classroom climate. The intersection of these dimensions is the *instructional zone*—a space that provides opportunities for activities and strategy instruction. The purpose of this chapter is to provide guidance to plan for teaching in the instructional zone.

PLANNING TO PLAN

Experienced teachers often claim to not spend much time planning. Teacher education programs, however, emphasize planning. This seeming contradiction results in the situation in which teacher education programs sometimes get a bad rap from both former and current students. Why is there this contradiction about planning? One reason is that expert teachers have learned from their experience and plan in a different way than a beginning teacher does (Housner & Griffey, 1985). Novice teachers lack the years of experience from which the experts have learned. You can bet that an experienced teacher trying something new or undergoing a major shift in beliefs or practices spends considerable time planning.

Planning begins long before a lesson plan is written. Recipes and formulas are offered to beginning teachers to help them "get their feet wet" and to "get off on the right foot," but they are never adequate. Teaching is difficult and teachers hold a number of considerations in mind while preparing. The more expert teacher balances all those considerations in his or her mind without having to write them all down.

Teacher education is partially to blame for the "to plan or not to plan" contradiction, because planning is sometimes presented as a simple and linear process: Begin with behavioral objectives, teach, test, reteach, and test again. There are two problems with this model. First, it downplays the nature of the ideas on which instruction is based. We teach to engage students in the construction of ideas. Deep thought is needed to make the selected ideas coherent and to imagine how the ideas can be connected to students' interests and prior experience. In addition, the behavioral model ignores the reality that planning is only a template for what might happen. Plans have to be flexible and adaptable (Arends, 2001). Teachers are sensitive to the part that students play—some plans go astray, not because they are poor plans, but because the plans don't jive with a particular group of students. An experienced teacher is able to predict students' reactions, interests, and backgrounds, which makes for more reliable planning.

In this chapter we offer the wisdom of experienced teachers and research-based practices, which helps to make up for some of the years of experience that naïve teachers lack. We also believe that mature teachers who are "burned out" can be invigorated by the suggestions found in this chapter. We recommend an organizational scheme, or template, to help prepare for planning a unit that incorporates literacy development and the learning of ideas. In some teacher preparation content area literacy classes, this template is called a *planning notebook*.

In the last part of the chapter we offer a menu of options for literacy strategies to help engage students in literacy learning. We offer these knowing full well that some options are more adequate than others. We also know, however, that there is no prescription for practice; rather, each teacher creates and constructs a teaching practice from menus such as ours, other professional literature and colleagues, and personal experience.

We theorize that the time invested in planning to plan makes up for a lack of experience. We suggest a system to organize concepts, materials, and activities as a basis for daily lesson plans. Daily lesson plans emerge naturally when the components are collected and organized in a coherent unit. We suspect that the planning that goes into making this unit plan is analogous to the kind of content and pedagogical knowledge that experienced teachers have.

Planning involves preparation to orchestrate ideas, resources, and activities. How does a teacher choose the ideas or concepts to use in planning? This question was one of our foci in chapter 3. To recap, there are at least four sources for conceptual objectives. One source of information is the content knowledge gained in college courses and in independent study and personal experiences. Considering the content topics about which you are passionate is a good place to start. Another source is available resources. In addition to the print and digital resources we have discussed, consider people resources in your community: parents and business people, colleagues, and your students. Curriculum guides are another source for finding possible concepts. Depending on where you teach, you may find that your department, district, or state offer standards and curriculum guides. In addition, knowledge standards are provided by content area professional organizations, which can be a rich source of conceptual objectives. By examining all of these sources, you should be able to plan several coherent units that will represent your content well. Pedagogical knowledge is how you orchestrate the ideas, resources, and activities with and for your students.

Box 6.1 provides directions for the planning notebook we recommend. Following these steps to keep track of your plans and materials in a notebook is helpful. That way, over time you can continue to develop the notebooks by adding new ideas and materials or by deleting activities and materials that didn't work with your students.

Teachers who follow this planning to plan template and create a notebook are set to decide which of the prose and digital reading assignments have to have the support of literacy instruction. Next, we share suggestions for choosing activities to support students' use of multiple literacies to learn concepts.

BOX 6.1. A Suggested Guide for Planning to Plan: Integrating Literacy Instruction and Content

1. Choose a title that is potentially interesting to your students and encapsulates the conceptual objectives.
2. Write the superordinate concept in a complete sentence.

   Note: A complete sentence is necessary because it provides a grammar for your unit and contributes to the coherence.

3. Make a conceptual map with the superordinate concept, coordinate concept, and subordinate concept.
4. Make a resource chart, relating print, digital, and other resources available for students.

   This chart is a matrix. The column headings are each of the coordinate concepts from the concept map. The row headings are the available resources. The boxes in the matrix provide space to make notes about the resource and to make visible which resource will provide an opportunity for students to engage which concepts.

   Note: Select the resources you believe to be critical or important for all or most students to read. Do an analysis of those materials so that reading strategies can be selected and developed to support students' reading of these key materials.

5. Make a strategies and activities chart, relating planned activities that include activities for supporting students' engagement with prose and digital text.

   Note: List many activities, such as experiments, field trips, guest lecturers, and so forth, and also the literacy strategies you intend to use with particular texts.

6. Design a rubric for evaluating students' engagement with concepts.

MENU OF INSTRUCTIONAL LITERACY STRATEGIES

Literacy strategies vary in terms of the amount of teacher direction and the purposes for which they are designed. We begin with highly structured and teacher-directed strategies and move toward more student-controlled strategies. We conclude with suggestions for ways you can help your students become more independent. The strategies we recommend have a research or theoretical basis, but we caution that not all strategies have been researched with a representative sample of all types of students. Hence, we know that, in practice, you will make changes and adaptations to the strategies to fit your students and your teaching goals. All teachers do that. What is important is that you have a sense of *why* you are doing the strategy. We offer the theoretical rationale for these strategies, and, in doing so, we hope that you will consider whether or not your changes are consistent with the theoretical rationale for which the strategy is designed. The theoretical reasons for using literacy strategies are related to the principles discussed in chapter 3. We state them again, this time as guidelines for selecting and evaluating the instructional literacy strategies that make the most sense for your content and students.

1. Learning has to be meaningful; strategies can be selected to help students perceive that what they are learning and reading about is meaningful and *relevant*, that it affects them and their world.
2. Meaningful learning is related to students' *interests*; strategies can be chosen to entice students to read the assignment.
3. Students' interests are *connected to prior knowledge* and experiences; reading strategies are designed to help students see this connection.
4. The *purpose* for studying, reading, and learning about a topic should be clear; literacy strategies help students select a purpose for the reading.
5. Reading strategies should help students *select* the information they need to construct meaning.
6. Learning takes place when students create a personally meaningful *organization* of the knowledge; literacy strategies can help to create that organization.
7. Learning is enhanced when students have opportunities to *apply* the knowledge being constructed; literacy strategies and a teacher's content-related activities can accomplish this.
8. Long-term memory is developed when students have regular opportunities to *review*.
9. Literacy is a *social* practice; learners need opportunities to collaborate and cooperatively develop their understanding.
10. Becoming an independent literacy user and learner is a developmental process and is enhanced when students engage in literacy reflectively, growing in their *metacognitive* awareness of themselves and their learning processes.

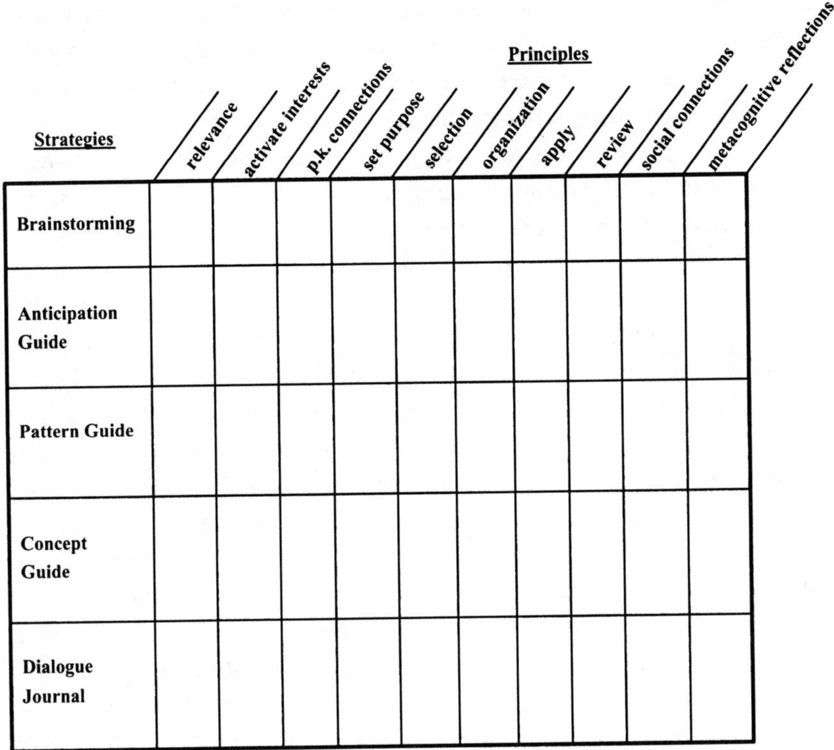

Strategies	relevance	activate interests	p.k. connections	set purpose	selection	organization	apply	review	social connections	metacognitive reflections
Brainstorming										
Anticipation Guide										
Pattern Guide										
Concept Guide										
Dialogue Journal										

FIG. 6.2. Instructional feature analysis.

Literacy strategies, both those taught and used instructionally and those used by learners, enact one or more of these principles. When selecting literacy strategies, we find it helpful to use an instructional feature analysis as a metapedagogical tool (a strategy for thinking about your teaching) for reflecting on the quality of the strategy. A sample chart, or matrix, is in Fig. 6.2.

Most content area literacy books include a stand-alone chapter about vocabulary. We have chosen not to include one because content area vocabulary development happens in the context of the concepts being engaged. Most strategies have a vocabulary component. The idea is that, as students engage in an activity, they learn the conceptual vocabulary that is necessary to read, write, and talk about the ideas. Having said that, however, we think that there are a few points that you should keep in mind. First, not all conceptual vocabulary terms are hard words to pronounce or to spell, but a conceptual word might be difficult because of the unique conceptual context in which it is used. For example, the word *root* is an easy word, but, depending on the unique context, it may be more difficult to understand. Consider Melissa as she goes to her first-period family studies class. Here she might learn about the food value of root vegetables. In her second-period biology class, she might learn about classification schemes that are based on the roots of plants. Moving on to math, she may need to calculate the square root, and during the next period in English, she may study the roots of words. Oh yes, in history, she could be discovering her roots, or, to make matters even more confusing, she could be figuring out the best route (which, in some dialects, is pronounced root) to drive between Phoenix and Boston. Clearly, helping students to become intimate with the key conceptual vocabulary is important and is best accomplished in the context of the content area class.

A second point to remember is that students must read, write, speak, and hear conceptual vocabulary many times before it becomes part of their working vocabulary. It is not enough to use a term being learned casually; it must be used in several different ways. One teacher we know begins each class period with a short concept-related vocabulary quiz. Other teachers have a "word wall" that changes as new words are introduced. This is an idea borrowed from primary-grade teachers, who post the words children are learning to read and write. In the upper grades, the word wall should post the words students are learning in their content studies. The point is, content area teachers who are cognizant of the related concept-related vocabulary intentionally provide systematic and regular opportunities for students to read, write, speak, and hear the terms. Students who learn to talk the talk of a discipline are able to formulate and represent their ideas through their newly acquired language.

Teacher-Directed Strategies

Harold and Joan Herber (1993) and their students (Alvermann & Moore, 1991; Conley, 1992; Estes & Vaughan, 1978; Vacca & Vacca, 2004) suggest a model, the instructional framework, for organizing literacy instruction in the content areas. There are three parts in the Instructional Framework: preparation, guidance, and independence. Herber and Herber explain that these "three parts follow the generally accepted logic of teaching. That is, students are *prepared* for the study of a conceptualization. They are *guided* in the acquisition of information and ideas related to the concept. They are then given opportunities to apply *independently* what they have learned relative to that concept" (p. 119). Box 6.2 shows the instructional strategies that have been presented earlier in this volume organized into the preparation, guidance,

BOX 6.2. Previously Introduced Instructional Strategies Organized by the Instructional Framework

Preparation	*Guidance*	*Independence*
In chapter 2:	In chapter 2:	In chapter 2:
Interactive discussions	Jounals	Interactive discussions
In chapter 3:	In chapter 3:	In chapter 3:
Langer's PREP	Mapping	Student strategy
A pretest of strategy use	Writing	Reflections
Mapping	Graphic organizers	Writing
Graphic organizers	Refutational text	Graphic organizers
Augmented activation	Think sheets	Cinquain
Think sheet	Bridging analogies	Think sheet
Bridging analogies	In chapter 4:	Discussion web
In chapter 4:	Connection questions	Bridging analogies
Text walk	Pattern guide	In chapter 4:
Extended anticipation	Extended anticipation guide	Connection questions
Guide	Double-entry notebook	Question–answer relationships
Prewriting	Think alouds	Extended anticipation guide
Think alouds		Relective dialogue journals
		Think alouds

and independence parts of the instructional framework. Some instructional strategies are adaptable and can be used in more than one of the time blocks; some of the strategies, therefore, are listed more than once.

Preparation Strategies. Preparing students for a reading assignment accomplishes several of the theoretical purposes that are fundamental to good comprehension. A before-reading strategy might help students to see that their interests are related to the reading assignment. A strategy accomplishing this also demonstrates to students that they already know about or have had experiences related to what they are reading and learning. The before-reading activity should also help students set a purpose for the reading. The more authentic and meaningful (related to ideas) that purpose is, the more likely it is that comprehension will occur.

Guiding Reading Strategies. Several types of study guides exist, including the concept guide, the three-level study guide, and the pattern guide.

BOX 6.3. Instructions for the Concept Guide

The concept guide consists of two parts. Part 1 helps to the student's attention to the subordinate concepts in the reading assignment. Part 2 facilitates the student's cognition by making connections to the coordinate concepts.

1. Read the assignment you wish to your students. After you have read the assignment, ascertain the superordinate, coordinate, and subordinate concepts. The superordinate concept is the title of the concept guide.
2. List the coordinate and subordinate concepts in a word or a phrase.
3. Choose statements from the reading assignment that represent the subordinate concepts. Create alternative statements, which do not represent the subordinate concepts (distracters). These statements are Part 1 of the concept guide.
4. Use the word or phrase representing the coordinate concepts for Part 2 of the guide.
5. Instruct students to respond to the guide by (a) indicating whether the statements in Part 1 actually occur in the passage and (b) categorizing the statements from Part 1 under the coordinate concept(s) to which they most clearly relate in Part 2.
6. After students have completed the guide, ask them to discuss and defend their categorizations. Typically these discussions are in small groups, followed by a class discussion summarizing the groups' conclusion. (See Box 6.4, which is an abbreviated concept guide for Chapter 6.)

Discussions of how to use these guides and their instructional advantages and disadvantages are available in several sources (see, e.g., Herber & Herber, 1993). Directions for the concept guide are provided in Box 6.3 and an example is provided in Box 6.4. Directions to make a Three-level guide are provided in Box 6.5. What we discuss in this section are the points about the Herber study guides that set them apart from what is usually thought of as study guides.

Most everyone has experience with study guides—much of it negative. The typical scenario involves a handout given to students to be used while they read. Most of these old-fashioned study guides are several pages long and

BOX 6.4. Sample Concept Guide

Instructional Strategies to Help Guide Students' Reading

Part 1

Planning is critical for literacy instruction in the content areas. As you read chapter 6, check the statements that follow that are congruent with what you read.

1. ______ Activities (i.e., reading, writing, discussing, experimenting) are the means by which students construct meaning in the content areas.
2. ______ The major problem for learning in the content areas is that students lack the reading ability.
3. ______ The teacher's content knowledge, pedagogical knowledge, and interests have little to do with planning.
4. ______ Behavioral theory may inform teachers about planning, but it is not a sufficient theory for planning.
5. ______ An often neglected resource for students and teachers are the experts who live in our community.
6. ______ Teachers should rely on standardized tests to learn about their students' interests and backgrounds.
7. ______ Educators agree that responsibility for planning and delivery of those plans rests with the teacher.

Part 2

Now, consider each of the statements just given, and place each under one or more of the following categories. Be prepared to justify why you placed the statement under the category(ies) you did and whether or not you agree with it and why.

Dimensions of Planning   *Theories of Planning*   *Resources*   *Students' Options*

are made up of questions to which students are expected to write answers, answers that are likely to come verbatim from the text being read.

Three things are wrong with this scenario. First, the guide suggests that meaning (what is to be learned) is *in* the text. This contradicts the reading and learning process: Meaning is constructed as a reader thinks about the author's

BOX 6.5. The Three-Level Study Guide

The steps for constructing a three-level study guide include the following:

1. Analyze the reading assignment for the subordinate, coordinate, and superordinate concepts you intend for the students to engage while reading the passage. List as many of each of these concepts as possible.
2. After listing all three types of concepts, select the factual, subordinate, and literal concepts that relate to the coordinate concepts and the superordinate concepts. These statements are representative of "reading the lines." List these for student response in level 1 of the guide.
3. Level 2 of the guide consists of statements that relate to the subordinate concepts but are representative of coordinate-type concepts. Hence, they should reflect reading between the lines, that is, inferences and interpretations of the reading that can be made by a reader.
4. Level 3 of the guide consists of statements that lead the reader to read beyond the lines, Write statements to demonstrate how the information in the reading assignment may be used.
5. Provide a copy of the guide to each student and ask each to agree or disagree with each statement. Responses to the third level of the guide should provide a good starting point for small group or whole class discussion.

writing. Meaning is a transaction that occurs as a reader and the text interact in a social context. The typical study guide sends a message to the student that reading in the content area is simply "getting the author's meaning" rather than constructing meaning.

A second problem with the typical study guide is that it requires students to copy from the reading, thereby encouraging students to read only those parts of the text that answer a particular question and copy these parts verbatim. Writing helps to construct meaning, but that kind of writing is creative and constructive, not simply an exercise in copying someone else's words and ideas. A study guide should help students to *think* about the ideas being presented in the prose; copying answers to someone else's questions is artificial and actually distracts students from thinking.

Further, in the current culture of testing, which is influencing teachers' practices, teachers and students alike are bound to think of the study guide as a test of whether or not the students read the assignment (Anders & Richardson, 1992). Teachers might grade the old-type study guide, which affirms the student's notion that learning is "getting someone else's ideas in my head" instead of constructing meaning. Likewise, students resort to playing the game of school rather than using the guide to help construct meaning. Evidence that students are playing the game is when they copy each others answers, lose the study guide, or simply write in something that looks like answers, whether the "answer" makes sense or not! Students are also quite capable of giving the teacher the answer the teacher wants without actually changing what they really think, particularly when they have misconceptions (Guzzetti et al., 1993).

The study guides suggested by Harold Herber do not require students to do much writing, because he theorizes that students should be thinking rather than producing. In addition, the last parts of the three-level and concept guides ask students to extend their thinking beyond the text in ways that promote critical and creative thinking. They also lead naturally to discussion by groups of students. For example, in a three-level guide, the last section asks students to agree with generalizations that are value statements or "rules," which may be controversial. After studying, students meet to discuss their reasoning for agreeing or disagreeing with the statements. Herber (1978) summarized the parts of the concept and three-level guides as "reading the lines," "reading between the lines," and "reading beyond the lines." This is a useful metaphor because it reminds us that students need to be involved with details (subordinate concepts), categories (coordinate concepts), and the big ideas (superordinate concepts) to construct meaning.

Literacy strategies, such as three-level guides, pattern guides, and concept guides, which guide students during reading, are an opportunity for the teacher to help students select the information needed to construct meaning. The guides also help students to create a personally meaningful organization of the knowledge. Both the concept guide and the three-level guide require discussion among the students after the guide is completed, which helps to affirm literacy as social practice. The guides are often related to the literacy activity the teacher used before the reading and also relate to the activity that students will be asked to do after the reading to develop independence.

The guides call for critical and creative thinking; it is not necessary or possible, therefore, to grade the answers. Depending on the meaning that a student has constructed, answers will vary. Hence, a teacher may give students points for completing the study guide, but it is not graded in the summative and normative sense of an A, B, C, and so forth. Rather, the teacher's evaluation of the guide is formative. By looking over the guide, the teacher gets an idea as to the progress students are making toward engaging and understanding a concept or concepts.

Independence Strategies. Independence activities involve students in synthesis, evaluative, critical, and creative thought. These are the activities that develop the schema that becomes prior knowledge the next time these ideas or related ideas are met. When students make presentations, write laboratory reports, describe either orally or in writing how they solved a problem, discuss issues, write term papers, and do projects, they are becoming independent. These sorts of activities provide students with opportunities to construct and create knowledge.

The discussion web is an example of an activity designed to help students gain independence. The discussion web requires students to persuade each other of their opinions in response to a central question by citing support with evidence from a text. This form of discussion addresses any alternative conceptions students may harbor and will provide the element of cognitive conflict that research has shown affects conceptual change (Guzzetti et al., 1993).

You can adapt the discussion web to any content area by altering the classification categories. Swafford (1990) provided examples of adaptations for mathematics, science, literature, and social studies. Here are some examples:

- When reading mathematical word problems, students may be asked to classify relevant and irrelevant information.
- When reading science material, including experiments, students may be asked to predict outcomes and find evidence from the text to support their predictions.
- When reading biographical books in social studies, students may be asked to determine how historical persons might stand on an issue and to support this stance with evidence from the trade books.
- When reading novels or short stories, students might be asked to infer information about the author or the narrator of the story (like positing whether or not the narrator of *The Tell-Tale Heart* was sane or insane) and to list their reasons for their determination by referring to illustrative excerpts from the text.

No matter what the content or classification scheme, discussion is structured around the central query. The discussion is interactive among students and between students and the teacher. The focus is on convincing group members of individual opinions based on evidence from the source. Alvermann, Dillon, and O'Brien (1987) describe the benefits of the discussion web. First, true discussion is characterized by the dominance of student talk in which students are talking to each other and putting forth multiple points of view. This kind of discussion is contrary to the common type of recitation discussion in which the teacher asks a question, the student gives a short answer, and the teacher responds. The authentic-type discussion enriches understanding as students consider each others' interpretations. These shared views contribute to a community and a common set of meanings, which develop as group members voice their opinions and listen to each other.

Second, true discussion can help to place concepts in long-term memory. Students who are required to articulate and to defend their points of view with evidence from the text, thereby eliminate inconsistencies and contradictions in their thinking. Learners will be better able to recall concepts that they have grappled with in a lively discussion because those concepts will have personal meaning.

Herber's model is the seminal foundation on which most theorists and practitioners base content area literacy instruction. The instructional framework is well accepted by content area teachers, because it begins with the concepts teachers need and want to teach. The advantage of the instructional framework is that it provides space in the teacher's planning to intentionally and systematically incorporate literacy and content instruction.

The Interactive Teaching Model

Patty and her colleague Candy Bos (Bos & Anders, 1993) base their instructional strategy research on Herber's instructional framework (preparation, guidance, and independence), but they investigated strategies that, by design, are integrated across a reading assignment; that is, each of the strategies is used *before* students read a content area assignment, again *during* reading, and also *after* reading. The practices are interactive because they provide students with occasions to put into practice the thinking processes that promote students' construction of meaning. The instructional strategies are *semantic mapping*, *semantic feature analysis*, and *semantic-syntactic feature analysis*. See Boxes 6.6, 6.7, and 6.8 for directions to create and use these instructional strategies.

BOX 6.6. Directions for Semantic Mapping

1. List concept-related vocabulary terms and phrases.
2. Tentatively map the selected words and phrases. You may find that the author does not use some words you believe to be important. Add those words or phrases to the list.
3. Prepare a handout for students that list the words and phrases on the left-hand margin of the handout, leaving most of the space on the paper for students to draw their maps. Prepare an overhead transparency identical to the handout or duplicate the handout on the whiteboard.
4. Distribute the handout to students and read the list of words and phrases aloud. Ask which word or phrase appears to be the biggest idea in the list (that is, which idea or phrase seems to include all the other ideas)?
5. Encourage discussion about why students believe that particular idea to be the most generalized statement. Guide students to draw that central idea either in the center of the page or at the top of the page; use the tentative map you drew to advise students as to the best place to put the biggest idea. (Note that the discussions are critical to the success of this strategy. All student predictions should be accepted as hypotheses about the relationships between and among ideas. Following the reading, all predicted relationships have to be justified either by information provided by the author or by student experiences that contact the author. When contradictions exist, students need to be directed to find further substantiation for their predictions.)
6. Ask students to predict and select other ideas that go together. Map those ideas that can be agreed on. Continually ask students why they believe ideas are related.
7. If there are terms or phrases the students are unable to map, put them aside in a Question Box—these are terms students will attempt to add to the map following their reading.
8. Ask students to read the assignment silently and to compare the author's use of and connection of the terms to the predictions made by the students.
9. Following the reading, lead students in a discussion comparing their predictions with what they read. Discuss whether or not the

author's connections confirm their predictions. Redraw the map to include the previously unknown terms. Sometimes students will disagree with the author and will need to seek further information to either confirm or disconfirm their predictions.

BOX 6.7. Directions for Semantic Feature Analysis

The semantic feature analysis is a matrix students use to predict the relationships between and among concepts in a reading assignment.

1. Begin by discerning the superordinate, coordinate, and subordinate concepts presented by the author.
2. Choose a title for the matrix that is related to the superordinate concept. Coordinate concepts are the categories across the top of the matrix, and the subordinate concepts are the details listed down the side of the matrix.
3. Prepare a copy of the matrix for each student and also prepare an overhead transparency that you can use to guide the students' use of the matrix.
4. Distribute the handout and place the overhead on the projector in front of the class.
5. Tell students about the concept they will be reading about. Ask students to relate prior knowledge or experiences about the topic.
6. Introduce the coordinate concepts that are at the top of the matrix. Provide information students need to begin to develop an understanding of each concept and ask them to relate their personal experiences relative to each of the concepts.
7. Tell the students that you want them to predict with you the nature of the relationship between each of these coordinate level ideas (major ideas), with each of the details listed down the side of the matrix. If they agee that a major idea and a detail are related, both you and the students will put a plus sign (+) in the corresponding box on the matrix; if there is a disagreement among the students in the class, each of you will put a question mark (?) in the box; and if students believe no relationship exists between the two terms, each of you put a zero (0) in the box. (Some teachers use a numbering system: 0 = no relationship, 1 = some relationship, 2 = a strong relationship, and? = relationship is unknown.)

8. Considering each term in turn, discuss the students' predictions of the relationship between each detail word or phrase and each major idea.
9. When each of the boxes in the matrix is filled in, ask students to read to confirm their predictions. While reading, a student may change a prediction or may change a question mark to either a plus or a zero.
10. When al students have completed reading, lead a discussion of the changes students have made on their charts. Ask students to explain their justifications for the changes thy have made. If students disagree among themselves or with the author, refer to additional sources for more information.

BOX 6.8. The Semantic–Syntactic Feature Analysis

This strategy is the same as the semantic feature analysis, except for one addition.

1. At the bottom of the chart, create fill-in-the-blank sentences. One blank represents a major idea from the top of the chart, and one or more of the other blanks represent the detail words from the side of the chart.
2. Ask students (on the basis of the completed chart and before reading) to predict the words that might fit in each of the blanks.
3. After reading, ask students to confirm or disconfirm the words or phrases they have inserted in the blanks. If they disconfirm, ask them to change their sentences to reflect their present understandings.

These three strategies were used in 47 classrooms at three grade levels and in three different content area classrooms: upper elementary students, many of whom were ESL students, reading social studies; middle-school students reading science; and high school students reading vocational materials. Candy and Patty (Bos & Anders, 1993) compared the interactive strategies with direct instruction of the conceptual vocabulary, asking students to memorize definitions of the vocabulary, which were the same terms used in the feature analysis charts and in the maps. In every case they found that the students participating in the interactive practices outperformed the direct-instruction students. To measure student's learning, Patty and Candy administered two tests before and after instruction; one test was a multiple-choice test of both vocabulary and comprehension, and the second was a "free write," which asked students to write everything they knew on the topic. This finding was incredible, but what was even more amazing was that students were tested with the same instruments 6 months later, and the scores improved for the students who were in the interactive instructional groups and declined for the students in the direct instruction groups. We theorize that the interactive strategies provided "slots" in the learner's schema for selecting and integrating new information.

Some points should be remembered regarding the use of these strategies. First, as with Herber's strategies, each is based on a conceptual analysis of the material being read. Patty and Candy did a concept map of each reading and analyzed the rhetorical structure of each reading assignment. (Recall the information about coherence and rhetorical patterns presented in chapter 4.)

Second, make allowances for students to create concepts as the lesson proceeds. If students are engaged in the topic, it is very likely that they will go beyond your expectations by making connections to their own experience that you could have not possibly foreseen. Although Patty and Candy did not do this in their research (because of constraints of the research design), teachers have adopted these practices and have done so. It is easy to do. When making the semantic feature analysis chart, leave blanks at the end across the top and at the bottom of the details column. Then, as students negotiate the meaning of the text they are reading, main ideas (coordinate concepts) and details can be added as they evolve from the discussions before, during, and after the reading. If a semantic map is being used, simply provide students the opportunity to add words and phrases to the list to be mapped.

It is also important to recognize that these strategies are interactive: students' prior knowledge is built on; students collaborate to make predictions before reading about concepts and about the potential relationships between and among concepts; and students are involved in confirming and justifying their reasoning throughout each part of each activity. Most of the predicting, confirming, and justifying is done in oral discussion—and sometimes that discussion is noisy and argumentative! Despite the noise, the notion that literacy is a social practice came through loudly and clearly while Patty and Candy led these lessons.

After Patty and Candy (Bos & Anders, 1993) confirmed that the strategies were efficacious, they taught them to teachers. The results were the same: Students learned more when using the interactive strategies than when using direct-instruction vocabulary strategies. The downside to these strategies, in a few teachers' judgment, was that some teachers were uncomfortable allowing students this much involvement during the lesson; these teachers reported being afraid of losing control. Others were concerned about misinformation students "put on the table" during discussion. We empathize with these concerns. In response to the first concern, however, teachers face very little risk of losing control if students are involved with substantive and interesting ideas. This is the sort of intellectual excitement, enthusiasm, and involvement that we want to encourage!

The second concern is important. We wrote in chapter 3 that alternative conceptions are difficult to change. The good news, however, is that we have evidence that these instructional strategies help to change naïve or incorrect conceptions. Saulawa (1990) studied the use of these strategies in light of students' misconceptions. He tracked students as their conceptions developed over the interactive lessons and found that the misconceptions at the beginning of the lesson were dispelled; these strategies provide sufficient opportunity for challenging and changing students' unconventional concepts.

Next, Candy and Patty adapted the strategies for student's use. The adaptations emphasized peer collaboration and required the students to reflect on the ways that the strategies helped them to be better readers and how the strategies might transfer to other contexts. In other words, they sought to increase student responsibility for quality collaboration and they also wanted to foreground metacognitive development.

The 2 years of intensive classroom investigations related to teacher-led interactive strategies caused us to think of ways that the strategies could be modified and used by students independently. We learned that students were capable and successful using semantic mapping as a before-, during, and after-reading strategy. The semantic feature analysis was too difficult to do before reading, but it worked well as a follow-up activity to mapping. The mapping strategy worked well with most types of text, and the semantic feature analysis worked best with text written in a compare-contrast rhetorical structure. The procedures Patty and Candy used to teach students to use these strategies are described in Box 6.9.

BOX 6.9. Student Use of Semantic Mapping and Semantic Feature Analysis

1. Students meet around a table with a large piece of newsprint between them. Each student is given two packets of sticky notes; one packet is one color and the other packet is a different color.
2. The teacher provides the topic to be studied in a word or two and students write the topic in a large circle in the middle of the newsprint. Using the notes of the same color, each student writes every word or phrase that comes to mind about the topic—one word or phrase per sticky note. The sticky notes are laid out on the newsprint and, through discussion and negotiation, students organize the notes into categories. If there are notes that do not relate to other notes, students make a special place on the newsprint labeled *Unknowns*—the students revisit these unknowns after studying to see if they can be categorized and, if not, they are rejected. These notes represent students' prior knowledge.
3. Next, students "survey" the related reading assignment, paying attention to boldfaced or italicized words, pictures, and subtitles. One student is asked to record on the second color of sticky notes the words and phrases students notice in the reading assignment. These sticky notes are then placed on the newsprint and integrated with the background-knowledge sticky notes. These notes represent initial impressions of the content and are parallel to the type of thinking that occurs when students preview or survey an assignment (a typical before-reading activity).
4. Each student reads the assignment. If necessary, some students may read the assignment aloud to each other as in shared reading. During the reading, new words or phrases representing new knowledge are recorded on the second color of sticky notes. This represents a closer reading of the "text knowledge."
5. After all students have completed the reading, they meet again at the newsprint, bringing the sticky notes written during the reading. They discuss each sticky note and integrate it onto the newsprint or place it in the Unknown bracket. In effect, the students are creating a giant map of ideas before the reading, and they are integrating those ideas with the ideas gleaned during the reading. Before finishing the map, the Unknown sticky notes should either be integrated into the map or deleted from the map.

6. Students work together to agree on categories and how the categories and sticky notes should be recorded on the map. Lines can be drawn on the newsprint to connect the categories and details on the sticky notes. When agreement has been reached, tape the sticky notes onto the newsprint before hanging the poster.
7. An alternative or extension of the mapping is to make a semantic feature analysis after reading. Students would use their tentative map as a resource for choosing categories of ideas, and, using another large sheet of newsprint, make a matrix with categories as the column headings on the chart. The subordinate vocabulary words and phrases are then listed on the side of the chart and students discuss the relationship between each category (column heading) and each vocabulary or detail word (line heading).

After hanging the posters on the wall, the teacher leads a discussion comparing and contrasting the meanings constructed by each small group of students. There may be differences between the maps, and that can help to add details and elaborations to student thinking. The teacher can also examine the maps for misconceptions and design subsequent lessons to confront those mistaken understandings. This activity provides an excellent opportunity to lead a discussion with students about metacognition. Students should have some new insights about their thinking as a result of doing these activities. Students of Patty and Candy did and, through discussion, they helped them to develop adaptations for similar types of study methods in other content areas.

Student-Directed Models

The instructional strategies described thus far are examples of teacher-controlled strategies. What we mean is that the teacher engages students in preselected activities and resource materials. There are other instructional frameworks, however, that we discuss in subsequent paragraphs that provide for much more student decision making and direction.

The Inquiry Cycle. The inquiry cycle is a plan that involves students as they investigate ideas and questions related to a particular content area or superordinate concept in the discipline. The role that language plays in this cycle is as a tool for constructing meaning. The idea underlying this cycle is that curriculum is a negotiated process among students, teachers, and the topics teachers are responsible for teaching. The cycle begins with these three conditions converging to negotiate the conduct of the cycle. During negotiation between teacher and students, the prior knowledge and interests of each and the teacher's perceptions of necessary content, questions, and goals are put on the table for discussion. The discussion provides a context for experiences to be shared, questions to be posed, and possible resources to be explored.

From this discussion, groups of students begin to focus on particular questions or goals. These questions and goals launch the cycle, providing a frame of reference for what will be investigated by a group of students during the inquiry cycle. It also indicates to the teacher and students the types of tasks, resources, and potential outcomes of the inquiry. Students consider and discuss these questions and goals until they are comfortable selecting topics for inquiry. Students form groups based on topics of common interest. Each group designs and carries out an investigation related to the chosen topic and its corresponding questions.

Getting a good question is not always easy; sometimes students ask questions they already know the answer to or they ask a question that is very literal. One instructional approach is to ask students in a group to first list and discuss everything they think they know or that they assume about a topic. From this discussion and by continuing to ask the question of why or how, a more sophisticated question may emerge.

Each group devises a plan for accomplishing its goal. The plan is analogous to a research proposal and reflects the students' best predictions about how they will address the topic and its related questions. The plan is written and should describe the students' thinking about how they will gather, analyze, and interpret information and also how they will present their findings. Each group usually presents its plan to the class and receives comments. On the basis of this commentary, some groups may revise their questions, goals, or plans. Group membership may also shift as students relate their interests, talents, and backgrounds to what their peers propose. Further, the teacher listens to each plan with an ear toward the sorts of instruction and resources students will need to carry out their plans.

For example, most students of any age have trouble analyzing and interpreting data to create a new understanding or synthesis. To help students, instruction about summarization, categorization, and organization is helpful. Other students may have trouble selecting sources of data. One group we worked with decided to include interviews as part of their data. This meant that the teacher needed to help the students develop and practice doing an interview, locate tape recorders, and provide instruction about how to transcribe and interpret an interview. The Internet provides another selection challenge. There are so many sources of information—how do students select which information to use to answer their question? In chapter 5, we discussed this issue. One suggestion is to ask students to not accept anything as fact unless three sources (triangulation) can be found to confirm the fact. After a group is tentatively satisfied with its plan, the next step is to gather data. Students are encouraged to use a variety of data sources and to record their findings. Possible data sources include various community resources, media, textbooks, trade books, and the students' own experiences.

Students record their findings in written form and share them with their group members, thereby making the findings accessible to all members of the group. Students usually need guidance as to the different forms that might be used for recording their findings. Teacher-designed minilessons are appropriate ways to offer this guidance. The minilessons teach about different forms of lists that students might use, note-taking strategies, various forms of charts, brief descriptions, quotes from informants, drawings of observations, and so on. These lessons appear to occur naturally as the students' need to portray data arises. We say *naturally* because the instruction is available when students need it, but careful planning is needed on the teacher's part to prepare that instruction for when students need it.

Minilessons may be implemented in several ways. One possibility is to announce to the class that you have noticed that several groups could use help on, for example, taking notes from the Internet. Perhaps you believe that having the students take their notes in a double-entry notebook would be helpful. Invite each group to send a student to the computer corner in the room to learn how to do this. Next provide a lesson, making sure that students understand well enough to teach the other students in their group. Another possibility is to present a minilesson to the whole class and then invite students who want to know more about the lesson or who want to make sure they understand it to meet in a small group with you. This allows for everyone to be introduced to a technique they might use, but only those who need it or are interested in it need to learn it well.

Teachers also need to notice opportunities for students to review and reflect on methods that work well and those that do not work so well. That is, because the inquiry cycle promotes the development of independent learning, students should be asked to reflect on the value of the research methods they use and to evaluate critically the success and limitation of particular organizational methods. This reflecting and revaluing could be accomplished by asking students to write about their processes, including a description of what was done and why and how well it worked. Then, during a discussion, students could share their processes. Perhaps a processes notebook would be appropriate for recording these reflections. This reflective writing and discussion would help students become more sophisticated thinkers and doers of research; the sharing time would also serve as an opportunity for everyone in the class to get additional ideas. The notebooks could be an important source for other students to use as they learn about research methods. This practice, or something like it, is well grounded in our theoretical understanding of literacy. The aspects of literacy that are highlighted here include literacy as a social practice, the creation of a personally meaningful organization, application, and reflectivity.

In the next step, students analyze and interpret the information, data, they have gathered. This process requires the use of language to evaluate data in terms of the original questions and topics and to construct new understandings related to those questions and topics. It is likely that the students' questions and interests will change during the analysis process. This is sometimes difficult for teachers to accept, because it means that the students' plans will change and that it will be difficult to predict the amount of time any inquiry cycle will take. Nonetheless, if students are to conduct an inquiry cycle, both they and their teacher need to value the right for the students to change their minds, to ask better questions, to return to the planning phase of the cycle, and to rethink their goals.

The process of analysis is one of the most challenging parts of the inquiry cycle. Students need to understand their findings well enough to negotiate with each other the various possibilities for organizing and presenting their findings. Furthermore, integrating each other's work to create a representation of that work is intellectually and socially challenging. These expectations, or something like them, are included in every set of educational standards developed by professional organizations. In most ases, teachers offer suggestions (as they did with the collecting and recording phase) for students to develop methods of analysis. The analysis process requires students to categorize and organize ideas and data. Charts, maps, and graphs are often good representational methods. As with collecting and recording, students should be asked to reflect on the process of analysis in writing. Whole class and small group class discussion time should be devoted to sharing and evaluating the methods used to analyze.

Finally, students present their findings and celebrate their work. Students explain their thinking, justify their approaches and findings, and create new understandings both for themselves and their classmates. Possibilities for presenting encompass all the language forms, including writing, demonstrations, plays, computer graphics, a Power Point presentation, and videos. Students could also use other forms of expression such as music and art. Ideally, the presentations lead students to ask new questions and wonder about new topics, thereby leading to topics for further inquiry cycles. We want to emphasize that the cycle is recursive; that is, at any one step, a group might decide to go back and redo or reconceptualize a phase of the cycle. This recursive nature promotes meaningful and authentic thinking and doing in two important ways. First, students must continually reflect on the value and direction of their work—they must use metacognitive processes. Second, students are required to entertain a variety of notions and hypotheses—to demonstrate cognitive flexibility (Spiro & Myers, 1984).

The inquiry cycle takes advantage of the students' social nature by providing a context for collaborative work. It also integrates content learning with language development. Students continue to develop their reading, writing, speaking, and listening skills as they engage in meaningful and authentic work. Notice also that students have more control over their inquiry than in either the instructional framework or the interactive teaching model.

Sometimes teachers are concerned with classroom management when they are implementing the inquiry cycle. Organizing the class period so that time and resources are available when students need them takes a special kind of planning and a different conceptualization of teaching than what is typically experienced in schools. Teachers who use the inquiry cycle report that they give up the need to control what everyone does and learns. They also find themselves trusting students to ask meaningful questions and to carry out substantive work. Moreover, teachers change their ways of assessment. Students' participation in the processes of learning becomes as important as the product, and so formative assessments are used as students engage in the process. Honoring students' need to change questions, change groups, and take the time to deeply investigate topics are also reported changes. Furthermore, teachers find themselves no longer the person with all the answers or the resources; rather, teachers find themselves asking questions of their own and often engaging in an inquiry process themselves. So a teacher no longer perceives herself or himself as a "sage on a stage," and labor, knowledge, and resources are distributed among all the members of the class. For these teachers, the concept of research comes alive. They see themselves as researchers, investigating both their content and their pedagogy as they join their students as researchers.

Barbara, who is a literacy teacher educator, and Tom McGowan, a social studies teacher educator, teamed with a graduate student at the university who was also a sixth-grade teacher, Barbara Kowalinski, to implement an inquiry cycle, utilizing trade books (Guzzetti, McGowan, & Kowalinski, 1992). The three selected a topic from the sixth-grade curriculum, China, and gathered relevant fiction and nonfiction from the children's section of neighboring public libraries. They compared the district and state objectives for sixth-grade social studies to the trade book's content and format, determining that the literature would meet the same objectives (and more).

This teacher researcher team then designed ways to measure the impact of this approach on students' learning. First, they created an 88-item multiple-choice test from the district and state objectives that measured literal comprehension (factual recall) and inferential comprehension (generalizations and inferences from facts). This test was constructed to demonstrate to the district that a literature-based approach could fulfill the requirements of the sixth-grade curriculum for reading and social studies. The test was given to both classes as a pretest, and the researchers found that there were no significant differences between students in either class in their knowledge of China before the unit began. The team also planned other more natural formative assessments, like brainstorming all the words the children associated with China before, during, and after the unit; interviewing students; and assessing students' projects.

Actual instruction began in a rather teacher-directed way. For example, the teacher member of the partnership selected four fictional books of children's literature about China and gave book talks about each one. A typical book talk consisted of a brief synopsis of the story (up to a dramatic or leading point) that would interest students to read the book to find out how it ended. The teacher also read aloud particularly poignant or moving sections of the book to generate students' curiosity and interest. On the basis of book talk, students selected the literature group they wanted to join.

The literature groups met to discuss mostly predetermined questions, like the story's setting, trouble or problem to resolve, order of events, resolution, ending, and vocabulary (students would mark unfamiliar words with sticky notes). Each day the teacher would read aloud to her students a book she selected (like *Lon Po Po*, the Chinese version of *Little Red Riding Hood*, a

Caldecott award winner). She then led a discussion of the book's vocabulary and content, and she helped the students consult maps to determine the book's geographical setting.

As the 5-week unit progressed, however, instruction became less teacher directed and more focused on the student's interests. Beginning with the preassessment, when students brainstormed all the words and phrases they could think of associated with China, individuals generated their own curiosities about China. Their naïve concepts were also revealed (e.g., that Hong Kong was the capital of China; that all Chinese women wear kimonos but no shoes), stimulating investigations to discover correct information. As the unit progressed, social studies instruction and activities were in response to a plethora of student curiosities generated by the literature they read and heard.

In response, instruction became less teacher directed and more student directed as the students investigated answers to their questions and began to make comparisons between the population, culture, climate, geography, and customs of China and those of the United States. For example, students formed groups based on their individual and mutual queries to create question-and-answer books about China. The teacher facilitated this effort by providing think sheets (as shown in chapter 3 and researched by Dole & Smith, 1987), reading guides that individuals used to record their central and personal queries (e.g., "How does the geography of china compare to the United States?"), their related questions (e.g., "Does china have mountains? lakes? rivers? oceans?), their ideas (e.g., "China has the highest mountain in the world"), and the answers they found from literature (e.g., China has rivers, like the Yangtze). This activity assisted students in clarifying their interests and in correcting their alternative conceptions by contrasting their prereading ideas with those in the trade books.

Barbara also encouraged students to respond in visual and verbal ways to the literature, thereby becoming personally involved with the text. For example, some students chose to create salt dough maps as they read *Young Fu of the Upper Yangtze* to help them picture the story's setting. Two other activities that were successfully used in high school English classes were adapted for comprehension of social studies literature—*character charts* and *paradigms* (Guzzetti, 1990). Some students chose to create a character chart, which is their visual representation of individual characters in a story. Students' illustrations, drawings, and photographs were supplemented by an explanation of why they selected those particular visuals to exemplify each character.

Creating character charts enabled students to bring to life the figures and characters they were reading about in literature.

Other students created a paradigm, a visual display on poster board of the relationship between the students' hobbies and interests to events in a fictional story (Guzzetti, 1990). For example, one student whose hobby was fishing read Laurence Yep's Newberry honor book *Dragonwings*, a story of an 8-year-old boy (Moonshadow) who sailed from China to live with his father in San Francisco. The reader chose to portray the dilemmas, fears, and successes that Moonshadow experienced while adapting to a new culture in terms of the life of the fish. Each of the major events in the story was illustrated by a parallel, like the fish choosing one fork in the river over another, avoiding being caught on a fisherman's hook, and finding a school of other fish to swim with. By constructing their paradigms, students became "co-creators" of meaning (Rosenblatt, 1978).

By implementing literature studies in an inquiry approach, students in the literature-based class performed significantly better on the end-of-unit test that did students in the school's other sixth-grade class who studied China through a traditional textbook-based teacher-directed approach. The students in the literature-based approach were better able to compare and contrast features of China to features of other nations, to evaluate China's economic and political policies, and to apply the concepts they had learned to new contexts. After comparing the responses of the two classes, the teacher who taught the unit on China by traditional methods expressed his desire for a literature-based program.

This study demonstrates that, by focusing instruction on students' interests, by offering students choice, and by emphasizing conceptual applications, teachers can affect learning that not only satisfies district objectives but has personal meaning to students as well. The teachers and researchers were more concerned that students come away from the unit on China with an understanding of and empathy for its culture and its people than with rote knowledge of facts concerning the country's population and history. Trade books allowed students to come to know China's people, culture, *and* facts about the country, its population, history, and geography.

Students' stereotypes about the people of China were also challenged and changed through reading and using the trade books. The teacher saw students share their concerns as they investigated concepts that were important to them. Their interests lay in how they thought about China and its people and how that view influenced their actions toward Chinese people. By facilitating

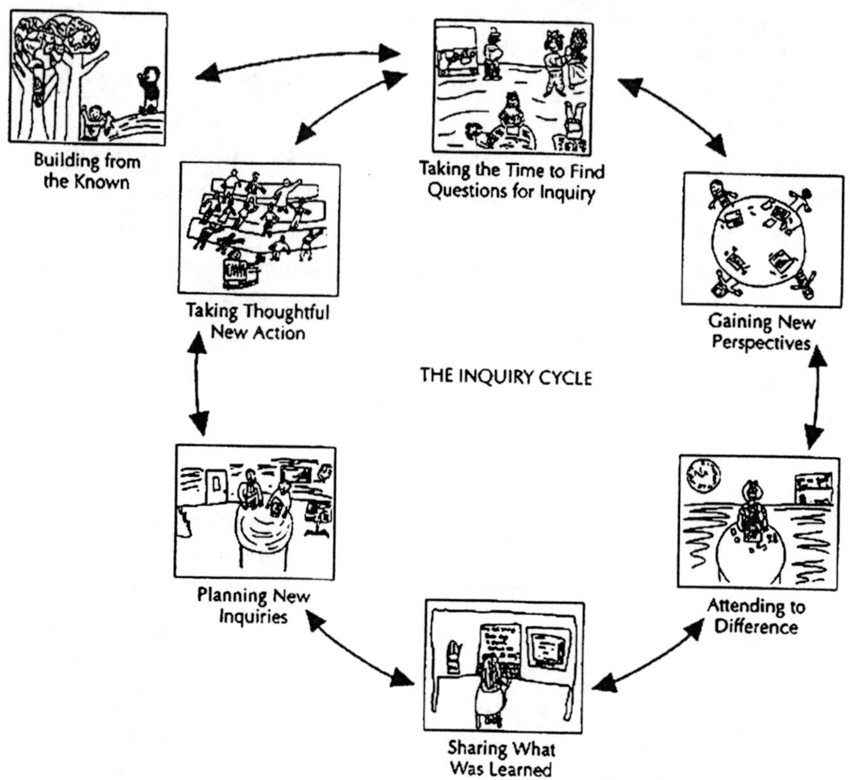

FIG. 6.3. Authoring cycle as a curricular framework for inquiry. (Reprinted with permission from Stenhouse Publishers.)

learners to pursue their own interests, the teacher found that the students surpassed the goals set by the state and the district, allowing them to realize their responsibilities as world citizens. This is not surprising. We find that learners of all ages exceed our expectations when given the opportunity to follow their own lead in learning what is meaningful.

The Authoring Cycle. Kathy Short and her colleagues (1996) discuss another plan, the authoring cycle, which is similar to the aforementioned inquiry cycle and the learning cycle described in chapter 3. These authors first developed the authoring cycle to support students' development as readers and writers. As it was implemented in several classrooms, they began to understand that the term *authoring* was a metaphor for learning. The authoring cycle is graphically produced in Fig. 6.3.

We are attracted to several features of the authoring cycle. For example, it makes clear that students need time to conduct sustained reading and writing. In contrast, the inquiry cycle devotes time to negotiation of questions about concepts and to collaboration, but it may not provide the amount of opportunity students may need for personal exploration.

Another attractive feature, similar to the inquiry cycle, is that students are encouraged to use all sorts of means to construct meaning. That is, students are often involved in doing art and making music and videos. The use of several sign systems to construct meaning is likely to include opportunities for far more students to construct meaning than if reading and writing are the only tools available.

Kathy and her colleagues (Short et al., 1996) report that, although conceptions have been important in their thinking, their emphasis is on providing opportunities for language development. Although they continue to acknowledge the power of language as a tool for constructing meaning, they are coming to believe that it is the powerful effects of ideas that motivate a learner to use language. We agree.

Bess Altwerger and her colleagues (Altwerger, Resta, & Kilarr, 1987) and Yetta Goodman and Carolyn Burke (1980) have long privileged the meaningfulness of engaging ideas. Each set of researchers describes planning and instruction in terms of theme cycles. Theme cycles, learning cycles, inquiry cycles, and authoring cycles are similar; the main difference is that both Altwerger and Goodman detail the initial negotiation process much more specifically than do those writing about the other cycles. Another difference is that the theme cycle seems to be more related to the whole class and its activities, whereas the inquiry cycle is oriented to small groups of students.

Theme cycles are typically inaugurated with a discussion of everything the students would like to learn in a semester or school year. The teacher also lists the ideas that the school curriculum expects. One topic is selected to focus on first. Following the selection of a topic, the teacher and students brainstorm everything they know about that topic. The ideas that students brainstorm are categorized and mapped. Then students generate questions they would like to answer, and the questions are prominently displayed in the classroom; there they stay for the duration of the theme study. Next, the class creates a list of possible means to answer those questions. Students work as a whole group, small groups, or individuals to explore the theme. As the theme cycle progresses, the initial web or map of "what we know" and "what we want to know" is redrawn to represent the developing and changing knowledge of the class.

Theme cycles are used in elementary classrooms with great success. Teachers report liking the flexibility that theme cycles allow for "going with" students' interests and for integrating the subject areas. Theme cycles are also appropriate for a middle school that integrates its curriculum.

The I-Search. The I-Search (Macrorie, 1988) extends student searches to the writing of a report. The I-Search could be incorporated into any of the cycles, as many of the principles underlying student-driven inquiry are the same. Macrorie writes this:

> [The problem with] most textbooks [is that they] present only the conclusions, the abstracted or generalized findings of experts, detached from the experience in which they were formed. And this for students who are novices in the field and often have never encountered its data or theories in any form. Reading such textbooks is not only difficult but discouraging. The discoveries of the express seem to be delivered by genius or the touch of god, and so students come to feel that they could never make such discoveries themselves. The expert is up there and they are down here taking notes. But if they were to see the experts at work—finding needs in their own lives and answering them, working brilliantly, working stupidly, making mistakes, stumbling into profitable answers—they would understand the true nature of productive women and men, and would come to believe that they might become such people themselves. (preface, n.p.)

The I-Search begins with a student describing something that he or she already knows. This introduction then concludes with a goal to learn something new. The second part of the I-Search is a written description of the process of learning the new information—the search. The third part, findings, tells the story of the information gathered and what it means. The paper ends with a conclusion, which is a reflection of the value of what has been learned and how the information may be used.

This framework is excellent for students who are becoming aware of and learning how to write research. Most of the professional content area organizations are including a standard that expresses expectations that students should be able to do research related to the content area. As a result, many districts are requiring that students conduct a research paper. The I-Search is a perfect first research-writing experience. It has all the parts of a research report, but it is closely related to a student's experiences and interests. Certainly, it is not the only model for research writing, but some teachers and students find it to be a good beginning.

Carol Jago (2002) writes a book that is a good companion to Macrorie. She points out that, to write well, student authors need to balance several things at once—they need to wrestle with ideas, balance form and function, push words this way and that, attend to syntax and diction, and employ imagery and metaphor until a coherent message emerges. The structure of the I-Search helps to lighten the load for student writers by providing an overall coherent framework for their writing.

Macrorie (1988) provides anecdotal and experiential evidence of the success of this method and leads teachers and students through the I-Search in a step-by-step way. The suggestions for both teaching writing and guiding students' efforts are consistent with writing and learning process principles that help students to advance their experiences with both literacy and content subject matter.

TOWARD STRATEGIC INDEPENDENCE THROUGH STUDY METHODS

The strategies in this chapter are those that promote students' engagement with ideas by scaffolding reading, writing, and discussing activities to engage content. As students mature, systematic study techniques are needed. Students may develop these techniques on their own as they engage in successful strategies provided by their teachers, but they should know, and so should their teachers, that there are research-based study systems.

Several examples of strategic approaches are published in how-to-study books and journal articles. Typically, few differences exist between specific approaches; rather, a strategy varies in emphasis. For example, one strategy might emphasize review and another strategy might emphasize setting a purpose for reading. All study approaches include some learning activity to involve students in getting ready to read, thinking about what they are reading, and thinking after the reading.

As we discussed in chapter 2, one study approach that is taught in many schools and presented in many how-to-study materials is SQRRR, which is an acronym for a five-step study system: Survey, Question, Read, Recite, and Review (Robinson, 1941). Research results on SQRRR are mixed, because it is difficult to test a strategy with five parts. Furthermore, a number of interpretations exist as to how the strategy should be implemented; thus, some experiments test the adaptations rather than the strategy as it was originally conceptualized. Our interpretation of the strategy is consistent with our understanding of psychological learning principles. Because the literature reports many different interpretations and adaptations of the strategy, we offer our use of the strategy step by step. We suggest you share this or a similar study strategy with your students.

SQRRR

The first step is to survey, which accomplishes two mental purposes. First, it provides an opportunity for making two important decisions: How much time should be devoted to studying and what is the best approach to use for a particular studying task? We have all had the experience, while studying, of reading to the bottom of the page, realizing that we can't remember a thing on the page, and wondering to ourselves, how long is this darn chapter, anyway? At that point, we usually page through the chapter, look to see where it ends and, if we decide to continue, begin to read the chapter again. A chapter survey negates this inefficient behavior and makes for strategic and focused study.

Regarding the second decision—choosing the best approach—a strategic student selects a study strategy that is appropriate for accomplishing the purpose at hand. For example, if the purpose is to read closely for details in material that is particularly dense and relatively unfamiliar, a student might decide to first read the chapter all the way through and then divide it into manageable units for note taking and close study. In contrast, if the purpose is to familiarize oneself with the topic in a general way, with less emphasis on details, and if the material is written in an inviting and considerate way (see chapter 4, this volume, for characteristics of text that is considerate) and if it is about a topic that is relatively familiar, a student might decide that a quick read with minimal notes is appropriate.

The survey step provides the reader with an opportunity to attend to the major ideas to be studied. The major ideas are usually signaled by cues such as subheadings, pictures, and graphic displays. Paying attention to those clues helps to create a mental map what is to be studied. In addition, during the survey, background knowledge is activated and the reader makes predictions about how prior knowledge might be connected with new information. Reflection on those potential connections indicates appropriate and possible

BOX 6.10. The ReQuest Procedure (Modified for Use in Content Area Classes)

1. The teacher and the students each read a paragraph or subheading together, either silently or orally.
2. Students prepare and ask the teacher all the questions they can think of on the material just read.
3. When the students have exhausted their supply of questions, the teacher then asks questions of the students, paying special attention to ask open-ended, thought-provoking questions that call for critical and creative thought.
4. The teacher and the students together then analyze the qualities of the questions asked by each.
5. The teacher concludes the strategy lesson by encouraging students to ask the more provocative and appropriate questions of themselves when studying.

purposes for reading the assignment, and, if prior knowledge conflicts with predicted text-based information, a purpose can be set to resolve that potential conflict.

Learning to survey is a special strategy. Many students have been taught to read carefully, following every word, and to read slowly when comprehension is difficult. For these students, the notion of skimming, which is required for surveying, is foreign and has to be taught. To teach surveying, demonstrate the process and provide opportunities for students to do it under supervision. To demonstrate the process, use an opaque or overhead projector and demonstrate physically (with your hand) and verbally what you would notice when skimming. After students have practiced skimming the text, review the purpose for the survey and ask students to discuss their experiences and difficulties with the step.

The second step is to question. This is another opportunity for the student to take *control* of learning. By thinking about the questions that the student wants answered, purposes for reading are made more clear and interest is likely to be stimulated and maintained. Some adaptations of the SQRRR method suggest that the student turn the subheadings of the reading assignment into questions. We have trouble with that recommendation because it is text based rather than student initiated. For questions to be meaningful, they have to be related to what the student really wants to know.

Some students have trouble asking authentic, meaningful questions. We don't think this is the students' fault; we know that possessing the ability to ask good questions is difficult. Nonetheless, a teacher may need to help students become good question askers. The ReQuest procedure (Manzo, 1969), when modified for group instruction, is a practice that has demonstrated good results. See Box 6.9 for ReQuest directions.

Earlier, in chapter 4, we suggested the use of the question–answer relationship (Raphael, 1984) as a strategy for helping students to ask good questions, and we reaffirm it as a viable strategy here also. When encouraging students to ask meaningful questions, we find that the culture of the classroom comes into play. If the teacher encourages a climate of inquisitiveness and divergent thinking, the students are more likely to adopt that spirit. We think it is important for students to realize that their questions are not always answered in a text and that other resources (such as educational videos, magazines, or trade books) may have to be accessed. Hence, developing students' ability to ask meaningful questions is a step toward developing independent learners who are more able to accept responsibility for their own learning.

It may seem like a good idea for students to write their questions so they can remind themselves later of what they wanted to know. We want to discourage this idea because writing questions takes time and decreases the efficient use of the strategy. Rather than writing questions, we suggest that less material be studied. That is, after the survey, if a student decides that the material being studied is particularly challenging and that questions are not likely to be held in short-term memory, the student might use the subsequent steps of SQRRR on a smaller amount of material, repeating the strategy until the assignment is completed.

Ideally, about 10% of the study time is devoted to the surveying and questioning steps. The idea is to skim over the material, simply looking over the lay of the land, so to speak. If more time is spent during the survey step than is necessary, two things are likely to happen. First, the student is likely to become discouraged by how long it takes to study the material. Second, the purpose of the survey will be defeated as too many details will be paid attention to and the important step of simply getting an overview will be ignored. Questions are a starting point for the reading, but readers need to be prepared to change their questions as they read. The questions set the stage, but if they are too narrow or not answered in the text, readers must be ready to adapt their questions or abandon the material for some other resource that does address their questions.

After the surveying and the questioning, the student is asked to read, which is the first *R* in SQRRR. The *way* that the material is read depends on three conditions: first, the quality of the material (well organized, well-written material is easier to read than poorly organized or poorly written material); second, the purpose for reading (if the material is being read to confirm information the reader already possesses, it can be read more quickly and lightly than if the purpose is to become familiar with relatively complex, obsure, and new material); and third, the extent of prior knowledge the reader has about the topic presented in the material. Hence, we see that reading to study is not simply a matter of beginning at the first word on the page and moving word by word across the page; rather, the strategic reader chooses to simply skim over some parts (those that are already familiar) and closely read other parts (those that conflict with prior knowledge or those that relate relatively new information). The text walk, introduced earlier, is a teacher-directed strategy that can help students learn how to make a plan for reading.

The second *R* represents the recite portion of SQRRR. The idea behind recitation is that, after reading, the student reflects on what has been learned. This is an opportune time to create maps or outlines of the material studied. Ideally, recitation should be done without returning to the resource material. The questions asked that helped to establish the purpose for reading might be consulted to guide the recitation. Teachers who use graphic organizers are helpful to students who are implementing this step in the study process. Students should be encouraged to draw maps or make charts during the recitation phase of the study system. One modification we have made is that we ask students to map from memory what they have read; then, during the next step, they fill in their maps with material they neglected to include during the recitation. We suggest that students use a different color marker to add material because that is the material that did not stay in short-term memory and is the material that will most likely be forgotten.

The third *R* represents review. This step involves going back over the material to compare what was recited with what was actually said in the text. It is also appropriate to reflect back on the questions, to attempt to answer those questions or to revise the original questions, to better match the constructed meaning.

The recite and review portions of SQRRR should be proportional to the amount of time spent reading. The formula for time distribution that we recommend is that 10% of the study time should be spent surveying and questioning, 70% of the study time spent reading, and the remaining 20% of the time spent reciting and reviewing. Imposing this sort of discipline on your time results in efficient use of the time available for studying.

One criticism that is often leveled at this or any other study strategy is that it is too linear, suggesting to some that these steps be carried out in a lock-step manner. That criticism has merit because in reality effective study is recursive. That is, a student should expect to revise the questions posed during the questioning stage and expect to develop new questions as the reading, reviewing, and reciting progresses. Hence, students should not be led to believe that any strategy should be employed in a lock step, mechanistic, or passive manner; rather, these steps simply provide opportunity for the conduct of active, efficient, and effective study.

Another criticism of SQRRR by some students is that it takes too much time. It is easy to understand why students might feel that way, especially if the time guidelines are not followed. Unfortunately, some students use SQRRR in a rigid way, like writing down the information gathered during the survey stage and writing down the questions. We think such concrete activities related to those initial processes negate the psychological processes they are designed to enhance. For many people, SQRRR is actually more efficient than the tedious reading and rereading that many students use.

The Reflective Journal

Another strategy for individual use is the writing of a reflective journal. This sort of a journal requires the student to regularly write about successful and less successful studying attempts. For example, one student we know, Karen, had difficulty in trigonometry and kept just such a journal. She had transferred schools late in the semester and had to catch up with the students in her new school. Each day, to initiate her studying, she wrote what she expected to learn from the daily assignment and how she was going to attack that material. At the conclusion of her studying, she reflected on what she had learned and the success of her attack. After keeping the journal for about 1 month, she gained confidence in her ability to complete the assignments and was able to internalize the type of thinking she had made explicit by keeping the journal. She then abandoned the journal but used the technique at other times when confronted with particularly challenging material.

Teachers who expect this sort of journaling activity help students. We previously described the double-entry note-taking system and reflective dialogue journals, which, when used in the classroom, help students to see the value of written reflection. Once success is enjoyed in the classroom with these sorts of strategies, students are more likely to use them on their own, as they become independent readers and learners.

Rate Flexibility

Middle-school and secondary students are often interested in being able to read faster and more efficiently. As we have stated before, to the layperson this is called speed reading, and to the reading specialist it is called rate flexibility. Fantastic claims are made about individuals reading several thousand words per minute. Instruction and research that is related to rate flexibility has a long history: Some of the very earliest reading research was conducted by Cattell (1886) and was designed to investigate eye movements. The idea was that, if he could figure out how fast the eye could move, he could estimate the number of words processed by the eye.

Much that we recommend regarding rate flexibility is gathered from conventional wisdom rather than empirical knowledge. Despite the lack of empirically based evidence, however, our recommendations are consistent with what is known about comprehending and learning.

The concept of rate flexibility is based on the reader being in *control* of choosing the strategy or strategies that will be used to construct meaning. The choice is made by the reader according to the purpose for reading, the quality and quantity of related prior knowledge, and the organization of the material being read. For example, most people read a grocery list by employing different strategies than they use when reading a scientific theory. As intuitively obvious as this concept might be, students sometimes believe that reading is a word-by-word process and that to successfully comprehend it is best to read each word slowly and carefully. In reality, mature readers read phrases of words rather than individual words. Other times, readers do not read line by line; rather they scoot ahead, skimming the material and then read in a seemingly backward pattern to confirm details.

In addition, some readers have firmly established habits that limit their flexibility. For example, some readers read each word aloud to themselves; others play with their hair or swing their leg to the rate of their reading. These habits signal that a reader is reading without flexibility, and in all likelihood their stance is more passive than active. Flexible reading that results in constructing meaning is active and vigorous.

Readers who read everything at about the same rate (usually about 250 words per minute), whether it is a grocery list, a scientific explanation, or a classical novel, should practice varying their rate to become more flexible. In this case, the analogy to physical fitness is appropriate: Exercise such as weight training or running results in increased strength and flexibility; systematic practice in reading at faster rates also increases a readers, reading flexibility. To help students develop their flexibility, teachers might discuss the role that purpose, background, and text organization has on the approach a reader uses to read. In addition, students need to be made aware of their reading rate and of the concept of flexibility. To accomplish this, provide students with 3-minute timed readings and then practice varying the rate depending on the variables of purpose, background, and text organization. To do a 3-minute timed reading, ask students to read a text for 3 minutes. At the conclusion of the timed reading, ask students to estimate the number of words on a page, to multiply that number by the number of pages read, and to divide by the total number of words read by the length of time reading. Becoming aware of one's typical reading rate and then intentionally choosing varied but appropriate rates will help to develop flexibility.

We imagine that the notion of rate flexibility is going to reemerge as an important area of reading education for two reasons: To use the Internet, one must be efficient. There is a lot of activity on the Internet (pop-ups, links, and so forth), and using it is nigh on to impossible if the reader only processes prose one word at a time in linear fashion. Second, recent reading tests are including measures of "fluency." The idea is that a "good" reader can read aloud in a fluent, accurate, and expressive manner. We do not support these sorts of tests because we know that mature reading for learning is done silently and that readers use skimming, scanning, and other recursive types of reading patterns when reading to study. Nonetheless, as professionals listen to students reading aloud and consider their reading rates, it will be natural for questions about reading rate to emerge.

Metacognition

In chapter 4 we discussed instructional strategies to help students become metacognitive—the ability to think about their thinking and reading processes. You may have noticed that we italicized the word *control* in the previous two sections. Students having a sense of control of their own reading strategies is an element in both metacognition and rate flexibility. Teachers can help students become more metacognitive by regularly employing and modeling think-aloud strategies. That is, when students are confronted with needing to learn new strategies to comprehend challenging material, it is a great help for the teacher to model how to do the strategy. Projecting the task and demonstrating how the reading and thinking is done is the best way to do this. Linda Robb, a middle-school teacher and reading expert, makes several helpful suggestions in her book, *Teaching Reading in Middle School* (2000, p. 71). Here is a synopsis of her suggestions that we like best.

1. Explain to students that good readers monitor their comprehension. As they read, they ask questions such as these: Does this passage make sense? Can I restate it in my own words? Can I say what part or parts were hard?
2. Present your demonstration. Prior to thinking aloud, place the passage and any accompanying materials like diagrams or maps on an overhead transparency and read the passage to the students. Robb shares a think aloud she presented on "Why don't I remember what I've read?" As you share the passage, talk about what you are thinking and the steps you take to make sense of the passage.
3. After several demonstrations, ask students to do think alouds in pairs, and ask them to share their reading strategies. Circulate among the students to lend support and make suggestions to help them become more metacognitively aware.

We suggest that each content area teacher regularly incorporate think-aloud strategies in his or her instruction. In addition to using materials that students are required to read, consider reading aloud to your students. Choose content-related materials that you admire and discuss your thinking as you do so. Judy Richardson's (2000) book, *Read It Aloud! Using Literature in the Secondary Content Classroom*, is a terrific source, which includes many appropriate, read-aloud materials for each content area.

Think alouds are likely to be very helpful for teaching young people to use the Internet and other technologies. True, many young people are increasingly facile with technology, but not necessarily with using technology to engage ideas in school; hence, it is likely that you can build on their prior knowledge and experience to help them learn to gather information and use it for content area learning purposes.

REFLECTION AND SUMMARY

At this point, we hope our readers are constructing a vision for themselves as teachers who help students read, write, and discuss in the content areas. We imagine that each of you can explain why it is important to do so and that you have lots of ideas to get started. In this chapter we have suggested a template to be used as you plan to plan, and we have provided several instructional strategies that represent a range of teacher and student direction. However, what we have presented is far from the whole story. The reality is that the ideas presented thus far will not be successful unless you spend time and energy conceptualizing the sort of environment you want in your classroom. The next chapter speaks to establishing a classroom culture that will support the literacy and learning of your students.

APPLICATION ACTIVITIES

1. Consider the ways that those who work in your content area discover new knowledge, the sorts of evidence that are required for knowing, and the conventions of your field for reporting new information. You might accomplish this by conducting interviews with professors in the content area you plan to teach (or are teaching). Summarize your findings and compare and contrast your findings with those of your colleagues. Do the "ways of knowing and doing" in your content area match the sorts of learning and literacy strategies and activities you plan to use? Why or why not? If not, could you make adaptations that would better suit your content area?
2. Write a "thought paper" on how you might involve students in the processes of your content area. What are the advantages you see for doing this and what are the drawbacks?
3. Choose one of the models for planning and begin a plan using a major concept or topic in your field. Be sure to incorporate the use of several of the practices and strategies from other chapters in this book or other resources you have read.
4. Create a list of all the resources you can find related to a particular concept you might teach. Be sure to search especially for materials that represent a diverse range of cultures, ethnicities, and genders.
5. Do a planning to plan notebook as described in this chapter.

6. Do an Internet search on concept-based instruction and on content area literacy (reading) strategies. Are the ideas in this book confirmed? Extended? Use the Instructional Feature Analysis chart to estimate the potential value of the strategies you find.

FROM OUR PROFESSIONAL LIBRARY

Buehl, D. (2001). *Classroom strategies for interactive learning* (2nd ed.). Newark, DE: International Reading Association.

Burke, J. (2002). *Helping all students read, write, speak, and think*. Portsmouth, NH: Heinemann.

Estes, T., & Vaughan, J. (1978). *Content area reading and learning*. Needham Heights, MA: Allyn & Bacon.

Guzzetti, B. J., McGowan, T., & Kowalinski, B. J. (1992). Using literature to promote social studies learning. *Journal of Reading, 36*, 114–122.

Herber, H. L., & Herber, J. N. (1993). *Teaching in content areas with reading, writing, and reasoning*. Neeham Heights, MA: Allyn & Bacon.

Jago, C. (2002). *Cohesive writing*. Portsmouth, NH: Heinemann.

Macrorie, K. (1988). *Searching writing*. New York: Boynton/Cook.

Richardson, J. S. *Read it aloud! Using literature in the secondary content classroom*. Newark, DE: International Reading Association.

Robb, L. (2000). *Teaching reading in the middle school*. New York: Scholastic.

Short, K. G., Schroeder, J., Kauffman, G., Ferguson, M. J., & Crawford, K. M. (1996). *Learning together through inquiry*. Portland, ME: Stenhouse.

Vacca, R., & Vacca, J. (2002). *Content area reading*. Boston: Allyn & Bacon.

7

Content Area Literacy Assessment and Classroom Climate

The conclusion of the previous chapter suggested that the theory and pedagogy presented thus far is necessary, but not sufficient for good content area literacy instruction. We encourage teachers to teach students to become independent, critical, and self-motivated learners. This is accomplished when teachers and students work together to construct an understanding of a particular content area. This is not a new idea. Our ideas are consistent with those promoted throughout American education by leaders such as Dewey (the father of progressive education), Huey (one of the first psychologists to write about reading), Thorndike (a psychologist of the early 1900s), Bruner (one of the greatest American psychologists of our time), and many other current educators (Stipek, 2004). Research has been presented and practices recommended throughout this volume to provide evidence that reading, writing, and discussing in the content areas is one important key to constructivist-type instruction and to developing the literacy and learning of your students.

Despite the long history of these ideas, they are not the norm in schools today. One reason is that research on characteristics of classrooms providing a context or space for engaged, constructivist literacy is in its infancy (Guthrie, 2004). In this chapter we provide some insights as to why constructivist literacy instruction is not the norm and make specific suggestions for actions to resist the status quo to create a constructivist classroom. There are three potential roadblocks, or constraints (Little, 1982), to using the suggestions in this volume: the culture of assessment and accountability, the school culture, and personal beliefs and vision. We discuss each of these so that you might better establish a space for supporting students as they engage in literacy practices to learn.

CULTURE OF ASSESSMENT AND ACCOUNTABILITY

As we write, educators are deeply affected by issues of assessment and accountability. The president of the United States, the Congress, governors, and state and local school boards are looking for ways to evaluate teachers and students in the nation's schools. Anders and Richardson (1992) wrote this: "We have now come to realize that a culture of testing permeates schools and classrooms to such an extent that teachers seemingly have great difficulty considering instruction and the improvement of instruction from outcome measures designed for purposes of accountability" (p. 383).

Teachers are continually challenged to be accountable for the instruction they offer. This demand for accountability is oppressive; teachers' curricula and practices are affected (Johnston, 1989). Darling-Hammond and Wise (1985) reported the following: "[Teachers are] alter[ing] curriculum emphasis, teaching students how to take tests, teaching students for the text [specific preparation for the test], having less time to teach and feeling under pressure. The most common effect reported by teachers about their own behavior was that they altered their curriculum emphasis" (p. 359).

This quote from more than 20 years ago is even truer today. We believe that accountability is important; what bothers us is that (a) the norm-referenced and criterion-referenced tests for which students and teachers are held accountable may not be valid for the curriculum and instruction in which the students are involved; (b) the tests may not be reliable and valid for the students who are taking them; and (c) the tests provide information for policymakers, but they provide precious little information for the teacher to use to inform and guide instruction.

Norm-referenced or standardized tests not only alter teachers' perceptions and delivery of curricula but also narrow modes of instruction, reduce the amount of time for instruction, and limit the teacher's ability to use methods and materials that are incongruent with standardized tests (Smith, 1991). The scenario in many schools is that, a few weeks before the mandated tests, gears in the curriculum shift. Instruction becomes a matter of practicing both the content and procedures of the standardized test. Emphasis is on efficiency and productivity. The process of learning (real school) is set aside to accommodate accountability demands.

In this way, testing programs significantly reduce the amount of time for instruction by 3 to 4 weeks as teachers prepare students and administer the standardized tests (Smith, Edelsky, Draper, Rottenberg, & Cherland, 1989). The time taken up by testing reduces the capacity of teachers to adjust their instruction to meet students' needs or to be flexible and responsive.

Efforts to improve scores on standardized, norm-referenced tests also belie the assumptions of the test. These tests are based on assumptions of randomization; they are designed to represent the performance of students in comparison with a normal sample, and students' performance is supposed to represent the bell-shaped curve. In other words, the test is designed so that, for it to be valid and reliable, half the students need to score below average. As districts across the country "prepare" students for the tests, the assumptions of the test are violated.

In addition, multiple-choice testing leads to multiple-choice teaching (Smith, 1991). Teaching becomes more testlike, as worksheet questions resemble standardized test items. Course content and methods of presentation increasingly match expectations of the tests. What effect does this have on teachers? Smith (1991) gave this report:

> Whatever the merits are for substituting geometry for metrics, map and graph skills for history and civics, study skills for science, or recognition of grammatical errors in worksheets for editing one's own work, the effects of such substitution on teachers seems obvious. If science, civics, or critical thinking is shifted out of the curriculum because it is not tested and if exploration, discovery, and integration methods fall out of use because they do not conform to the format of the mandated test, teachers will lose their capacities to teach these topics and subjects, use new methods, or even imagine them as possibilities. A teacher who is able to teach only that which is determined from above and can teach only by worksheets is an unskilled worker. (p. 11)

We quote Mary Smith from more than 15 years ago, because we fear that her predictions have, in many districts across the country, come true. This is a devastating quote for what it portends for teachers, students, and the future of education in a democratic society.

We know that a teacher's beliefs about teaching and learning affect student outcomes (Bos & Anders, 1994). Does a teacher's compliance with the testing culture also affect students? Shepard and Smith (1989) report that students learn from these tests "that there is one right answer to every question, that the right answer resides in the head of the teacher or test maker, and that their job is to get that answer by guessing if necessary" (p. 23). In other words, not only do multiple-choice tests lead to a multiple-choice style of teaching, but worse, with an unbalanced emphasis on simplistic tests, students are likely to believe that multiple-choice thinking is the sine qua non of learning. These are neither attributes that support the development of students as constructors of understanding attributes that are consistent with critical thinking, creativity, or responsibility for one's own learning—all goals that most educators value.

In addition to standardized, norm-referenced tests, states and local districts are creating and mandating criterion-referenced tests, many of which are developed as "high-stakes" tests; students need to pass them to graduate from high school. These tests are more likely to be representative of what students are taught because they are supposedly linked to the state or district standards, which are one of the resources teachers use when developing curriculum. That's the good news. The bad news is that the tests may not be reliable. In other words, the test items may not measure what they claim to measure. Test development is expensive and presents a high level of challenge to the best of psychometric test developers. These local tests are also likely to be influenced by politics, which does not bode well for the creation of a sound test. Another issue with criterion (standards)-referenced tests is whether or not a test can truly measure what it means to be a high school graduate. Some students are gifted in the arts but perform poorly on tests of reading and mathematics. If those students receive passing grades in their courses, should they fail high school because they do not score well enough on the "privileged" knowledge—knowledge that is deemed more valuable (reading and math) to society than the arts? Policymakers and society as a whole seem to be galloping toward accepting tests as the only way to know that students are learning and that teachers are teaching. We look forward to the day that other options are available. See the companion volume to this one by Sheila Valencia for alternatives.

Additional Artifacts of the Culture of Accountability

Externally imposed accountability is not the only contributor to the culture of accountability. Educators' expectations and practices related to grading students' work are also indicative of the influence of the culture of accountability. For example, Peggy, a fifth-grade teacher, reported showing her grade book to her principal as proof that she knew what grade her students were earning, that she had enough separate grades to average for each item on the report card, and that certain material had been presented (Anders & Richardson, 1992). A norm existed in Peggy's school that teachers needed to prove to their principal and to parents that sufficient individual grades had been recorded and that averaging those grades equaled a grade that was representative of what each child was learning. This is nuts! It doesn't represent what we know about the teaching and learning.

This is not an isolated case. What is wrong with it? The problem is at least threefold. First, it assumes that learning is product oriented, that it can be quantified, and that each step can be measured as successful or not successful. These are values suggesting an information-transfer theory of teaching and learning rather than a constructivist theory.

Further, it puts teachers on the defensive. Teachers are able to describe the processes in which their students are engaged, and they can describe the quality of that process. That is very different, however, from assigning a normative-type grade (A for outstanding, C for average, and F for failure) to students' everyday performance. Normative grades may be appropriate in the sense of marking the end of one time period, but they are not appropriate on a daily basis as students are involved in the process of learning—a process that requires that errors be made and be learned from. In a constructivist classroom, errors are used as an opportunity to learn, not as an opportunity for punishment.

Moreover, this view of teaching and learning turns grading into a means for controlling student behavior. When teachers were asked what would happen if they did not give daily grades, they responded, "we might as well go home" (Anders & Richardson, 1992, p. 387). Hence, grading is not perceived as a means of providing feedback to students so they may improve, or to teachers so they can make better instructional decisions, but as a means of management and control. We know management and control are important, but consider this: If students are engaged in meaningful and valued curricula, the discipline problems are few and usually all but disappear.

Systems of accountability are influential because the public and many educators are looking for objective measures to evaluate students' learning and teachers' teaching. In this climate, teachers mistrust their judgment, and so does the public. Wirth (1989) points out that this mistrust is indicative of the dehumanizing nature of schools. Tests that are developed elsewhere are considered more credible than the judgment of the teacher who works closely with the learner.

Suffice it to say that all evaluations are subjective. Evaluations necessarily require that someone's values be taken into account—even the test company's executive's values! Test makers who ascribe to an information-transfer perspective of teaching and learning develop standardized measures. We are on a collision course. As educators continue to develop constructivist perspectives and practices of teaching and learning, the testing industry races on to create tests that are representative of another paradigm, the information-transfer model.

The standards movement, as represented by professional organizations, is an example of an effort to hold students and teachers accountable but by providing standards that represent processes as well as products. Criterion-referenced tests are designed to measure the degree to which students are able to reach criteria on certain measurable standards. These tests are, of course, not perfect—no test is—but at least they attempt to measure curricular goals that can be discussed, agreed on, and taught.

Policy makers and the testing companies are the main beneficiaries of the norm-referenced and standards-based criterion-referenced tests; they are examples of summative evaluations. They are not particularly useful to the classroom or content area teacher, because the tests are not linked to curriculum or, as in the case of criterion-referenced tests developed to align with state standards, the results arrive at school after the subject has been taught and students are on their way to new classes. Besides, how reliable can a few multiple-choice items be on a subject you taught for 6 weeks? Not very. No, what every teacher needs is a repertoire of assessment strategies, which can be used continuously and will inform the decisions she or he makes about instruction and will also help students know how well they are doing.

Suggestions for Assessment

It is important to distinguished between summative and formative assessment. Summative assessment methods "sum up" where the learner is at in terms of engaging a set of concepts or processes at a particular point in time. It is the summary; it is part of what gets recorded on the report card as a "final" grade for the grading period. Summative evaluations can be the total number of points earned during a grading period, projects, tests, and demonstrations—a major culminating activity that provides students an opportunity to show their "new" learning. These summative evaluations are most often graded with a rubric.

Another summative evaluation that informs both teacher and student is the portfolio. Portfolios are analogous to an artist's collection of representative work. How portfolios are actually done vary by classroom. Some organizational strategies exist, however, that most teachers will find helpful. Students' portfolios need to be related to conceptual goals; if they are not, they are likely to be an unfocused collection of student work that is difficult to evaluate. The sorts of instructional activities done in the classroom are good products to be included in the portfolio. For example, if semantic maps are used to engage concepts in the content area, students could be asked to include the map in their portfolio. It is important to remember that students play an active role in the development of the portfolio. The portfolio is an opportunity for the student to reflect on the learning process, to present what has been learned, and to help establish goals for the future. Portfolios are discussed in detail in Sheila Valencia's book, *Classroom Based Literacy Assessment* (forthcoming).

Formative assessments, in contrast to summative assessments, provide teachers with information that is *informative* about the *form* of student's progress toward engaging ideas. In effect, formative evaluation techniques are helpful to a teacher in two ways. First, as a teacher considers formative evaluation, it is natural for her or him to ask a self-question: What can I ask students to do that will help them to process or engage these ideas? The sorts of before-, during, and after-reading activities discussed throughout this volume are examples of ways to engage students in activities that involve reading and writing to engage concepts. Your content area also suggests activities such as lab experiments and lab reports in the sciences, problem-solving activities in mathematics, including writing explanations to how problems are solved, making and explaining projects in the various arts courses, and playing games and such in physical education. Another idea is to ask students, at the end of each class period, questions such as these: What did you learn today? What gave you problems with today's lesson? What do you expect we will do tomorrow? Students answer these questions, or others that you would like to know the answer to, on 4 in. × 8 in. (~10 cm × 20 cm) index cards the last few minutes of the class period. These "exit cards" are helpful formative assessments: The cards let you know what went well during the class period, who needs more time or opportunity to learn, and whether or not students' predictions for where the learning is headed matches your own. Some teachers even report getting better ideas for what should happen the next day than what they had thought of doing.

Second, formative assessments address the need for teachers to be able to analyze and evaluate the data gathered from students, the evidence students provide, indicating that they have indeed engaged concepts and have integrated new information and experiences in their schema. In other words, when students write an explanation of a particular concept engagement, how does the teacher know that learning has in fact taken place? Here are some suggestions for this type of evaluation.

One idea is to borrow the analytical procedures described in the prose chapter. We suggest that you do a concept map of what your students write. What are the similarities and differences between the conceptual map used to construct the unit and the writing that your students do? Another idea is to look for your students' use of the conceptual vocabulary (the words and phrases that are part of your conceptual map). Do they use that vocabulary in ways that are consistent with the concepts being developed?

Patty makes this recommendation from personal experience. Working closely with student teachers in science education, she provided samples of writing done by high school students in the student teachers' classes. In most cases, the student teachers gave the high school students credit for their writing about concepts. On closer evaluation, using the concept map analysis, she found it clear that the high school students had only superficially engaged the concepts; they actually had made inappropriate connections between and among the concepts.

Remember the prewriting and postwriting that Barbara and her colleagues collected from students in the literature-based inquiry described in chapter 6? Collect a writing sample from your students at the beginning of a unit of study—ask them to write everything they know about the conceptualization you are about to study—and then ask them to do a postunit writing sample, asking them to again write everything they know; you would have a comparison to analyze that would describe student progress. Your analysis of their taking up the concepts would indicate the quality and quantity of learning and the areas of study that had to be retaught or reengaged by you and your students.

Other teachers do not ask their students to compose; they simply ask each student to brainstorm everything that comes to mind when a certain word or phrase is heard. At the end of the unit, each student is asked to do that again. The difference between the two lists suggests growth.

The time you spend learning about aspects of accountability and the part you play in that culture is time and energy well spent. Be aware that strong political forces devalue authentic assessment in the classroom, but that this type of assessment is what informs you as the teacher and should be what you value. We hope that we are conveying the message that your values and beliefs are critical to being the kind of teacher to which you aspire.

TEACHERS' BELIEFS AND THEORIES

Beliefs are an individual's understandings of the world and the way it works or should work (Richardson, 1994); hence, as teachers picture their classroom, their students, and the school and society in which they work, their beliefs about school and schooling are brought to bear. Reflecting on beliefs raises to consciousness the picture we have in our minds about what a classroom should be like. This is important because the picture we form is likely to affect the ways we choose to teach.

Study of beliefs is grounded in the investigations and writings of anthropologists (e.g., Goodenough, 1963), social psychologists (e.g., Rokeach, 1968), and philosophers (e.g., Green, 1971). In the mid-1980s, teacher educators began to study the relationship of teachers' beliefs and practices with particular attention to how teachers change.

Three conceptions of that relationship emerged. First, Guskey (1986) suggests that teachers develop their beliefs after they adopt particular practices; hence, if teachers attempt and subsequently approved of a teaching method, they are likely to adjust their belief system to accommodate that way of teaching. The second conception suggests that changes in beliefs precede changes in practices. Richardson, Anders, Tidwell, and Lloyd (1991) theorized that such was the case in their study, which showed a strong and fairly consistent relationship between teachers' stated beliefs and their observed reading comprehension instructional practices. The third conception suggests that the process of changing beliefs and practices is interactive; and, depending on the types of changes and the teachers themselves, the change process may begin with changes in beliefs or changes in practice (Richardson, 1994). Which conception best reflects the change process? The answer to this question is unresolved; however, we are of the mind that reflecting on beliefs in terms of practices is a good starting point.

Contrasting Content Area Teachers' Beliefs and Practices

Beliefs about teaching and learning in the content areas can be categorized in terms of two extreme perspectives. One perspective is a transmission or information-transfer model, and the other is a social constructivist model. The former is briefly described in the paragraphs that follow, and the latter is represented by the ideas we have presented in this volume.

The transmission model is based on particular assumptions about the nature of learning, students, curriculum, pedagogy, and evaluation. A few of those assumptions are presented here for two reasons. First, we hope that if we provide a few of the assumptions from this model, you will begin to distinguish evaluation and instructional practices as being more similar to one of the models or the other. Second, we want you to begin to reflect on your beliefs in terms of these two categories. Where do your beliefs lie between these two extremes?

One assumption inherent in the transmission model is that students' minds are viewed as blank slates, and the teacher's responsibility is to inscribe new information on the slate. Another assumption is that knowledge exists in sources of authority such as the textbook, and that students read and study to get information. In terms of curriculum, this model assumes that knowledge can be organized into scope and sequence charts of skills and ideas—that first one idea must be learned before another and that certain skills must be learned before the next skill can be learned. Another example, in terms of pedagogy, is that students are encouraged to work alone and to demonstrate mastery of certain skills or understandings. Mastery is evaluated by student accuracy when a student responds to questions in prescribed ways.

In contrast, constructivist teachers believe that instructional decisions are made on the basis of the unique and particular interactions and transactions that take place in the culture of the classroom. In other words, the content to be studied is negotiated by the teacher and the students as available resources, expectations of others in the school community, and the backgrounds of the teacher and the students are considered. Furthermore, teachers holding a social constructivist belief system "take students where they are," offering them opportunities to develop skills and strategies needed to interact with and construct new ideas. Moreover, critical and creative thinking is likely to occur on a regular basis in a social constructivist classroom because it is a condition for success in the culture of that classroom. The climate promoted by the constructivist teacher honors and celebrates the questions students ask and creative ways of using the information gathered.

On the surface, a social constructivist type of teaching may appear scary because it challenges the norms most of us have experienced in school; steps can be taken to create a constructivist classroom, however. Over time and with experience, a teacher can come close to providing optimum teaching and learning opportunities. Recognizing and acknowledging the power that our belief systems have over what we do is a good step (see Activity 1 at the end of the chapter). Other suggestions for bringing beliefs and practices into correspondence follow.

Discovering Beliefs

Secondary teachers are taking responsibility for their own intellectual and professional practice through programs such as "critical friends" (Dunne, Nave, & Lewis, 2000). Essentially, this is a study group that meets so that members can offer each other support in increasing professionalism and improved practice. Lortie (1975) revealed the isolation many teachers sense in their schools, and the critical friends groups are a response to that isolation as well as an effort to improve practice.

Teachers who write regularly about their practice are more likely to be aware of their beliefs and more able to reflect on and change their practices. Putting thoughts and experiences down on paper provides an opportunity to think critically about those ideas and events.

Challenging and Changing Beliefs

How do teachers change their beliefs about teaching and learning? Like schemata, beliefs are difficult to change; however, recent research on the relationship of beliefs and practices (Richardson & Anders, 1990) suggests that preservice and in-service teachers can examine their beliefs and choose to change them. This research was based on Fenstermacher's (1986, 1987) notions of the practical argument. The practical argument is a way for teachers (or any professional) to think about why they teach the way they do. The practical argument takes place in a conversation, or a series of conversations, between the teach and an "other." This other person serves the role of a critical friend, who is at least as knowledgeable about teaching and learning as is the teacher doing the practical argument. The purpose of the conversation is to elicit four kinds of reasons for the teaching action:

- valuative reasons, which relate to definitions of poor, and right and wrong;
- stipulative reasons, which relate to definitions of terms or events;
- situational reasons, which relate to the context in which the action takes place; and
- empirical reasons, which are based on evidence that can be tested.

This analytical tool "provide(s) a means of transforming teachers' beliefs from being subjectively to objectively reasonable" (Richardson & Anders, 1990, p. 3).

The practical argument is related to something that a teacher does. Richardson and Anders (1990) videotaped each teacher while he or she taught a reading comprehension lesson. Both the teacher and the "others" (Richardson & Anders) viewed and discussed the videotapes together. The discussion focused on why the instruction was conducted in the manner it was. The reasons the teacher gave were categorized as being one or more of the four types just listed here. For example, if a teacher said "I ask students to read aloud a lot because that is reading," it would be categorized as a stipulative belief because he or she provided a definition. An example of a valuative reason is the following: "I love stories with human drama and so I make sure students have lots of opportunity to read those sorts of stories." A situational reason is related to the environment, such as, "when it rains, kids always act like this, and so I always do thus." An empirical reason is one related to a testable hypothesis, such as if a teacher said the following: "Research shows that prior knowledge affects reading comprehension. I begin a lesson with an activity that lets me know something about my students' prior knowledge related to the information being read. I decide how to teach a particular reading assignment depending on what I find out about my students." This reason for why a reading assignment is taught a certain way is an empirical premise. Richardson and Anders transcribed the discussions about the videotapes. They then studied and analyzed these transcriptions for the types of reasons given for the instructional practices. This process of analysis is powerful for coming to terms with beliefs and practices. However, there is no magic combination of reasons. It is not known whether or not a particular combination of beliefs and practices is superior to another combination. It is, though, a process of reflection that seems to affect practices (Klaussen & Short, 1992; Lloyd & Anders, 1994). The question as to whether the practical argument can be done casually and informally between teachers or if it needs to be carried out formally is not resolved.

We find particular value in the practical argument framework as a way to listen. The level of conversation is almost always raised when, during a collegial or professional discussion, empirical evidence is asked for and examined. For example, in a department meeting, as a crucial decision is being made, the colleague who asks about the quality and quantity of the evidence is a colleague who advances the conversation in productive ways. A colleague who justifies an action because "that's how it is always done" (a stipulative premise) or "we don't have the space" (a situational premise) tends to shut down conversations rather than advance them. Valuative statements often wield a lot of power in a discussion and sometimes cause a breakdown, because conversants simply agree to disagree on the basis of their values. By recognizing that the values we each hold is what is dominating the conversation, however, the participants can decide to resolve the issue in a way that honors the varying values.

The challenge of considering beliefs in relationship to teaching practices seems to be well worth the effort. As beliefs and practices are considered and sometimes questioned, we are a better able to think more deeply and objectively about what is being done (Anders & Evans, 1994; Costa & Garmston, 1985). We encourage you to develop this sort of self-analysis as you teach and learn. The instructional feature analysis (mentioned in chap. 6) is a good tool to integrate into your self-analysis.

We predict that involving yourself in processes of reflection will affect the instruction you offer because you will be led to conduct critical inquiry in your classroom, and, concurrently, you will see opportunities for inviting your students to also conduct inquiry. For yourself, the critical inquiry will be about the quality and effectiveness of the opportunities you provide to students. Students' critical inquiry may involve evaluating the top quality and effectiveness of their learning and also conducting inquiry about topics in the curriculum. This way of thinking—a penchant for critical inquiry—is contributing to a growing interest among teachers to conduct research (Patterson, Santa, Short, & Smith, 1993), and it seems to be a natural outgrowth of constructivist teaching. Moreover, if critical inquiry is a way of life in the classroom, critical thinking is promoted and rewarded. This is an important example of how theory and practice connect.

Picture the Classroom. Imagining how your classroom will look, sound, and feel is another good way to begin reflecting on your beliefs and practices. Usually, there is a correspondence between how the classroom looks and feels and the type of instruction that take place. The imagined classroom is likely to include physical considerations, such as the arrangement of the furniture, possible uses of bulletin board and whiteboard space, and students' personal artifacts, as well as your own. In addition, despite the quality or extent of furnishings, a teacher is likely to imagine the social climate. In other words, the teacher pictures and hears the types of interaction that occur between teacher and student(s) and among students.

In a constructivist classroom, the teacher needs flexible space and movable furnishings. The students and teacher need room to work, to carry out activities, to meet in groups, and to present or display their work. To be as well organized as a constructivist teacher needs to be, he or she must have storage space, shelves, and cupboards. Carts are helpful for moving resources; tubs and baskets are needed for holding work in progress; and tables are useful for holding small group meetings. We recommend that computers connected to the Internet be available in the classroom (rather than in a lab down the hall), because students need ready access to find information, they need to store data and information they have collected, and they also need to be encouraged to compose on the computer.

There is likely to be a hum of activity and a comparable amount of noise in the classroom as students and the teacher carry out their activities. To facilitate communication, the teacher must develop systems so that not all messages have to be delivered orally. For example, in New Zealand, Patty observed teachers using magnets that students had designed. Activities were listed on a whiteboard, and as students moved to various activities, they put their magnets next to that activity on the board. That way, without asking, the teacher could see what each student was doing. Other teachers might use signs, such a lag put on the desk when a student has a question or needs help. That way, the student can continue working without keeping a hand in the air. Constructivist teachers and their students may establish mail systems, computer networking, journal activities, and common meeting times to keep in touch with each other.

Time is not used in a constructivist classroom in the same way that it is used in an information-transfer or transmission classroom. Negotiation is a critical attribute of the constructivist classroom. It is typical for the teacher and student to negotiate how their time together will be spent. Fore example, the first few moments of class time may be spent setting an agenda for the class period. Alternatively, in some classrooms, a particular day may be set aside for organizing time and tasks, thereby establishing a work agenda for several days with a set time for reporting and evaluating progress. It occurs to us that involving students in these processes of negotiation is also likely to increase the extent that students take responsibility for their own learning and also contribute to their developing independence as learners.

Picture the Students. A constructivist classroom also presents challenges for students, which means that the teacher has some extra work to do preparing students for this different type of classroom. Students' perceptions, usually based on experiences in information-transfer classrooms, are likely to clash with the expectations of a constructivist teacher. Class meetings are a good way to begin to develop community in the classroom. The teacher and students need to create and negotiate norms for behavior, student and teacher responsibility, and learning outcomes. In addition, most teachers find it necessary to directly teach appropriate group behavior, sometimes going so far as deciding who may work together in a group and who may not. As students increase in their capacity to take responsibility, the amount of structure or control imposed by the teacher is gently released. Distributing group membership so that students vary by ability, interests, talents, gender, and popularity is important so that all students have opportunities to share their talents, to learn from each other, and to practice the principles and processes of democracy (Calkins, 1991; Evans, 1993).

We believe there are attributes of constructivist teachers that are critical for creating a successful and positive relationship with students. For example, respect for students ranks very high. Students are a diverse lot and are likely to come from cultural and socioeconomic backgrounds different from those of their teachers. These differences can be threatening; however, the constructivist teacher sincerely believes that differences among people represent a learning opportunity. This fundamental belief is translated into action when a teachers is working with students. A second attribute is one of flexibility. Because modern society is complex, a teacher cannot hang on to preconceived or inflexible notions; rather, she or he needs to be able to go with the flow and adjust to circumstances. This requirement of flexibility is true for all matters relating to students and curricula. Barbara read aloud the book *The Geraniums on the Windowsill Just Died, But Teacher You Went Right On* (Cullum, 1971) to her fifth-grade students. This trade book illustrates the relevance of caring and flexibility. When teaching seventh graders, Patty once set aside the content for a class period because the students came to school overwrought as a result of a reported rapist in the neighborhood. Patty spent time talking about safety precautions and strategies to control fear. As a result of that conversation, Tanya (a pseudonym) approached Patty after class in tears. She was afraid she was pregnant because her cousin had raped her a month before. It is very likely that Tanya never would have confided this terrible truth to an inflexible teacher, and she may not have gotten the help and support she needed.

Flexibility is also related to curriculum. A major theme throughout this volume is that curriculum is created and constructed by the teacher and the students; hence, both the interests and backgrounds of students must be acknowledged and accepted in a constructivist classroom. This does not mean that whatever the students bring to the classroom must be accepted. Teachers are responsible for socializing students to appropriate school behavior, which means that illegal activities and marginal social behavior are not acceptable. What is required is a spirit of negotiation. Inherent in this attribute is regular and systematic methods of *member checking*—students and teacher regularly give each other feedback and offer constructive criticism.

Member checking can take place in dialogue journals. These journals provide opportunities for students to reflect on the quality of their participation in activities and the success of those activities for achieving particular learning goals. The teacher reads and reacts to these journals in positive, encouraging, and thoughtful ways. As explained in Chapter 5, Patty uses dialogue journals in her college classes. Students can choose to write either e-journals or paper-and-pencil journals. These journals are not graded in the sense of a student product. Rather, students receive credit for engaging in the process, but not in the normative sense of "good" or "poor."

Another idea for member checking is to spend a couple days at each grading period evaluating both the teacher's and the students' performance during the previous grading period. The teacher might have individual conferences with each student to discuss that student's progress. Although individual conferences are conducted, students organize themselves into committees: one committee would be charged with evaluating the teacher, another the curriculum, and a third the activities of the previous time period. The committees could survey the class, interview each other, and come up with a grade for each of the three categories. After the individual conferences, a class meeting could be used to report the results of the committees to each other and to the teacher. From this activity, goals could be set for the next grading period.

This activity has advantages in addition to member checking: Students use a research process to assess the work that was accomplished and participate in creating what comes next, which increases their motivation.

Constructivist teachers have a sense of humor too. A teacher who has the ability to laugh at herself or himself, to enjoy what is going on, and to do so with the rhythms of student life is likely to enjoy a great deal of success with students. We are often impressed with the culture of children and adolescents. They have particular forms of humor, interests, and social life that teachers need not necessarily participate in, but the extent that we adults can be aware of and appreciate that culture is a predictor of how successful we will be.

Our final recommendation for interacting with students is that constructivist teachers have and demonstrate a driving and compelling need to learn. Not knowing an answer and wondering how to find it out is of more value than having answers and providing them. The teacher who says, "What a good question!" "I never thought of that before!" "I wonder how we could find out?" "What made you think of that?" and "What do you already know that could help us find out?" is promoting critical inquiry and a love for learning that is contagious.

Picture the School and Society. You, your classroom, and your students exist in a school culture and in society. Many teachers' beliefs and practices are influenced by the perceptions of others in the school, district, education profession, and society at large. Thinking about those perceptions in terms of your beliefs and practices is worthwhile.

One perception that can limit teaching, as we believe we should, is a fear of students with backgrounds with which we are unfamiliar. In such a complex society, the list of possible differences is long, including those students for whom English is a second language, students of homelessness and poverty, students of varying religious orientations, students of widely differing ethnic backgrounds, and students whose family composition is different from your own. To relate to students with such varying backgrounds (and to recognize personal biases and prejudices), it is important to avail yourself of every opportunity possible to become familiar with people from whom you differ. This can be accomplished by wide reading, by travel, and by field studies into communities where your students live.

A second constraint to implementing the ideas discussed in this volume is the culture of the school in which you work. We think of three speed bumps, so to speak, that you may appreciate being warned about.

First, most of your colleagues will be well attuned to psychological models of teaching. They may have had a content area reading course, which has historically been grounded in the psychology of learning. Psychological understandings are important, but they do not provide a sufficient foundation of knowledge for making instructional decisions related to literacy.

Knowledge of the nature of language is also important. Language develops as students are involved in authentic and meaningful content area activities. As students try new activities and meet new concepts, their language develops to describe and express those new understandings. Further, literacy processes are embedded in what Gee (2001) identifies as Discourses (the capital *D* indicates words and practices of a particular community, which are learned as a consequence of being a member of that community. Learning the Discourse is intentional and requires "taking on" a new or different identity). Thus, for youth to comprehend, interpret, or challenge the texts of classroom content area Discourse communities, they need to become aware of how the Discourse operates and how knowledge is produced in that content area (Moje et al., 2004). This understanding involves much more than simply doing strategies; it means students take on whole new identities as people who belongs to a particular Discourse community. Anyone who understands the complexities of adolescents recognizes the challenge this poses. Kids don't easily buy into communities or cultures that are foreign to them; that doesn't mean they won't or can't, it just means that we teachers need to strategically plan how to get kids to join.

Ellen Spitler, the teacher referred to in previous chapters, is a model teacher who persuades kids to join the club. She makes it interesting, fun, and challenging. She tells the students that others perceive as "losers" that they can do this and that she will help them. She tells them they are smart. Responsible adults must recognize that inviting a young person into new Discourse communities affects the student's identity (Gee, 2001). This is unchartered territory. Elizabeth Moje and her colleagues (Moje et al., 2004) explain some of the complexities involved and ask all of us to engage in inquiry to help better understand the issues of identity development—which they call The Third Space—in content area learning.

Your colleagues and administrators are likely neither to be familiar with these concepts nor to understand your emphasis on language development. This is not problematic; it is an opportunity for you to initiate discussions about teaching and learning that can improve the learning culture of your school.

Lortie's research (1975) and our experiences (Anders & Richardson, 1992; Guzzetti, 1989) suggest that many teachers feel isolated in their schools, particularly when they are implementing innovative practices like these. This climate of isolation contributes to a feeling that taking instructional risks is not worth the effort, and it also contributes to a sense of teacher burnout. The circumstances many teachers find themselves in often contribute to this sense of loneliness. Teachers in one middle school with whom Patty is familiar agreed to teach without a preparation period so that they could have smaller class sizes. Smaller class sizes are very important to these teachers; however, without any planning time there is little opportunity to confer with colleagues, to team plan or teach, or to share resources. With limited available resources, most teachers need to help each other.

We encourage you to find time and opportunities to work with like-minded colleagues. If you find yourself working in a climate of isolation, take steps to change the norms of that culture. Perhaps you could start a study group, meeting with colleagues during off-school hours to discuss professional literature or to address common professional concerns. If finding like-minded colleagues in your school is a problem, local professional organizations such as the local council of the International Reading Association or your content professional group are a few possibilities.

If collaborating with others is not possible, rely on your personal reading and writing to help advance your understandings. Subscribe to professional journals that provide fresh ideas and the experiences of others. Write about the issues you are dealing with, integrating your experiences and concerns to better understand them and yourself. Conduct action research in your classroom, and casually share what you learn in the teacher's lounge. Your efforts will pay off; you will find that, as you better understand yourself as an educator, others will want to be associated with you because chances are very good that they are experiencing the same concerns.

It is common for teachers to shut their doors and teach the way they want to. We blame the information-transfer model of teaching (often promulgated in teacher education programs) for this unfortunate norm. Staff development programs sometimes consist of an "expert" brought in to deliver information and practices to teachers, and the teachers, in turn, are supposed to implement those "good ideas." Teachers may resent these sorts of presentations and expectations for good reasons. Outside experts are likely to be unaware of the issues and realities the regular classroom teacher faces; hence, the expert's advice does not ring true. Although a teacher might be polite and nod in agreement, once the expert leaves and the classroom door is closed, the teacher resumes instruction as before.

We suggest that you influence your colleagues and administrators by insisting on staff development that is responsive to the realities of your school. This happens most often when the consultant has an opportunity to meet with teachers to learn what their concerns and needs are. It also happens when the consultant is attuned to the ideas of connections between teachers' beliefs and practices. In other words, you and your colleagues need not be victims of norms that limit your professional development and instructional effectiveness. We look forward to a generation of teachers who take instructional and curricular matters into their own hands.

We may be overly sensitive, but it seems that teachers and schools are the scapegoat for many of society's supposed ills. We will not list all those problems here, but they appear regularly in the press. Rather, we challenge you to think about your response.

When thinking about those criticisms, consider that, as a profession, we may be particularly vulnerable for having adopted a theory of learning and teaching (information transfer) that corresponds to a trend among educational publishers and policymakers. Within the information-transfer model, the teacher is less important than the instructional materials. Hence, publishers believe themselves justified in creating materials described as "teacher proof." Likewise, policy-makers tend to focus on changes in material and program changes as if teachers play no role in instruction.

This is a dangerous trend for those of us who believe that the teacher is the heart of the school and that the curriculum is constructed and created through the interaction between and among teachers and students! A constructivist theoretical framework puts responsibility for teaching students where it belongs—with teachers and students. As teachers recognize their power and begin to talk among themselves and to the public about teaching and learning, education will change.

The pictures we paint of ourselves as teachers interacting with students, working in a classroom, and living in a school and society are important for the kinds of teachers we become. This section has discussed some of the more formidable potential blotches on our pictures—our own conception of teaching and learning, our view of students, and our view of society's expectations. Thinking about these considerations and reflecting on them relative to your own position will make a difference in the quality of your professional life.

SUMMARY AND REFLECTION

This chapter has broadened the case for content area literacy instruction in two ways: First, we have argued that literacy instructional strategies are not in and of themselves sufficient for developing mature literacy learners. Rather, it is necessary that teacher's beliefs and practices acknowledge that literacy development changes students' identities and that engaging in literacy to learn is a life-changing event. We also acknowledge that this sort of teaching and the concomitant expectations for young people are not the norm. We considered three potential obstacles to embracing these notions: the culture of assessment and accountability, teacher's beliefs, and the culture of the school and society. We included suggestions for individual teachers, which may help to ameliorate these barriers and improve the climate for teachers and students.

The next chapter is written for literacy leaders in schools and districts. There is a movement toward a position called a *literacy coach* in secondary schools, and we hope to join the conversation of what a literacy coach does.

APPLICATION ACTIVITIES

1. Return to the literacy autobiography or memoir you wrote earlier. Use it as a starting point for developing an action plan to incorporate your beliefs and knowledge about content area literacy in your classroom.

2. Choose a community that is different from the one you grew up in or the one in which you presently live. Visit stores, churches, and other community buildings in that neighborhood. Observe and talk to people to learn about their goals for their children and youth, their opinions about their local school, and their history in that community.

3. Read books that describes the culture of communities different from those with which you are familiar. These are usually found in the categories of anthropology and sociology in the library or in bookstores.

4. Read novels that portray the lives of those who are unfamiliar to you. Some current suggestions are listed in the subsequent From Our Professional Library section.

5. Imagine yourself at a social gathering where the topic is bashing education, bashing teachers, or bemoaning the state of youth. Write or act out the issues that would likely be raised, and describe your informed response.

FROM OUR PROFESSIONAL LIBRARY

Ayers, W. (2004). *Teaching the personal and the political*. New York: Teachers College Press.

Clandinin, D. J., & Connelly, M. F. (1995). *Teachers' professional knowledge landscapes*. New York: Teachers College Press.

Cochran-Smith, M. (2004). *Walking the road: Race, diversity and social justice in teacher education*. New York: Teachers College Press.

Emery, K., & Ohanian, S. (2004). *Why is corporate America bashing our public schools?* Portsmouth, NH: Heinemann.

Hargreaves, A. (2003). *Teaching in the knowledge society*. New York: Teachers College Press.

Moje, E. B., Ciechanowski, K. M., Kramer, K., Ellis, L., Carrillo, R., & Tehani, C. (2004). Working toward third space in content area literacy: An examination of everyday funds of knowledge and discourse. *Reading Research Quarterly, 39*, 38-70.

8

Promising Principles and Practices for Adolescent Literacy Programs

This chapter is intended to respond to a growing and exciting trend: the expansion of adolescent literacy programs. As we look out over the landscape of schooling in the United States, we are convinced that secondary schools are likely to be looking for ways to respond to the continuing literacy needs of their adolescent learners. The Alliance for Education, a national policy, advocacy, and research organization, claims that over 6 million secondary students are not being adequately taught in secondary schools and that developing their literacy should be a high priority. In addition, professional organizations such as the National Council of Teachers of English (www.ncte.org), the International Reading Association (www.reading.org), and the National Middle School Association (www.nmsa.org), publish position statements justifying and calling for attention to adolescent literacy. It is quite likely, then, that funds will be available and priorities will shift toward supporting adolescent literacy programs.

During the sixties and seventies, adolescent literacy programs were common across the United States, but with increased attention to early reading by the federal government and declining resources allocated to the upper grades, adolescent literacy programs suffered a decline from their heyday (Anders, 2002). Given the strong possibility of new programs, our purpose is to provide principles, practices, and related policies for establishing a secondary literacy program. Examples of published programs and commercial packages are included.

PRINCIPLES AND PRACTICES

Barbara and Patty were secondary reading specialists and found the position to be professionally exciting and fulfilling. We worked with teachers, administrators, and students in ways that were not possible as classroom teachers. We had opportunities to creatively provide for teachers' and students' success in literacy and for the development of community through literacy. We look forward to the reestablishment of secondary literacy programs and hope to make a small contribution to the shape of programs created in the next few years.

Universities and colleges typically provide graduate-level course work toward the endorsement or certification of reading specialists. We strongly maintain that anyone providing literacy leadership be endorsed and that the literacy principles and understandings learned in graduate school be held as sacrosanct in practice. The International Reading Association publishes standards describing the knowledge and performance base required for these endorsements or certifications.

Recently, a new term has been introduced, the *literacy coach*, which in some quarters is replacing the term *reading specialist*. A literacy coach possesses deep knowledge of the reading process (Sturtevant, 2004):

> [Literacy coaches know about] literacy theories and appropriate teaching strategies in order to serve as models and curriculum leaders. They must understand the adolescent learner, as well as the middle or high school context of teaching. Skills in program leadership and in working with other professionals are critical to the coach's effectiveness. Without all three qualities, literacy coaches are unlikely to be successful in helping to reform middle and high school education. They will not only lack the knowledge base to provide appropriate guidance and advice, but they will be unable to gain the respect of the teachers and administrators with whom they work. (p. 17)

This description of literacy coaches is very similar to that recommended by the professional organizations and is borne out by our experiences as high school reading specialists. This chapter identifies those who carry out the functions of either a literacy coach or a reading specialist as a *literacy leader*.

Principles and Goals

A good place to begin is with the principles and goals of an adolescent literacy program. What is it that has to be accomplished? Why are these objectives the chosen goals?

There are four key goals of any adolescent literacy program: to create and maintain *a literate environment* in the school; to create an environment where the *tools* of reading and writing are used to engage *meaningful ideas*; to energize colleagues to solve problems through *reflection and inquiry*; and to create and maintain an environment for the development of *literacy for all*.

What do we mean by a *literate environment*? We mean that literacy is an integral part of the school, and that everyone is engaged in literate activity. For example, the principal may regularly share the personal or professional reading he or she is doing at faculty meetings; each department head may regularly distribute meaningful professional articles to the faculty; and the president of the student body might edit a series in the school newspaper that includes book or Web cite reviews (see Box 8.1 for further ideas). The idea is that the literacy leader seizes every opportunity to make literacy activity visible so that it is honored and perceived as valuable and precious.

The ideas in Box 8.1 are just a few examples of ways that a literate environment can be established in a secondary school. Every school is likely to provide other opportunities not described here. The point is that, with this, goal as a priority, literacy and literacy activity permeates the school and affects the environment, providing space for members of the community to participate in literacy activity. Recall that literacy is social: Making literacy socially visible in the school will enhance the literacy development of the community.

The second goal, to create an environment where the tools of literacy are used to engage ideas, is a natural extension of the first goal. Unfortunately, a myth persists that one must know the intricacies of successful literacy skills *before* one is able to engage ideas. This is nonsense. Consider the apprentice working with a carpenter to build a house. The carpenter demonstrates to the apprentice how to do a task when that task is required for the job at hand. Imagine trying to teach each detail of holding a nail and hammer and then pounding the nail into a beam out of context, with no purpose or tool at hand. That's exactly what we do when we teach literacy skills isolated from the authentic material to be read, the context for the reading, and the purpose for doing so. The bottom line is that a high priority of any adolescent literacy program is that *all* members of the school community engage in literacy to better understand themselves and their world by using literacy tools.

A school environment that uses literacy to engage ideas includes the professional staff as well. It means that the processes and activities associated with reflection and inquiry are tools used to address a topic or question that a

BOX 8.1. Ways to Promote a Literate Environment

- Involve athletic coaches by asking them to write or present "book talks," reviews of magazine articles and Web sites related to athleticism or a sport for the school newspaper or posters in the hallway.
- Establish a "take and share" book exchange in the teacher's lounge or in the faculty cafeteria.
- Invite local authors to present at assemblies or in classes.
- Choose a student as "poet laureate" and celebrate his or her work through programs and rewards.
- Use student clubs to promote literacy: ideas include poetry clubs, author circles, and book clubs.
- Encourage all members of the staff, both professional and support staff, to join school-sponsored book clubs.
- Hold regular book and magazine sales.
- Have the librarian maintain a list of "best sellers" in the library, which are the top 10 titles checked out during a month. Publish this by posters on the walls, the school Web site, and announcements over the intercom.
- Institute an all-school reading time, often called sustained silent reading (SSR) or drop everything and read (DEAR), a time period when everyone in the school is reading something of their choice (Allington, 2002).
- Institute a similar program for writing (sustained silent writing, or SSW)—a few minutes every day—dedicated to giving each person in the school a time to do personal writing.

teacher or faculty group perceives as a barrier or issue related to curriculum, instruction, or programs. Terese Dennison (2004), a teacher and graduate student, wondered about her students' reading habits both in school and out of school. Recognizing that she and many of her teacher colleagues believed that adolescents' literacy experiences were few, she conducted a survey and interviewed her students to learn first hand about their literacy experiences. She found that her students' out-of-school reading far surpassed her expectations. Students read and wrote broadly for their social and personal interests, but they had difficulty finding connections between out-of-school and in-school literacy activities. Students claimed that teachers seemed unaware of the out-of-school literacy practices and were not very helpful in making connections between the two. In addition, the students she surveyed and interviewed exclaimed over opportunities in school to choose reading material related to the topics being taught in their content area classes. They decried lack of choice, feeling that their interests and abilities were squelched when no choice was offered. Students also related that they believed what they read and the literacy-related activities contributed to their developing sense of self—indeed, students commented that their identity was reflected in their perceptions of themselves as literacy users.

This study completely turned the heads of Terese and her colleagues. Imagine—students valued literacy and resented the reductionist and narrow ways that many of their teachers used literacy in the classroom. These young people seemed to be saying to their teachers that they can, could, would, and, in real life, actually do engage in more literacy practices than they have an opportunity to express in school. This is an example of a teacher examining and reflecting on her beliefs and assumptions about her students: She did an inquiry project to test those beliefs and assumptions. A literacy leader with an attitude toward inquiry would support and encourage his or her colleagues to do the same.

The fourth goal a literacy leader works to attain is to create and maintain opportunities for all students to continue to develop their literacy. In some schools, only those students who demonstrate the poorest literacy achievement receive benefits of the program. We are suggesting that all categories of students need opportunities to advance their use of literacy tools. Box 8.2 is a diagram of the components of an all-school literacy program.

There are three aspects to a developmental literacy program, a program dedicated to achieving the goal that all students have opportunity to develop literacy: (a) a targeted program for students who need instruction to meet their particular needs, like ESL students and those whose reading development is very immature; (b) a program to expand literacy capacities; and (c) a developmental program, including content area literacy and the development of reading and writing generally.

The Targeted Program. A word of caution: Classes or programs that set adolescents apart from the mainstream are very difficult for both students and teachers. The special opportunities must be designed in such a way that students sense their value and meaningfulness. Deborah Dillon, and her colleagues (Dillon, O'Brien, Wellinski, Springs, & Smith, 1996) argue persuasively

BOX 8.2. An All-School Literacy Program

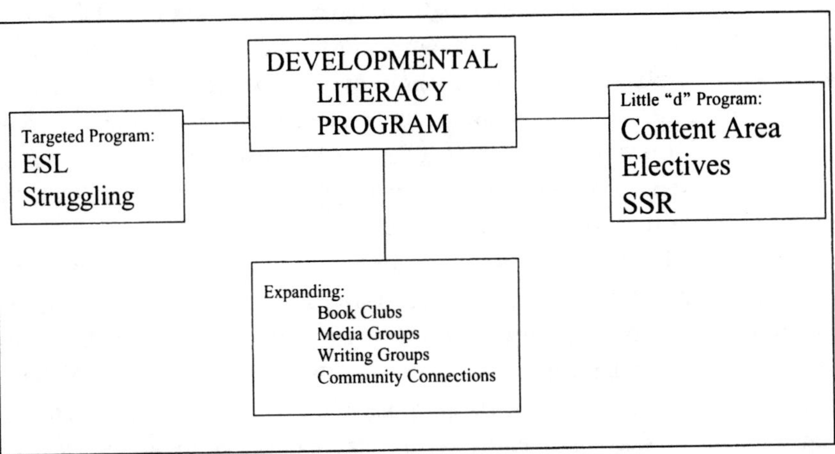

and passionately that "traditional programs that isolate students and label them on the basis of psychometric tests have seriously diminished students' self worth as they face tasks they believe they are incompetent to attain. By high school, the result can be devastating" (p. 243). These researchers find that adolescents "respond to programs and opportunities that maintain students' engagement from day to day by capitalizing on their free choice and balancing their daily hallenges and successes through the use of tasks that are possible by using technology tools typically reserved for high track, more privileged students" (pp. 242–243).

It is not possible to offer a prescription for how to establish positive programs for targeted students; each school varies and the leaders in the school are in the best position to create programs or opportunities. Listed in the following paragraphs, however, are suggestions that may be adaptable to different school contexts and for ESL students or English language learners (ELL students).

First, establish a tutoring program. Solicit volunteers from the community such as teachers in preparation and retired teachers. Train the tutors about literacy processes and practices. Match high school students who want to improve their literacy skills with a tutor. The students might be excused from one of their content area classes two times a week to work with their tutor. Students should choose to participate in this program and should agree to the terms of the tutoring, which might include signing a contract to fully participate and to work toward the fulfillment of the plan for improvement.

To create the plan, the literacy leader interviews each student as to his or her interests and perceived literacy strengths and weaknesses. Through diagnostic tools such as an informal reading inventory or miscue analysis, develop, with the student, a plan for how to best improve that student's literacy. Share the plan with the tutor and monitor each student's progress through regular meetings with the tutor. If the student has been excused from a content area class to pursue improvement in literacy, a system has to be established to report progress to the classroom teacher.

Second, establish language seminars for ESL and ELL students. These seminars should focus on the discourse and literacy of particular content areas, probably the content area of most interest to the ELL student. Teachers in preparation or bilingual subject matter teachers or community members could conduct these seminars. The purpose of the seminar would be to teach cognates, phrases, and conceptual terms related to the content area.

Third, offer language classes for all students that are organized in a manner to let the speakers of one language teach those who speak a second language. We can imagine classes in which half the students are Spanish speakers (or another language) and half are English speakers. Pairing students to practice conversation in both languages or to learn the discourse of a particular content area would be beneficial to all.

Fourth, establish a cross-age tutoring program for high school students to work with elementary students in second language development (O'Byrne, 2003).

Fifth, create a Newcomers Club to help immigrant youth find their way in the school and community. Include activities that the students say they need.

The following additional suggestions are adapted from those by Eliane Rubinstein-Avila (2003–2004, pp. 299–300):

- Place ELL students in small content area classes, so they receive more one-on-one attention from the teacher;
- Encourage discussions and collaboration among students to stimulate oral language use and development;
- Support collaborative planning by subject area teachers and ESL or bilingual teachers; and
- Build into the all-school professional development program sound, research-based strategies for curriculum adaptation, as well as modifications of participation structures that encourage the participation of ELL students.

Ovando, Collier, and Combs (2003) offer outstanding strategy and resource suggestions, which emphasize language across the curriculum by utilizing many of the same ideas suggested in this volume (also see Ernst-Slavit, Moore, & Maloney, 2002, for an excellent overview of programs and resources.)

Students who are targeted as needing special attention are sometimes thought to need "basic" or watered-down curriculum and activities. This is a serious error. A recent summary of conventional approaches to teaching academic skills to at-risk students, offered by a group of national experts in reading, writing, and mathematics education, concluded that such approaches tend to (a) underestimate what students are capable of doing; (b) postpone more challenging and interesting work for too long—in many cases, forever; and (c) deprive students of a meaningful or motivating context for learning or for employing the skills that are taught (Means & Knapp, 1991, pp. 283–284).

Larry Johannessen (2004, p. 638) summarizes eight principles of literacy instruction recommended for struggling secondary students. These principles are similar to those we recommend for all students, but it is well worth stating them here as we consider the literacy needs of those students who need special attention.

1. Focus on complex, meaningful questions and problems so that students' reading and writing can be in service of genuine inquiry (Hillocks, 2002). Keep the level of tasks high enough that the purpose is apparent and makes sense to students.
2. Embed basic skills instruction in the context of more global tasks, such as including reading comprehension and composing skills in introductory reading and writing activities or instruction (Johannessen, Kahn, & Walter, 1984; McCann, 1996).
3. Make connections with students' out-of-school experiences and cultures.
4. Model powerful thinking strategies for students; for example, lead the class through a discussion aimed at figuring out a difficult text passage before you ask them to try it on their own (Langer 2001a, 2001b).
5. Encourage students to use multiple approaches to academic tasks and have students describe their answers aloud to the class so that all students hear different ways to solve the same problem.
6. Provide scaffolding to enable students to accomplish complex tasks; for example, provide prewriting activities designed to help students learn

to use specific sensory details before you ask them to write a personal narrative (Hillocks, 1975).

7. Make dialogue with students the central medium for teaching and learning (Hillocks, 2002; Langer, 2001a, 2001b). One example of this is reciprocal questioning in which groups of two or three students ask and answer one another's questions after a lesson or presentation (King, 1990, 1994).
8. Use teaching strategies that will help students internalize the questions that good readers ask when they read (interpret) literature and good writers ask when they tackle complex writing tasks.

These guidelines and suggestions are fundamental to the "target component" of the all-school literacy program.

The Little "d" Component. The second component is the little "d" program, which is the instruction that all students receive in their content area classes, electives from which all students may choose, and the SSR and SSW programs. In some schools, there are flexible class periods dedicated to exploring special topics. In one school in which Patty worked, the second period of the day was dedicated to short courses in special topics. Students could choose two such electives, each lasting half the semester, each semester. The reading specialist in that school offered short courses such as "test taking skills," "speed reading," "children's literature," "study skills," and so forth. The children's literature short course was particularly interesting: The course introduced terrific books that could be read to young children, and it was of great instructional value to those students who were already parents or who cared for younger siblings. We can also imagine similar electives, perhaps focusing on multicultural children's literature.

The literacy leader provides support and guidance for teachers as they integrate literacy and content area instruction. The literacy instruction in the content areas offered in this book is a good starting point. It is, however, only a beginning point; once teachers try to implement these ideas, lots of questions arise. The literacy leader collaborates with content teachers to resolve issues and to think of solutions. The literacy leader also demonstrates lessons that incorporate literacy instructional strategies for content area teachers.

The literacy leader organizes and helps to sustain the SSW and SSR programs. Two current concerns among educators is that students do not dedicate enough time to reading and writing and that students lack models of readers and writers. For that reason, several schools are implementing the SSW and SSR programs. For these programs to be successful, the entire school community must be committed to spending a specific few minutes each day reading and writing. Everyone in the school—secretaries, janitors, principals, counselors, teachers, staff, and students—all read or write for the designated 15 or 20 minutes a day. The reading and writing done during that time period is not graded, but students may receive points for participating.

The Expanding Component. The expanding program is the third component. In this part, opportunities are offered to all students to expand their literacy capacities through social networks in clubs and with the community. Most likely, clubs would meet outside the regular school day or during lunch period. Clubs or interest groups could also be formed with community members. A member of the local community with a special hobby or interest area could be invited to spend time with a small group of adolescents interested in the same topic. At one of the high schools in Tucson, the Poetry Club is very popular. The teacher who takes responsibility for that club meets with the students one night a week at a local coffee shop and students share the poetry they are writing. At another school, a community member advises the Spelunking Club and regularly asks students to write about their experiences, observations, and feelings when crawling about local caves. These writings—poems, essays, and stories—are published on the club's Web site. Book clubs could focus on contemporary adolescent literature or on reading materials related to a particular theme. The idea is that students choose to participate in literacy activities related to topics and activities of their choice and related to their interests.

There are five guiding principles that are helpful for achieving these goals:

- Literacy is a developmental process enacted in a social context;
- Everyone reads and writes to better understand themselves and the world, to experience the world vicariously and aesthetically, to gain information to improve the quality of their life, and to fulfill societal obligations;
- Secondary students need to learn the discourses of the content area courses they take; and
- Adolescent literacy learners deserve respect.

These underlying principles provide guidelines or standards for a literacy leader to develop and select activities for the literacy program. By holding any activity or aspect of the program to these standards of principles, the literacy leader can be assured that progress is being made toward a good adolescent literacy program.

LITERACY LEADER'S QUALIFICATIONS

The literacy leader is a particularly well-prepared professional. Successful literacy leaders are prepared as reading specialists, but they have other attributes like creativity, confidence, and humor. In other words, the literacy leader is a "people person" who is respected by his or her peers. Additional attributes of the literacy leader include a personal love of reading, writing, and learning and an approach to life that models inquiry and problem solving. In many ways, a literacy leader possesses characteristics similar to good constructivist teachers. The literacy leader does not need to know the answer to every question, or even most questions; rather, he or she has to be willing to ponder, saying "hmmm, what an interesting question, I wonder how we could find out?" Or, "I know how we can find that out! Let's do a study."

This is especially important in the content area part of the program. The literacy leader is working with others, content area teachers, who are experts in their own right. Content area teachers have instructional priorities, well-developed content and pedagogical knowledge, and established routines. If a literacy leader is not careful, he or she can make the content area teacher feel that this teacher's expertise is diminished, and the result will be a bruised relationship. That's the last thing a literacy leader wants to do! Literacy leaders can nurture relationships with content area teachers by remembering that the content area literacy program is built on a foundation of mutual respect and that the goals of the program can be reached through a partnership between the literacy leader and each teacher.

We know this sounds idealistic, so here is a reality test: School reform happens very slowly. Common wisdom suggests that it takes 5 years to establish an all-school secondary literacy program. Good things can be happening along the way, but do not expect that everyone will be on board right away. A good rule of thumb is that your expectations will be met by *about half* of the teachers at any given time. For example, say that you speak at a mandatory meeting of 100 teachers and you invite them to a follow-up nonrequired discussion; you can expect that about 50 teachers will show. Then, if at that meeting of 50, you ask them to *do* something, about 25 will agree and 12 or 13 will actually do the task. This may seem discouraging at first, but it all works out. What happens is that those few who *do* become involved influence others who thought they were not interested; so, within a couple years, most everyone is involved at least to some extent in the program.

The literacy leader is a patient and flexible professional. This leader knows where she or he is going and has a plan for getting there but realizes that her or his key resource is the people with whom this leader works. Communicating well, keeping colleagues involved, and continual distribution of shared responsibility are all key. Oh yes, one other point. Every literacy leader we know is well equipped with a coffee pot and can be counted on to provide snacks and other foods. This is just a small example of the spirit and attitude of literacy leaders—committed, well-prepared professionals who care for their colleagues and do their best to support them.

LITERACY PROGRAM PREPARATIONS

A literacy leader with the responsibility for establishing and maintaining a secondary literacy program has a daunting task. A beginning place is to collect data so that the first steps taken are justified on the basis of hard information. We like to think of this as conducting an audit. In effect, you are asking yourself this question: Okay, what exists here, and what do I have to work with?

The Audit

Collecting data is analogous to taking stock of the resources available for the literacy program. There are three sources for the audit. The first is the available testing data, the second is the capital resources, and the third is the available human capital. Each of these is discussed in the paragraphs that follow.

Testing Data. Look at the norm-referenced test performance of students in the school and find answers to the following questions: What is the range of scores? How many students are in each stanine? Is there a normal distribution of scores in your school? How different is the school's distribution from the national norm? Now look at the numbers of students who score in the first and second stanines and the students who score in the eighth and ninth stanines. On one hand, if the scores are significantly lower than the national norm, radical changes in the school may be warranted; on the other hand, if they are similar to the national norm or higher than the national norm, the existing program may need a little refinement or sprucing up, but the work of the literacy leader will be less challenging. If the number of students at the high end of the distribution and at the low end of the distribution are roughly the same, the literacy leader can assume that the program is stable; although a literacy program is likely needed, equal numbers of students at the top and the bottom suggest a "normal" program. At this point, you might want to pull the names of students at each end of the distribution. These are students that need to receive special attention in the school program, and so it is well worth your time to get their names in a file folder to look at later.

Look more closely at the norm-referenced test the students take. What does it measure? What is the standard error of measurement? We have two stories that demonstrate the importance of these questions. In the first story, Patty was asked to analyze the scores of ninth-grade students on a norm-referenced test. Scores in vocabulary were particularly low, and the principal wanted to know why. When she examined the test, Patty found that the vocabulary score was determined by the students' ability to select the correct antonym for the vocabulary word. The directions, of course, were read silently by each student; in this particular school, where most students are ESL student or bilingual students, it is unclear as to whether or not they even knew what an antonym is. The point is that this supposed vocabulary test was really a test of whether or not students read the directions and knew what an antonym was.

The second story took place in an urban high school where students were tracked into their ninth-grade English classes based on their eighth-grade standardized test scores; those students who scored 2 or more years below the mean were placed in "low classes," students who scored 2 or more years above the mean were placed in "high classes," and students who scored near the mean were placed in "average" classes. Walking down the hall, an observer could find it clear which level each class was: The low track was predominately made up of students of color, the average track was a heterogeneous group, and the advanced track was mostly upper-middle-class white students. To an observer, it looked like a clear example of institutional racism—students were segregated by skin color and social class. The standard error of measurement for the particular standardized test the students took was 23 months: That meant that the test publisher recognized that the grade-equivalent scores on the standardized test were a ballpark figure that could fluctuate plus or minus 23 months!—2 school years and 5 months! The school was tracking students within the standard error of measurement. This plan was separating kids, but not on the basis of their reading abilities. One of the reading specialist's objectives for that school was to find a way to detrack the students. For several reasons, students should *not* be placed in particular classes or programs on the basis of norm-referenced tests; this type of test can, however, be used as an initial screening tool, and so do make lists of student names whose scores are significantly different from the mean and follow up on the adequacy of the services they receive.

If your school gives a criterion-referenced test, analyze that test and the items that were missed by your students. The quality of criterion-referenced tests is highly variable, and so taking the time to analyze the quality of items missed by more than 50% of your students is well worth the time. It could be that several items are invalid or unreliable rather than a problem with your students. Consider the curriculum in your school and the criterion-referenced test and ask yourself if there is congruence. Unbelievable as it may seem, we have both worked in schools where students are tested on content they have not been taught.

Capital Resources. Your analysis of the available testing data is only a beginning point in the audit. The second source of data is in terms of capital resources. What equipment and space is available for the administration and activities of the literacy program? Is there storage space for the literacy program? What is the library like? Are there enough books? Are there books in the holdings that are representative of the student population? Are there content area instructional resource centers? What is the status of those collections? Are there learning laboratories? Are the technological tools up to date and available to students? Does the school have a Web site? Can you contribute to it? What other means does the school have to communicate both in the school and to the school community? As you conduct this audit, your plans will begin to take shape. You will think of how you can use existing capital resources and what you will need to negotiate to purchase or to get donated.

As the first questions suggested, space is needed. The literacy leader is not likely to be teaching very many classes of students, but meeting space is needed, like a conference room or at least a round table, a desk, bookshelves, filing cabinets, and storage. The office and meeting space should be in a central location, where teachers and students alike are likely to congregate; space off the library is good, but an office with the administration is not good.

The quality and quantity of reading material in the school is critical. The library and other repositories of resource materials should be well kept, current, and accessible to the school community. One particular issue to be checked out is the diversity of the collection. Are there materials in the library to which all students in the school can relate? In one school we know, over 20% of the student body was African American, but there were no current titles that reflected that heritage and only a couple that were very old. In this case, the literacy leader devoted part of his budget to purchase diverse adolescent literature.

Human Capital. The last stage of the audit is to take an accounting of the human capital in your building and in the community. What is the literacy background of the professionals in the building? It is always surprising for us to work in a building and learn that several teachers, counselors, or principals have had substantial graduate work in literacy. Sometimes these people don't come forward and volunteer their expertise because it isn't their job or because they don't want to tread on the literacy leader's territory, but our point is that we need as many people as possible to contribute to the all-school literacy program and so any expertise is delightfully accepted.

What is the librarian's background? Theoretically, the librarian should be the literacy leader's best partner. More often than not, we find the librarian is waiting to be asked to participate. If the librarian has graduated from an accredited college, she or he is most likely prepared to be a teaching librarian. This professional is prepared to provide a variety of resources to classroom teachers in all the content areas and often has terrific ideas to share.

Is there a college or university in your community? Are there teacher educators who are knowledgeable about adolescent literacy? The school literacy leader often needs someone else to deliver the message, and a professor can be a guest speaker. You might also team with a professor to offer a course for college credit on a topic related to adolescent literacy—"adolescent literature," "content area literacy," or "reading for alienated readers" are likely to be topics of interest to the teachers. The university professor can also help to design teacher–action research projects. Often independent studies can be negotiated so that teachers are rewarded for participating in the literacy program by receiving university credit.

The local college might also be a good source of volunteers. College preservice teachers in preparation are often looking for places to observe, work with youth, or do field research. If you are willing to provide a site for this work, you can probably work out an exchange so that the students also contribute to the literacy program. Service clubs and businesses might also be a source of volunteers.

Conducting the audit, establishing goals, and reflecting on the principles you want to enact provide the information needed to begin to plan possibilities for the ideas for each aspect of the program you will work toward establishing. Looking over the audit, you will quickly find it apparent that making a literacy program a reality is not a one-person job. Fortunately, you do not have to do it by yourself. The next step is to establish a *Literacy Council* (Anders, 1998), sometimes also called a *Literacy Team* or a *Literacy Committee*. The Literacy Council is made up of teachers and others in the building or community who are committed to developing an all-school literacy program. The council advises the literacy leader and helps to carry out activities to develop the program.

The Literacy Council

The Literacy Council has several advantages: It is a means for distributing responsibility across various members and programs in the school community; it can help to increase the faculty and staff buy-in to the literacy program; and the program can be adapted and grow according to input and suggestions made by the council members. Members of the council are extensions of the literacy leader's influence and serve as the literacy leader's ears, eyes, and helping hands.

Your school administrative structure will suggest how best to recruit members of the Literacy Council. In one school, volunteers from the professional staff were called for and the principal wrote a letter of invitation to one teacher from each content area who volunteered. In another school, each department decided who would be best to serve. The member needs to be well respected by his or her peers, be interested in contributing to the all-school literacy program, and be willing to learn and pass that learning on to others. Some schools also involve student representatives from each class, counselors and other nonteaching staff, and the community, including business leaders.

The Literacy Council receives intensive in-service from the literacy leader. The in-service program consists of information to respond to the most pressing questions of the faculty. The council members are expected to take this information back to their departments to help "spread the word." Along the way, the literacy leader also provides the results of the audit and the council members respond with suggestions and additional data. In some cases, through these discussions, other ideas for collecting data are generated. Once the members of the Literacy Council have some common experiences and knowledge, the literacy leader and council members can develop specific objectives to be achieved in the short term (1-year objectives) and in the long term (a strategic plan with goals and objectives for the next 5 years). These plans are shared with the departments and other constituents in the community, and a response is requested. The objective here is to get as many members of the community as possible to buy into the program. Their personal investment will pay off as the program gets underway.

One other responsibility of the council is to help develop an evaluation plan for the literacy program. What sorts of data will show the progress that is being made? The plan will include testing data, which are most likely being collected anyway, but it might also include data on student interests and attitudes toward literacy, teacher participation in the program, the number of books checked out of the library, and the individual progress of students who need the program the most.

THE LITERACY LEADER'S WORK

Thus far, we have suggested a few aspects of the literacy leaders work; this section expands on those ideas. The literacy leader's work varies by school and by the priorities set by the Literacy Council. Most likely, however, there are several tasks that most every literacy leader will do. For example, the literacy leader must pay attention to the needs of students. He or she must make it a high priority to know the struggling literacy users very well and ensure that the best services possible are being provided. These students deserve individual assessments and instruction designed for their needs.

Another task falls under the broad category of public relations. The literacy leader should meet with community groups; regularly publish press releases about the wonderful literacy-related events in the school; and sponsor activities and events to promote literacy, with highly visible advertising. One reading specialist we know publishes a newsletter called "From the Reading Lady" that is distributed throughout the community to people, agencies, organizations, and institutions that are interested in literacy. This publication not only informs the public about what is going on at the high school, but also gives some very hard-working teachers well-deserved credit. She describes teachers' lessons and activities that incorporate and promote literacy development.

The literacy leader works closely with the librarian to ensure that materials in the school are numerous and accessible. Some types of literature, especially appealing to adolescents like young adult popular literature or ethnic literature, may be sparse in the collection. As a literacy leader, you might want to use some of your materials budget to purchase materials that the librarian is unable to justify.

Typically, it is worthwhile for the literacy leader to spend time with counselors and principals. It is likely that these members of the school community have very little knowledge about literacy processes and practices. Helping those who advise students to better understand literacy will provide suggestions for them to use when counseling students and will help to make the program more coherent.

The literacy leader is a key resource person for the school community. In this role, he or she should be an active member of the International Reading Association, which has publications and provides other resources for the secondary school literacy leader. This organization has special memberships for schools that want to receive publications and send teachers to the annual conference. We cannot emphasize enough the importance of professional organizations for the continued education of the literacy leader and the faculty. For example, Arlene Barry (2002) reports on a study of the reading strategies teachers say they use. This article is of tremendous help to the literacy leader who is trying to promote discussions about literacy strategies, and it would be useful to share and discuss with teachers. Other organizations, like the National Council of Teachers of English, are also committed to providing materials and other resources to secondary teachers and literacy leaders. Most literacy leaders also belong to the National Council of Teachers of English. Literacy leaders simply cannot afford to be without these resources.

The most important people in the building with whom the literacy leader works are the content area teachers (Vogt & Shearer, 2003). Here are some suggestions:

- Model instruction in teacher's classrooms that incorporates literacy and content;
- Make digital or videotapes of your instruction to use in professional development;
- Do concept unit planning with teachers;
- Help to find materials and other resources that vary by difficulty and relate to students' varying background knowledge, and make these resources available to content area teachers;

- Develop activities that make resource material more accessible and friendly to the students;
- Use the instructional strategies described in this book for modeling and coplanning with teachers.

This close, one-on-one type of collaboration is one form of professional development. It is important to offer teachers choices among an array of professional development opportunities. Think of the professional development program as including three strands: (a) the one-on-one encounters; (b) opportunities according to themes, which include anyone who is interested in the topic; and (c) systematic presentations and opportunities within the organizational structure of the school.

Professional development organized by theme is interesting and often attracts colleagues who want to study that theme for a short time. For example, a professional development program based on motivating students might be one theme. Another idea is to borrow from the critical friends professional development model and organize participants around a topic or question that has to be dealt with in your school (*Horace*, 1996). An alternative model, which has enjoyed great success, is the "study group" (Klaussen & Short, 1992). Again, a particular topic is focused on and the literacy leader provides participants with professional and scholarly resources so that, through reading, writing, and discussing, the topic is studied. These theme-related programs are voluntary and provided as conveniently as possible for the teachers.

The third strand is planned around the organizational structure of the school. The literacy leader, with the help of the Literacy Council, should decide which units in the school should receive which sort of professional development. We can imagine that individuals in a particular content area department might allocate time at their department meetings to a series of topics related to literacy. Or, perhaps, the ninth-grade teachers want to plan a strategic intervention with all of their students to provide a curriculum of metacognitive practices.

There may be several teachers or other professionals in your building who are quite sophisticated in terms of literacy processes and development. You might want to form a special cadre of these colleagues with whom to discuss new and emerging literature. For example, William Kist (2002) describes an action research study to investigate the "broadening of our definition of literacy in this technological age" (p. 368). An article such as this would be a good source for helping teachers to think about an "updated" definition of literacy.

Conceptualizing and planning professional development with these three strands in mind helps you to provide a coherent program with something available to most everyone most of the time. Like all aspects of the literacy leader's work, each of the three strands should be evaluated with both formative and summative methods. Literacy leaders collect data at every opportunity: ask for and record feedback on the one-on-one meetings with teachers; use Likert scales to collect attitude and interest data from teachers after group meetings; and record your observations of teachers' implementing practices. Keep track of students' progress, both informally and formally, on standardized and criterion-referenced tests as the program grows.

The literacy leader should *not* be involved in evaluating the teachers. Most principals will ask for the literacy leader's input regarding how well a particular teacher is cooperating with the literacy program or how well she or he teaches. Avoid this role if at all possible. Remember, a literacy leader is supportive of all teachers, and credibility will be lost if the literacy leader is also reporting to the principal as an evaluator of teachers.

Finally, no literacy program survives or thrives without the support of the principal and other school and district leaders. Administrators need to be aware of the extensive demands the literacy program places on teachers, and they should be prepared to offer a system of support and reward for teachers' efforts (Gove, 1981; Little, 1982). In a study of secondary reading programs in the seventies, Patty (Anders, 2002) found that a consistent feature of successful programs was that administrators collaborated with the reading specialist and provided consistent support. Time has to be spent helping the principal to see your vision of literacy in the school. Those who know little about the possibilities of an all-school literacy program are likely to envision a reading teacher working with a small number of students to help students attain skills. This conception is diametrically different from what we are suggesting. Most principals will welcome your vision; many reform efforts are based on establishing just these sorts of learning communities (Miller, 2000).

Commercial materials are available for the secondary school. We are of the mind that a secondary literacy program is far more than the particular purchased materials—the literacy program we visualize is a program based on people, not materials. Nonetheless, a literacy leader needs to be aware of these commercial materials, be able to offer a critique of them, and perhaps choose one or two as components of the literacy program.

READY-MADE PROGRAMS

We are reluctant to strongly recommend ready-made programs[1] because we are committed to the idea that people make programs, not commercial materials. There is, however, a range of published materials and some of them may be helpful for establishing a secondary literacy program. The range represents a continuum that, at one end, includes commercial programs that come as a package and claim that little or no teacher expertise is needed; rather the students can progress in their literacy by "doing the program." At the other end of the continuum are programs that require adjustments in secondary curriculum and instruction and also involve a teacher's participation.

One ready-made program requiring a teacher to monitor student involvement rather than teach is the Accelerated Reader. This is a program that provides students with a self-assessment of reading comprehension on the computer. After completing the STAR, the self-assessment test, students are given options of thousands of books written at their "grade level" from which they may choose. When they finish reading a self-selected book, they take a test on the computer of literal comprehension questions and they receive points for completing the book and test. The computer also keeps track of students' performance. This program is purported to be the most popular pre-K to Grade 12 reading software in the nation (School Renaissance Institute, 2001), but little independent empirical data demonstrates its efficacy. One claim made by the publisher is that the program is highly motivating, but a recent report (Mallette, Henk, & Melnick, 2004) found that intermediate grade boys with both low performance and low self-perceptions of reading efficacy did not gain much from the program.

Another computerized program is Read 180, which targets students in Grades 4–12 who are reading below expectation. This program is also literature oriented and has built-in videos, activities, audio books, and paperbacks for independent reading. The authors of the program have conducted their own research and found that elementary students made significant progress; research is not yet available on the high school program.

[1]Donna E. Alvermann and Leslie S. Rush graciously shared a chapter they authored that is in press and that provides a summary and critical review of key intervention programs designed for middle and high schools. The basic information about the programs described here are from the Alvermann and Rush chapter.

Reading is FAME, designed by Mary Beth Curtis and Anne Marie Longo (2001), aims to teach adolescents in Grades 7 through 12 reading skills, according to Chall's (1983) stages of reading development. Curtis and Longo created the program for Flanagan's Boys and Girls Town in Nebraska, where adolescents live in a residence program because of "chronic neglect and abuse, illegal and antisocial behaviors, and academic failure" (Curtis & Longo, 2001, p. 1, as cited by Alvermann & Rush, in press) The program consists of four courses, each 16 weeks long. Research on Reading is FAME at its initial site found that "students gained about a year in reading achievement, as measured by the Woodcock-Johnson Psycho-Educational Battery, for every semester's worth of instruction. Similar gains were found in a public high school implementation of the program" (Curtis & Longo, 1999, as cited by Alvermann & Rush, in press).

The Supported Literacy Approach (SLA) and the next two programs require considerable teacher participation. The SLA is designed to support middle-school students identified as learning disabled as they read and discuss adolescent literature. The program is based on the idea that students learn to read by participating in group activities that are mediated by students' and teachers' uses of language in whole class, small group, and peer-led discussions. Catherine Morocco, Alisa Hindin, and their associates developed the program. Their research shows that integrating peer-led discussions with reading and writing about young adult literature enables special education students to perform similarly to peers in regular education (Hindin, Morocco, & Aguilar, 2001; Morocco & Hindin, 2002).

The Strategic Literacy Initiative focuses on improving adolescents' literacy by providing professional development to content area teachers. Ruth Schoenback, Cynthia Greenleaf, and their WestEd colleagues (Schoenbach, Greenleaf, Cziko, & Hurwitz, 1999) use a set of strategies they call a "reading apprenticeship," which includes guided reading, reciprocal teaching, vocabulary, and metacognition as the core strategies. Several studies have been conducted and are ongoing that show substantial growth for students, especially those who are the poorest achieving. The program and various adaptations of it are regularly shared at national conferences, like the International Reading Association, as the presenters demonstrate the strategies and methods they use to teach them.

Project CRISS, Creating Independence through Student-owned Strategies, is another literacy program based on content area that is focused on professional development. Carol Santa and her content area colleagues in Kalispell, Montana met to read research and professional literature about cognitive psychology and how the key principles they learned about could be applied to classroom reading and content instruction. Project CRISS was the outcome. The teachers and Santa also conducted teacher research to investigate the effectiveness of Project CRISS in the classroom.

The U.S. Department of Education designated Project CRISS as an exemplary high school program in 1985. The project was named as part of the National Diffusion Network because it used research-based reading and writing strategies to help students improve their learning in content area classes. Most recently, *Project* CRISS has been expanded to include several additional aspects of professional development, including engagement and school change. There is also a professional development component for parents, including a workbook available in English and Spanish, and soon in Vietnamese.

Research on Project CRISS is quite extensive and has been conducted in several states in various part of the country. Studies indicate that students who participate in CRISS classrooms significantly outperform students in comparison classes. The project participants regularly present their program at national and international conferences, and they share the materials, methods, and strategies they employ.

The last program we summarize is the Talent Development High School Literacy Program (TDHS Literacy Program), which is designed to "accelerate the literacy growth of under-prepared high school students" (Alvermann & Rush, in press). A high school reform team at the Center for Education of Students Placed at Risk (CRESPAR) and the Center for Social Organization of Schools at Johns Hopkins University created the program, which is currently available for ninth-grade students and consists of four components. The program involves block scheduling, teacher professional development, and instruction targeted to overcome students' lack of preparation for high school. The program has been tested in experimental schools and compared with control schools with similar scheduling, but with no specific program. The TDHS students significantly outperformed students in control schools on standardized measures of reading.

As a literacy leader, you might consider any of these programs as additions to one of the components of your developmental literacy program. Before adopting any one of these programs, however, please carefully consider the assumptions given within it. Align the assumptions of the commercial program with the goals and guiding principles discussed in this chapter. The following questions might be helpful:

- Does this program contribute to establishing and maintaining a literate environment in this school?
- Will this program help to create an environment that uses the tools of reading and writing to engage meaningful ideas?
- Will this program help to energize colleagues to solve problems through reflection and inquiry?
- Will this program contribute to a program that provides everyone access to the gifts of literacy?
- Does this program treat literacy as a developmental process enacted in a social context?
- Will this program engage students in reading and writing to better understand themselves and the world? to experience the world vicariously and aesthetically? to gain information that improves the quality of life and to fulfill societal obligations?
- Will this program help students to learn the discourses of the various content areas?
- Is this program respectful of adolescent literacy learners?

SUMMARY

In this chapter we provide a starting point for those who accept the challenge of being a literacy leader. We hope that the information and experiences shared will help the new literacy leader to get started, provide ideas for a practicing literacy leader to expand a program, and provide ways for teachers to contribute to the all-school literacy program.

We began the chapter by relating goals and principles that are fundamental to the work that a literacy leader does. Using a flow chart, we showed the components of the literacy program and suggested ideas for enacting each component. We described the personal and professional characteristics of a good literacy leader, and we explored commercial programs.

Of all the ideas discussed in this chapter, the most important is that a knowledgeable and qualified literacy leader recognizes the value of personal relationships with colleagues, students, and authors. The program is constructed within those relationships; it is not something that is imposed or laid on top of what already exists. It is integrated with the values and practices of the members of the community. Those who are the stakeholders negotiate it. These words are "counter culture" to the status quo of educational policy in the United States. The powerful voices today declare that programs need to be "scaled up"—that if there is a good idea, it should be good for all. Literacy is good for all and all schools have to provide excellent literacy development opportunities, but the generalizations end there: Literacy and learning opportunities happen when committed and knowledgeable professionals create and construct the space and relationships that allow for literacy and learning to thrive.

CONCLUSION

As we bring this volume to a close, we reflect on what we have written and what we have not written. We believe we have promoted and provided evidence for the ideas that follow.

First, teachers of the different content areas have the privilege, challenge, and responsibility to help all their students discover the universe. This discovery is mediated by the use of language. When students talk, listen, read, and write about their world, their understandings are increasingly elaborate and are likely to become part of their long-term memory, or schema.

Second, meanings are constructed in content area classrooms where the social nature of students is honored, celebrated, and used to find and interpret multiple resources, conduct activities, and report on the developed or developing understandings. Hence, meaning is not transmitted from the knower to the naïve; rather, meaning is constructed as the naïve question, challenge, dig, and create understandings.

Third, although reading in the content areas has a legitimate history of scholarship, it has not been widely accepted by the teachers of content areas. We have tried to explain why that might be. We have also suggested means by which those who work in the realms of language might connect with those who work in the realms of content-related ideas.

Fourth, we have provided knowledge and practices that we, and others, have found useful in our experiences working in content area literacy. We have by no means included all that is available. Other textbooks do that, and sources abound in the professional literature for current ideas. Our purpose was to share the information that has stood us in good stead across many circumstances.

Finally, this book has been written from our hearts, as well as our heads. We care deeply about the quality of instruction that students receive. We are concerned that classrooms parallel the ideals we dream of for society. We believe that this will happen when teachers adopt a constructivist perspective of teaching and learning and when a broader definition of literacy is the norm. This perspective enacts democratic ideals by engaging in negotiation; by accepting, honoring, and celebrating differences; and by recognizing that, although knowledge grows and changes on the basis of previous knowledge, all knowledge is open to challenge and question. We also care deeply about the quality of teachers' lives. As these ideals are enacted, we believe both teachers and students will benefit. We wish you well.

APPLICATION ACTIVITIES

1. Visit the Web sites dedicated to adolescent literacy at both the International Reading Association and the National Council of Teachers of English. Analyze the similarities and differences at the Web sites in comparison with this chapter.
2. Interview leaders in local secondary schools and find out what they think about the ideas presented in this chapter.
3. What appears to be the greatest barriers to establishing the type of program described in this chapter?
4. Gather information about the materials and programs summarized in this chapter. Which programs would you be interested in purchasing and why?

FROM OUR PROFESSIONAL LIBRARY

Ovando, C. J., Collier, V. P., & Combs, M. C. (2003). *Bilingual and ESL classrooms: Teaching in multicultural contexts.* New York: McGraw-Hill.

Vogt, M. E., & Shearer, B. (2003). *Reading specialists in the real world: A sociocultural view.* Boston, MA: Allyn & Bacon.

Wepner, S. B., Feeley, J. T., & Strickland, R. (Eds.). (1995). *The administration and supervision of reading programs* (2nd ed.) Newark, DE: International Reading Association.

References

A

Abisdris, G., & Casuga, A. (2001). Using poetry to teach Rutherford's discovery of the nucleus. *The Science Teacher, 68*, 58–62.

Afflerbach, P., & Pressley, M. (1995). *Verbal protocols of reading, the nature of constructively responsive reading.* Hillsdale, NJ: Lawrence Erlbaum Associates.

Ahrends, R. I. (1988). *Learning to teach*. New York: Random House.

Aldrich, C. (2003). *Simulations and the future of learning.* San Francisco: Pheiffer.

Allington, R. L. (2002). What I've learned about effective reading instruction. *Phi Delta Kappan, 85,* 740–474.

Altwerger, B., Resta, V., & Kilarr, G. (1987). The theme cycle: Creating contexts for whole language strategies. Katonah, NY: Richard C. Qwen.

Alvermann, D. E. (1991). The discussion web: A graphic aid for learning across the curriculum. *The Reading Teacher, 45,* 92–95.

Alvermann, D. E. (2004). Multiliteracies and self-questioning in the service of science learning. In W. Saul (Ed.), *Crossing Borders* (pp. x–x). Newark, DE: IRA.

Alvermann, D. E., Dillon, D., & O'Brien, D. (1987). *Using discussion to promote reading comprehension.* Newark, DE: International Reading Association.

Alvermann, D. E., & Heron, A. (2001). Literacy identity work: Playing to learn with popular media. *Journal of Adolescent and Adult Literacy, 45,* 118–122.

Alvermann, D. E., Hinchman, K. A., Moore, D. W., Phelps, S. F., & Waff, D. R. (Eds.). (1998). *Reconceptualizing the literacies in adolescents' lives.* Mahwah, NJ: Lawrence Erlbaum Associates.

Alvermann, D. E., & Hynd, C. R. (1989, December). *The influence of discussion and text on the learning of counterintuitive science concepts.* Paper presented at the annual meeting of the National Reading Conference, Austin, TX.

Alvermann, D. E., Hynd, C. R., & Qian, G. (1990, November). *Preservice teachers' comprehension and teaching of a physics principle: An experimental intervention*. Paper presented at the annual meeting of the National Reading Conference, Miami, FL.

Alvermann, D. E., Moon, J. S., & Hagood, M. C. (1999). *Popular culture in the classroom: Teaching and researching critical media literacy*. Newark, DE: International Reading Association.

Alvermann, D., & Moore, D. (1991). Secondary school reading. In R. Barr, M. L. Kamil, P. B. Mosenthal, & P. D. Pearson (Eds.), *Handbook of reading research* (Vol. 2, pp. 951–983). New York: Longman.

Alvermann, D. E., & Rush, L. S. (in press). Literacy intervention programs at the middle and high school levels. In J. Dole & T. Jetton (Eds.), *Handbook of adolescent literacy.* Chicago: Guilford.

Alvermann, D. E., Smith, L. C., & Readence, J. E. (1985). Prior knowledge activation and the comprehension of compatible and incompatible text. *Reading Research Quarterly, 20,* 420-436.

Alvermann, D. E., & Swafford, D. (1989). Do content area strategies have a research base? *Journal of Reading, 32,* 388-394.

Anders, P. L. (1998). The Literacy Council: People are the key to an effective program. *NASSP Bulletin, 82*(600), 16-23.

Anders, P. L. (2002). Secondary reading programs: A story of what was. In D. L. Schallert, C. M. Fairbanks, J. Worthy, B. Maloch, & J. V. Hoffman (Eds.), *51st yearbook of the National Reading Conference* (pp. 82-93). Oak Creek, WI: National Reading Conference.

Anders, P. L., & Commeyras, M. (1998). An educational feminist view of four vignettes about science education. In B. J. Guzzetti & C. Hynd (Eds.), *Theoretical perspectives on conceptual change* (pp. 133-145). Mahwah, NJ: Lawrence Erlbaum Associates.

Anders, P. L., & Evans, K. (1994). Relationship between teachers' beliefs and their instructional practice in reading. In R. Garner & P. A. Alexander (Eds.), *Beliefs about text and about instruction with text* (pp. 137-154). Hillsdale, NJ: Lawrence Erlbaum Associates.

Anders, P. L., & Richardson, V. (1991). Research currents: Staff development that empowers teachers' reflection and enhances instruction. *Language Arts, 68*(iv), 316-321.

Anders, P. L., & Richardson, V. (Winter, 1992). Game show host, bookkeeper or judge? Challenges, contradictions, and consequences of accountability. *Teachers College Record, 94*(2), 382-396.

Anderson, R. C. (1977). The notion of schemata and the educational enterprise: General discussion of the conference. In R. C. Anderson, R. J. Spiro & W. F. Montague (Eds.), *Schooling and the acquisition of knowledge* (pp. 415-431). Hillsdale, NJ: Lawrence Erlbaum Associates.

Anderson, R. C., Reynolds, R. E., Schallert, D. L., & Goetz, E. T. (1977). Frameworks for comprehending discourse. *American Educational Research Journal, 14,* 367-382.

Anderson, R. C., Shirey, L., Wilson, P., & Fielding, L. (1986). Interestingness of children's reading material. In R. Snow & M. Farr (Eds.), *Aptitude learning and instruction.* (pp. x-x). Hillsdale, NJ: Lawrence Erlbaum Associates.

Anderson-Inman, L., & Horney, M. (1997). Electronic books for secondary students. *Journal of Adolescent and Adult Literacy, 40,* 486-491.

Applebee, A. N. (1978). *The child's concept of story.* Chicago: University of Chicago Press.

Arends, R. I. (2001). *Learning to teach* (5th ed.). Boston: McGraw-Hill.

Aristotle. (1960). *The rhetoric of Aristotle* (L. Cooper, Trans.). New York: Appleton-Century-Crofts.

Armbruster, B. B. (1984). The problem of "inconsiderate text." In G. G. Duffy, L. R. Roehler, & J. Mason (Eds.), *Comprehension instruction: Perspectives and suggestions* (pp. 202-217). New York: Longman.

Armbruster, B. B. (1989). *Science.* Menlo Park, CA: Addison-Wesley.

Armbruster, B. B., & Anderson, T. H. (1981). *Content-area textbooks* (Reading Education Rep. No. 23). Urbana: University of Illinois, Center for the Study of Reading.

Artley, A. S. (1942). *A study of certain relationships existing between general reading comprehension and reading comprehension in a specific subject matter area.* Unpublished doctoral dissertation, Pennsylvania State College, University Park.

Atkin, J. M., & Karplus, R. (1962). Discovery or invention? *Science Teacher, 29*(5), 45-48.

Au, K. H. (1993). *Literacy instruction in multicultural settings.* Fort Worth, TX: Harcourt Brace Jovanovitch.

Au, K. (2005). *Multicultural issues and literacy achievement.* Mahwah, NJ: Lawrence Erlbaum Associates.

B

Baker, L., Afflerbach, P., & Reinking, D. (Eds.). (1995). *Developing engaged readers in school and home communities*. Mahwah, NJ: Lawrence Erlbaum Associates.

Barman, C., DiSpezio, M., Guthrie, V., Leyden, M. B., Mercier, S., Ostlund, K., & Armbruster, B. (1989). *Science*. Menlo Park, CA: Addison Wesley.

Barry, A. (2002). Reading strategies teachers say they use. *Journal of Adolescent and Adult Literacy, 46*, 132–141.

Barth, J. (1972). *Chimera*. New York: Random House.

Barton, D., Hamilton, M., & Ivanic, R. (Eds.). (2000). *Situated literacies: Reading and writing in context*. London: Routledge.

Bean, T. W., Bean, S. K., & Bean, K. F. (1999). Intergenerational conversations and two adolescents' multiple literacies: Implications for redefining content area literacy. *Journal of Adolescent and Adult Literacy, 42*, 438–448.

Beck, I., McCaslin, E., & McKeown, M. G. (1980). *The rational design of a program to teach vocabulary to fourth-grade students*. Pittsburgh, PA: University of Pittsburgh, Learning Research and Development Center.

Bertot, J. C., & McClure, C. R. (2000). *Public libraries and the Intenet 2000: Summary findings and data tables*. Washington, DC: National Commission on Libraries and Information Science.

Betts, J. D. (2000). A seed is planted: Multimedia data and analysis of an after school multimedia arts education program. *Proceeding of Ed-Media 2000 World Conference on Educational Multimedia, Hypermedia, and Telecommunications*. Montreal, CA: Ex-Media.

Betts, J. D. (2002). *Pascua Yaqui connection: Community resource lab study*. Washington, DC: National Telecommunications and Information Administration, U.S. Department of Commerce. Indexed online at http://ntiaotian2.ntia.doc.gov/top/details.cfm?oeam=046098039 and http://ntiaotiant2.ntia.doc.gov/top/docs/eval/pdf/046098030e.pdf

Betts, J. D. (2003). Art + technology integration: Developing an after school curriculum. *Afterschool Matters, 2*, 13–22.

Bishop, A. P. (2003). Communities for the new century. In B. C. Bruce (Ed.), *Literacy in the information age: Inquiries into meaning making with new technologies* (pp. 317–326). Newark, DE: International Reading Association.

Blanchard, J. (1989). An exploratory inquiry: The milieu of research in secondary, content-area reading methodology textbooks. *Teacher Education Quarterly, 16*, 51–63.

Blanton, W. E., Greene, M. W., & Cole, M. (2003). Computer mediation for learning and play: The fifth Dimension—A construction zone for literacies. In B. C. Bruce (Ed.), *Literacy in the information age: Inquiries into meaning making with new technologies* (pp. 247–257). Newark, DE: International Reading Association.

Bloom, J. W. (1992, April). *Conceptual change or contextual flexibility: The myth of restructuring and replacing conceptions*. Paper presented at the annual meeting of the American Educational Research Association, San Francisco, CA.

Bond, E. (1941). *Reading and ninth grade achievement*. New York: Columbia University Press.

Bond, G. L., & Bond, E. (1941). *Developmental reading in high school*. New York: Macmillan.

Bond, G. L., & Tinker, M. A. (1967). *Reading difficulties: Their diagnosis and correction*. New York: Appleton-Century-Crofts.

Bos, C. S., & Anders, P. L. (1993). Using interactive teaching and learning strategies to promote text comprehension and content learning for students with learning disabilities. *International Journal of Disability, Development and Education, 39*(3), 224–238.

Bos, C. S., & Anders, P. L. (1994). The study of student change. In V. Richardson (Ed.), *Teacher change and the staff development process: A case in reading instruction* (pp. 181–199). New York: Teachers College Press.

Bott, C. (2002). Zines—the ultimate creative writing project. *English Journal, 92,* 27–34.

Bransford, J., Brown, A., & Cocking, R. (Eds.). (1999). *How people learn: Brain, mind, experience, and school.* Washington, DC: National Academy Press.

Brewer, W. F., & Lichtenstein, E. H. (1980). Event schemas, story schemas, and story grammars. In J. Long & A. D. Baddeley (Eds.), *Attention and performance IX* (pp. 00–00). Hillsdale, NJ: Lawrence Erlbaum Associates.

Brown, D. E., & Clement, J. (1987). *Overcoming misconceptions in mechanics: A comparison of two example-based teaching strategies* (Report No. 143). Washington, DC: National Science Foundation. (ERIC Document Reproduction Service No. ED 283 712)

Bruce, B. C. (1987). Literacy technologies: What stance should we take? *Journal of Literacy Research, 29,* 289–309.

Bruce, B. C. (2003). (Ed.). *Literacy in the information age*. Newark, DE: International Reading Association.

Bruce, B. C., & Levin, J. A. (1997). Educational technology: Media for inquiry, communication, construction, and expression. *Journal of Educational Computing Research, 17*(1), 79–102.

Bruner, J. (1986). *Actual minds, possible worlds.* Cambridge, MA: Harvard University Press.

Bruner, J. (1990). *Acts of meaning.* Cambridge, MA: Harvard University Press.

Buehl, D. (2001). *Classroom strategies for interactive learning* (2nd ed.). Newark, DE: International Reading Association.

C

Calkins, L. (1991). *Living between the lines.* Portsmouth, NH: Heinemann.

Cambourne, B. (1988). *The whole story: Natural learning and the acquisition of literacy in the classroom.* New York: Scholastic.

Carlson, K. L. (1971). A psycholinguistic description of selected fourth grade children reading a variety of contextual material. *Dissertation Abstracts International, 32,* 158A–159A. (University Microfilms No. 71-17, 243)

Carroll, J. B., Davies, P., & Richman, B. (1972). *The American Heritage word frequency book.* Boston: Houghton Mifflin.

Cattell, J. M. (1886). The time it takes to see and name objects. *Mind, 11,* 63–65.

Cervetti, G., Pardales, M. J., & Damico, J. S. (2004). *A tale of differences: Comparing the traditions, perspectives, and educational goals of critical reading and critical literacy.* Retrieved October 23, 2004, from http://www.readingonline.org/articles/

Cicero. (1954). *De inventione of topica* (H. M. Hubbell, Trans.). London: Heinemann.

Chalklin, S., & Lave, J. (1995). *Understanding practice*. Cambridge, England: Cambridge University Press.

Chall, J. S. (1983). *Stages of reading development*. New York: Harcourt Brace.

Chall, J. S., & Squire, J. R. (1991). The publishing industry and textbooks. In R. Barr, M. Kamil, P. Mosenthal, & P. D. Pearson (Eds.), *Handbook of reading research* (Vol. II, pp. 120–146). New York: Longman.

Champagne, A. B., Gunstone, R. F., & Klopfer, L. E. (1983). Naive knowledge and science learning. *Research in Science & Technological Education, 1,* 173–183.

Chandler-Olcott, K., & Mahar, D. (2001). Considering genre in the digital literacy classroom. *Reading Online, 5*. Retrieved June 18, 2004, from http://wwwreading online.org/electronic/elecindex.asp?HREF=/electronic/chandler/index.html

Chandler-Olcott, K. & Mahar, D. (2003). "Techsaviness" meets multiliteracies: Exploring adolescent girls' technology-related literacy practices. *Journal of Adolescent and Adult Literacy, 46,* 556–568.

Clement, J. (1987, April). *The use of analogies and anchoring intuitions to remediate misconceptions in mechanics.* Paper presented at the annual meeting of the American Educational Research Association, Washington, DC.

Clement, J. (1991). Students' preconceptions in introductory mechanics. *American Journal of Physics, 50,* 66–71.

Coiro, J. (2003). Reading comprehension on the Internet: Expanding our understandings of reading comprehension to encompass new literacies. *The Reading Teacher, 55,* 103–115.

Coles, G. (1998). *Reading lessons: The debate over literacy*. New York: Hill & Wang.

Conley, M. (1992). *Content reading instruction. A communication approach.* New York: McGraw Hill.

Cope, B., & Kalantzis, M. (Eds.). (2000). *Multiliteracies: Literacy learning and the design of social futures*. London: Routledge.

Costa, A. L. (2000). Describing habits of mind. In A. Costa & B. Kallick (Eds.), *Discovering and exploring habits of mind*. Alexandria, VA: Association for Supervision and Curriculum Development.

Costa, A. L., & Garmston, R. (1985). Supervision for intelligent teaching. *Educational Leadership, 43,* 72–80.

Cullum, A. (1971). *The geraniums on the windowsill just died, but teacher you went right on.* Amsterdam: Harlan Quist.

Curtis, M. B., & Longo, A. M. (1999). When adolescents can't read: Methods and materials that work. Cambridge, MA: Brookline Books.

Curtis, M. B., & Longo, A. M. (2001). Teaching vocabulary to adolescents to improve comprehension. *Reading Online.* Retrieved March 11, 2004 from http://www.readingonline.org/articles/art_index.asp?HREF=/articles/curtis/index.html

D

D'Amasio, A. (1999). *The feeling of what happens: Body and emotion in the making of consciousness*. New York: Harcourt.

Darder, A. (1995). *Buscando* America: The contributions of critical Latino educators to the academic development and empowerment of Latino students in the U.S. In C. E. Sleeter & P. L. McLaren (Eds.), *Multicultural education, critical pedagogy and the politics of difference* (pp. 101–133). New York: State University of New York Press.

Darling-Hammond, L., & Wise, A. (1985). Beyond standardization: State standards and school improvement. *The Elementary School Journal, 85,* 349.

Davis, A., Clarke, M., Rhodes, L. K., Shanklin, N. L., Nathenson-Mejia, S., Selkirk, M., Commins, N., Bookman, M., & Sanders, N. (1992, September). Using multiple indicators to identify effective classroom practices for minority children in reading and writing. (Grant No. R 117E00188-90). Washington, DC: U.S. Department of Education, Office of Educational Research and Improvement.

Delattre, D. (1983). The insiders. In R. Bailey & C. Fosheim (Eds.), *Literacy for life* (pp. 52–59). New York: The Modern Language Association of America.

Dennison, T. (2004). Examining student self-perception and identity construction through adolescent multiple literacies. Unpublished master's thesis, The University of Arizona, Tucson.

Dewey, J. (1938). *Experience and education*. New York: Macmillan.

Dewey, J. (1943). *The child and the curriculum/The school and society.* Chicago: University of Chicago Press.

Diehl, W. A. (1980). *Functional literacy as a variable construct: An examination of attitudes, behaviors and strategies related to occupational literacy.* Unpublished doctoral dissertation, Indiana University, Bloomington.

DiGisi, L. L., & Willett, J. B. (1995). What high school biology teachers say about their textbook use: A descriptive study. *Journal of Research in Science Teaching, 32,* 123–142.

Dillon, D. (2000). *Reconsidering how to meet the literacy needs of all students.* Newark, DE: International Reading Association.

Dillon, D. R., O'Brien, D. G., Wellinski, S. A., Springs, R., & Smith, D. (1996). Engaging "at-risk" high school students: The creation of an innovative program. In D. J. Leu, C. K. Kinzer, and K. A. Hinchman (Eds.), *Literacies for the 21st century: Research and practice. 45th Yearbook of the National Reading Conference* (pp. 231-244). Chicago: National Reading Conference.

Dixon-Kraus, L. (1996). *Vygotsky in the classroom: Mediated literacy instruction and assessment.* White Plains, NY: Longman.

Doherty, C., & Mayer, D. (2003). E-mail as a "contact zone" for teacher-student relationships. *Journal of Adolescent and Adult Literacy, 46,* 592-600.

Dole, J. A. (1978). A validation of the construct of critical reading and of the three tests designed to measure critical reading ability. *Dissertation Abstracts International, 38,* 7135-A (University Microfilms No. 780 8892).

Dole, J. A. (1988, November). *Remarks on the symposium, Prior knowledge research: Misconceptions and multiple measures.* Paper presented at the annual meeting of the National Reading Conference, Tucson, AZ.

Dole, J. A., Niederhauser, D. S., & Hayes, M. T. (1990, November). *Learning from science text: Students' reliance on prior knowledge for familiar and unfamiliar topics.* Paper presented at the annual meeting of the National Reading Conference, Miami, FL.

Dole, J. A., & Smith, E. L. (1987, December). *When prior knowledge is wrong: Reading and learning from science text.* Paper presented at the annual meeting of the National Reading Conference, St. Petersburg, FL.

Donaldson, D. P. (2001). Teaching Geography's four traditions with poetry. *Journal of Geograpy, 100,* 24-31.

Donanue, D. (2003). Reading across the great divide: English and math teachers apprentice one another as readers and disciplinary insiders. *Journal of Adolescent and Adult Literacy, 47,* 24-38.

Dressman, M. (1997). Preference as performance: Doing social class and gender in three school libraries. *Journal of Literacy Research, 29*(3), 319-361.

Duchastel, P. C. (1978). *Selective learning: An interpretive review of orienting factors in prose learning.* (ERIC Document Reproduction Service No. ED 215 325)

Duffelmeyer, F. A., Baum, D. D., & Merkley, D. J. (1987, November). Maximizing reader-text confrontation with an Extended Anticipation Guide. *Journal of Reading, 31,* 146-150.

Dunne, F., Nave, B., & Lewis, A. (2000, December). Critical friends groups: Teachers helping teachers to improve student learning. *Phi Delta Kappa International,* Center for Evaluation, Development, and Research. Retrived June 4, 2004. from www.pdkint'l.org/edres/

Dwight, J., & Garrison, J. (2003). A manifesto for instructional technology: Hyperpedagogy. *Teachers College Record, 105,* 699-728.

Durkin, D. (1979). What classroom observations reveal about reading comprehension instruction. *Reading Research Quarterly, 14,* 481-533.

E

Ernst-Slavit, G., Moore, M., & Maloney, C. (2002). Changing lives: Teaching English and literature to ESL students. *Journal of Adolescent and Adult Literacy, 46,* 116-128.

Estes, T., & Vaughan, J. (1978). *Reading and learning in the content classroom.* Boston: Allyn & Bacon.

Evans, J. (2004). From Sheryl Crow to Homer Simpson: Literature and composition through pop culture. *English Journal, 93,* 32-38.

Evans, K. (1993). *Just when you thought it was complicated enough: Literature discussions meet critical theory.* Unpublished doctoral dissertation, University of Arizona, Tucson.

F

Falk-Ross, F. C. (2001). Classroom discourse routines: Changing the rules. *American Reading Forum Yearbook, 21* (243–253). Boone, NC: Appalachian State University.

Fay, L. (1956). *Reading in the high school.* Washington, DC: National Education Association.

Feathers, K., & Smith, F. (1987). Meeting the reading demands of the real world. *Journal of Reading, 30*(6), 506–511.

Feirro, E., & Teberosky, A. (1982). *Literacy before schooling*. Portsmouth, NH: Heinemann.

Fenstermacher, G. D. (1986). Philosophy of teaching: Thee aspects. In M. Wittrock (Ed.), *Handbook of research on teaching* (3rd ed., pp. 37–49). New York: Macmillan.

Fenstermacher, G. D (1987). Prologue to my critics. *Educational Theory, 37*(4), 357–360.

Ferguson, E. S. (1977). The mind's eye: Nonverbal thought in technology. *Science, 197,* 827–836.

Feynman, R. (1985). *Surely, you must be joking Mr. Feynman!* New York: Norton.

Finders, M. (1996). Queens and teen zines: Early adolescent females reading their way toward adulthood. *Anthropology & Education Quarterly, 27*(1), 71–89.

Finders, M. (1997). *Just girls: Hidden literacies and life in junior high*. New York: Teachers College Press.

Fry, E. (1968). A readability formula that saves time. *Journal of Reading, 11,* 513–516.

Fry, E. (1977). Fry's readability graph: Clarifications, validity, and extension to Level 17. *Journal of Reading, 21*, 249.

Fuller, R. G. (1982). *Piagetian based programs for college freshmen* [Accent on Developing Advanced Processes of Thought (ADAPT) Program]. Lincoln: University of Nebraska.

G

Gaskins, I. W., & Elliott, T. T. (1991). *Implementing cognitive strategy instruction across the school: The Benchmark manual for teachers*. Cambridge, MA: Brookline Books.

Gee, J. P. (2000). The New Literacy studies: From "socially situated" to the work of the social. In D. Barton, M. Hamilton, & R. Ivanic. (2000). *Situated literacies: Reading and writing in context*. London: Routledge.

Gee, J. P. (2001). Reading as situated action: A Sociocultural perspective. *Journal of Adolescent and Adult Literacy, 44*, 714–745.

Gee, J. P. (2001, December). *Reading in "new times."* Paper presented at the annual meeting of the National Reading Conference, San Antonio, TX.

Gee, J. P. (2003). *What video games have to teach us about learning and literacy*. New York: Palgrave Macmillan.

Gibson, E., & Levin, H. (1975). *The psychology of reading*. Cambridge, MA: MIT Press.

Giroux, H. A. (1994). *Disturbing pleasures: Learning popular culture*. New York: Routledge.

Giroux, H. A., & McLaren, P. (Eds.). (1994). *Between borders: Pedagogy and the politics of cultural studies.* New York: Routledge.

Glass, G. V. (1976). Primary, secondary and meta-analysis of research. *Educational Researcher, 5,* 3–8.

Goldman, S. R., & Rakestraw, J. A., Jr. (2000). Structural aspects of constructing meaning from text. In M. L. Kamil, P. B. Mosenthal, P. David Pearson, & R. Barr (Eds.), *Handbook of reading research* (Vol. 3, pp. 311–336). Mahwah, NJ: Lawrence Erlbaum Associates.

Good, R. (1991, October). *Constructivism's many faces.* Paper presented at the 13th conference on Curriculum, Theory and Classroom Practice, Dayton, OH.

Goodenough, W. H. (1963). *Cooperation in change*. New York: Russell Sage Foundation.

Goodlad, J. I. (1976). Facing the future: Issues in education and schooling. New York: McGraw-Hill.

Goodman, K. (1994). *Ken Goodman on reading*. Toronto: Scholastic Canada.

Goodman, K. S. (1976). Reading: A psycholinguistic guessing game. In H. Singer & R. Ruddell (Eds.), *Theoretical models and processes of reading* (pp. 497-518). Newark, DE: International Reading Association.

Goodman, S. (2003). *Teaching youth media: A critical guide to literacy, video production and social change.* New York: Teachers College Press.

Goodman, Y., & Burke, C. (1980). *Reading strategies focus on comprehension.* New York: Macmillan.

Goodman, Y. S. (2003). *Valuing language study: Inquiry into language for elementary and middle schools.* Urbana, IL: National Council of Teachers of English.

Gordon, C. J. (1991, December). *A case study of conceptual change.* Paper presented at the annual meeting of the National Reading Conference, Palm Springs, CA.

Graves, D. H. (1990). *Discover your own literacy.* Portsmouth, NH: Heinemann.

Gray, W. S. (1948). *On their own in reading.* Chicago: Scott, Foresman.

Gray, W. S. (1960). Reading. In C. W. Harris (Ed.), *Encyclopedia of educational research* (pp. 00-00). New York: Macmillan.

Green, T. (1971). *The activities of teaching.* New York: McGraw-Hill.

Guskey, T. R. (1986). Staff development and the process of teacher change. *Educational Researcher, 15,* 5-12.

Guthrie, J. (2004). Viewpoint: Teaching for literacy engagement. *Journal of Literacy Research, 36*(1), 1-28.

Guthrie, J., & Cox, K. (2001). Classroom conditions for motivation and engagement in reading. *Educational Psychology Review, 13*(3), 283-302.

Guthrie, J., Van Meter, P., Hancock, G., Anderson, A. E., & McCann, A. (1998). Does concept-oriented reading instruction increase strategy use and conceptual learning from text? *Journal of Educational Psychology, 90*(2), 261-278.

Guzzetti, B. J. (1982). A psycholinguistic analysis of the reading strategies of high, average, and low ability readers across selected content areas. *Dissertation Abstracts International, 43*(4), 1026-A. (University Microfilms No. DA 8211081)

Guzzetti, B. (1984). The reading process in content fields: A psycholinguistic investigation. *American Educational Research Journal, 21,* 659-668.

Guzzetti, B. J. (1989). From preservice to inservice: A naturalistic inquiry of beginning teachers' practices in content reading. *Teacher Education Quarterly, 16,* 65-71.

Guzzetti, B. J. (1990). Effects of textual and instructional manipulations on concept acquisition. *Reading Psychology, 11,* 49-62.

Guzzetti, B. J. (2001). Learning counter-intuitive science concepts: What have we learned from a decade of research? *Reading and Writing Quarterly, 16,* pp. 64-75.

Guzzetti, B. J. (2002, September). *"This place has no atmosphere": Secondary students' reports of and suggestions for literacy in science.* Paper presented at the conference on Ontological, Epistemological, Linguistic and Pedagogical Considerations of Language and Science Literacy: Empowering research and informing instruction, Victoria, BC, Canada.

Guzzetti, B. J., & Gamboa, M. (2003a, November). *Online journaling: The informal literacy practice of two adolescents.* Paper presented at the annual meeting of the National Council of Teachers of English, San Francisco, CA.

Guzzetti, B. J., & Gamboa, M. (2003b, December). *Interacting on the web: Technology, adolescents and literacies.* Paper presented at the annual meeting of the National Reading Conference, Scottsdale, AZ.

Guzzetti, B. J., & Gamboa, M. (2004). *Online journaling: The informal writings of two adolescents.* Paper presented at the annual meeting of the National Council of Teachers of English, San Francisco, CA.

Guzzetti, B. J., & Gamboa, M. (2004). Zines for social justice: Adolescent girls writing on their own. *Reading Research Quarterly, 39,* 408-437.

Guzzetti, B. J., & Gamboa, M. (2004). Zining: The unsanctioned literacy practice of adolescents. *53rd Yearbook, of the National Reading Conference*. Oak Creek, WI: National Reading Conference.

Guzzetti, B. J., Hynd, C. R., & Williams, W. (1995). Improving science texts: Students speak out. *Journal of Reading, 38*(6), 656-663.

Guzzetti, B. J., Snyder, T. E., Glass, G. V., & Gamas, W. S. (1993). Promoting conceptual change in science: A comparative meta-analysis of instructional interventions from reading education and science education. *Reading Research Quarterly, 28*, 116-159.

Guzzetti, B. J., & Taylor, J. C. (1988, December). *Effects of textual and instructional manipulations on concept acquisition.* Paper presented at the annual meeting of the National Reading Conference, Tucson, AZ.

Guzzetti, B. J., Young, J. P., Gritsavage, M., Fyfe, L. M., & Hardenbrook, M. (2002). *Reading, writing and talking gender in literacy learning*. Newark, DE: International Reading Association/ National Reading Conference.

H

Hartman, D. K. (1997). *Doing things with texts: Mapping the textual practices of two African American male high school students* (Final Report). Newark, DE: International Reading Association.

Havelock, E. (1991). The oral-literate equation: A formula for the modern mind. In D. R. Olson & N. Torrance (Eds.), *Literacy and orality* (pp. 00-00). Cambridge, MA: Cambridge University Press.

Heath, S. B. (1991). The functions and uses of literacy. In R. Barr, M. Kamil, P. Mosenthal, & P. D. Pearson (Eds.), *Handbook of reading research* (Vol. 2, pp. 15-29). New York: Longman.

Hegarty, M., Carpenter, P. A., & Just, M. A. (1991). Diagrams in the comprehension of scientific texts. In R. Barr, M. L. Kamil, P. Mosenthal, & P. D. Pearson (Eds.), *Handbook of reading research* (Vol. 2, pp. 641-668). New York: Longman.

Herber, H. L. (1970). *Teaching reading in the content areas*. Englewood Cliffs, NJ: Prentice-Hall.

Herber, H. L. (1978). *Teaching reading in content areas* (2nd ed.). Englewood Cliffs, NJ: Prentice-Hall.

Herber, H. L., & Barron, R. (Eds.). (1979). *Research in reading in the content areas: Second year report.* Syracuse, NY: Syracuse University.

Herber, H. L., & Herber, J. N. (1993). *Teaching in content areas with reading, writing and reasoning*. Boston: Allyn & Bacon.

Herber H. L., & Riley, J. (Eds.). (1979). *Research in reading in the content areas: Fourth year report.* Syracuse, NY: Syracuse University.

Herber, H. L., & Sanders, P. (Eds.). (1969). *Research in reading in the content areas: First year report.* Syracuse, NY: Syracuse University.

Herber, H. L., & Vacca, R. (Eds.). (1977). *Research in reading in the content areas: Third year report.* Syracuse, NY: Syracuse University.

Hewson, M. G., & Hewson, P. W. (1983). Effect of instruction using students' prior knowledge and conceptual change strategies on science learning. *Journal of Research in Science Teaching, 20,* 731-743.

Hinchman, K. A., Alvermann, D. E., Boyd, F. E., Brozo, W. G., & Vacca, R. T. (2004). Supporting older students' in- and out-of-school literacies. *Journal of Adolescent and Adult Literacy, 47,* 304-310.

Hinchman, K. A., & Zalewski, P. (1996). Reading for success in a tenth grade global studies class: A qualitative study. *Journal of Literacy Research, 28*, 91-106.

Hillocks, G., Jr. (1975). *Observing and writing.* Urbana, IL: National Council of Teachers of English.

Hillocks, G., Jr. (2002). *The testing trap: How state writing assessments control learning.* New York: Teachers College Press.

Hindin, A., Morocco, C. C., & Aguilar, C. M. (2001). "This book *lives* in our school": Teaching middle school students to understand literature. *Remedial and Special Education, 22,* 204-213.

Hirsch, S. A., & Bacon, P. (Eds.). (1988). *Communities.* Orlando, FL: Harcourt Brace Jovanovitch.

Holloway, J. H. (2000). Research Link/Preparing teachers for differentiated instruction. *Educational Leadership, 58*(1), 82-83.

Horace, 13 (1996). What does a critical friends group do? Retrieved June 11, 2004, from http://ces/edgateway.net/cs/resources/view/ces_res/40

Housner, L. D., & Griffey, D. C. (1985). Teacher cognition. Differences in planning and interactive decision making between experienced and inexperienced teachers. *Research Quarterly for Exercise and Sport, 56,* 45-53.

Huey, E. B. (1908). *The psychology and pedagogy of reading.* Cambridge, MA: MIT Press.

Hurd, D., Johnson, S., Matthias, G., McLaughlin, C., Snyder, E., & Wright, J. (1986). *General science.* Englewood Cliffs, NJ: Prentice-Hall.

Hurd, P. D. (1970). *New directions in teaching secondary school science.* Chicago: Rand McNally.

Hynd, C. R., McWhorter, Y., Phares, G., & Suttles, B. (1991, December). *The role of social, cognitive and affective factors in conceptual change.* Paper presented at the annual meeting of the National Reading Conference, Palm Springs, CA.

Hynd, C. R., Qian, G. Q., Ridgeway, V. G., & Pickle, M. (1991). Promoting conceptual change with science texts and discussion. *Journal of Reading, 34,* 596-601.

I

Iona, M. (1990). Would you believe? Artistic blunders. *The Physics Teacher, 17,* 116-117.

J

Jago, C. (2002). *Cohesive writing.* Portsmouth, NH: Heinemann.

Johannessen, L. R. (2004). Helping "struggling" students achieve success. *Journal of Adolescent and Adult Literacy, 47,* 638-647.

Johannessen, L. R., & Kahn, E. A., & Walter, S. (1984). The art of introducing literature. *The Clearing House, 57,* 263-266.

Johnston, P. (1989). Constructive evaluation and the improvement of teaching and learning. *Teachers College Record, 90,* 535-549.

Jonassen, D. H. (1996). *Computers in the classroom: Mindtools for critical thinking.* Columbus, OH: Merrill.

Judd, C. H., & Buswell, G. T. (1922). *Silent reading: A study of the various types* (Supplementary Educational Monograph No. 23). Chicago: University of Chicago Press.

K

Kajder, S. B. (2004). Enter here: Personal narrative and digital storytelling. *English Journal, 93*(3), 64-68.

Kane, S., & Rule, A. (2004). Poetry connections can enhance content area learning. *Journal of Adolescent and Adult Literacy, 47,* 658-672.

Kaplan, R. B. (1966). Cultural thought patterns in intercultural education. *Language Learning, 1*(2), 1-20.

Karchner, R. A. (2001). The journey ahead: Thirteen teachers report how the Internet influences literacy and literacy instruction in their K-12 classrooms. *Reading Research Quarterly, 36,* 442-466.

Karplus, R., & Thier, H. D. (1967). *A new look at elementary school science.* Chicago: Rand McNally.

King, A. (1990). Enhancing peer interaction and learning in the classroom through reciprocal questions. *American Educational Research Journal, 27*, 664-687.

King, A. (1994). Guiding knowledge construction in the classroom: Effects of teaching children how to question and how to explain. *American Educational Research Journal, 31*, 338-368.

Kintsch, W. (1986). Learning from text. *Cognition and Instruction, 3*, 87-108.

Kintsch, W., & Vipond, D. (1979). Reading comprehension and readability in educational practice and psychological theory. In L. G. Nielsen (Ed.), *Perspectives of memory research* (pp. 363-394). Hillsdale, NJ: Lawrence Erlbaum Associates.

Kisjord, P. T. (1986). *The american nation* Dallas, TX: Holt, Rinehart, & Winston.

Kist, W. (2002). Finding "new literacy" in action: An interdisciplinary high school Western Civilization class. *Journal of Adolescent and Adult Literacy, 45*, 368-377.

Klausmeier, H. J. (1984). Conceptual learning and development. In R. Corsini (Ed.), *Encyclopedia of psychology* (Vol. 1, pp. 266-269).

Klausmeier, H. J., Ghatatla, E. S., & Frayer, D. A. (1974). *Conceptual learning and development: A cognitive review*. New York: Academic Press.

Klausmeier, H. J., & Sipple, T. S. (1980). *Learning and teaching process concepts: A strategy for testing applications of theory.* New York: Academic Press.

Klaussen, C., & Short, K. G. (1992). Collaborative research on teacher study groups: Embracing the complexities. In C. K. Kinzer & D. J. Leu (Eds.), *Literacy research, theory, and practice: views from many perspectives. 41st Yearbook of the National Reading Conference* (pp. 341-348). Chicago: National Reading Conference.

Knobel, M. (2001). "I'm not a pencil man": How one student challenges our notions of literacy "failure" in school. *Journal of Adolescent and Adult Literacy, 44*, 404-414.

Kolczynski, R. G. (1974). A psycholinguistic analysis of oral reading miscues in selected passages from science, social studies, mathematics and literature. *Dissertation Abstracts International, 34*, 7108-A. (University Microfilms No. 11,984)

Kowanliski, B. J. (1992). *Using children's literature to foster learning in the social studies curriculum.* Unpublished manuscript, Arizona State University, Tempe.

Krantz, L. L. (1955). The relationship of reading abilities and basic skills of the elementary school to success in the high school. *Dissertation Abstracts, 15*, 1001 (University Microfilms No. 11,984)

Kress, G. (2003). *Literacy in the new media age*. New York: Routledge.

Kristeva, J. (1986). Word, dialogue, and novel. In T. Moi (Ed. and Trans.), *The Kristeva reader* (pp. 34-61). Oxford, England: Basil Blackwell.

L

Lam, Wan Shun E. (2000). L2 literacy and the design of the self: A case study of a teenager writing on the Internet. *TESOL Quarterly, 34*, 457-483.

Langer, J. (1984). Examining background knowledge and text comprehension. *Reading Research Quarterly, 19*, 468-481.

Langer, J. (2001a). Beating the odds: Teaching middle and high school students to read and write well. *American Educational Research Journal, 38*, 837-880.

Langer, J. (2001b). Succeeding against the odds in English. *English Journal, 91*, 37-42.

Langer, J., & Applebee, A. (1984). *How writing shapes thinking*. Urbana, IL: The National Council of Teachers of English.

Lankshear, C., & Knobel, M. (2002). Do we have your attention? New literacies, digital technologies and the education of adolescents. In D. Alvermann (Ed.), *Adolescents and literacies in a digital world*. New York: Peter Lang.

Lave, J. (1988). *Cognition in practice*. Cambridge, England: Cambridge University Press.

Lave, J., & Wenger, E. (1991). *Situated learning: Legitimate peripheral participation*. Cambridge, England: Cambridge University Press.

Lawson, A. E., & Kral, E. A. (1985). Developing formal reasoning through the study of English. *The Educational Forum, 49*, 211-226.

Lawson, A. E., & Thompson, L. D. (1988). Formal reasoning ability and misconceptions concerning genetics and natural selection. *Journal of Research in Science Teaching, 25*, 733-746.

Lawson, A. E., & Worsnop, W. (1992). Learning about evolution and rejecting a belief in special creation: Effects of reflective reasoning skill, prior knowledge, prior belief and religious commitment. *Journal of Research in Science Teaching, 29*, 143-166.

Lawson, C. A. (1967). *Brain mechanisms and human learning*. Boston: Houghton Mifflin.

Leu, D. J. (2002). The new literacies: Research on reading instruction with the Internet and other digital technologies. In A. E. Farstrup & S. J. Samuels (Eds.), *What research has to say about reading instruction* (3rd ed., pp. 393-417). Newark, DE: International Reading Association.

Leu, D. J., Jr., & Kinzer, C. K. (2000). The convergence of literacy instruction with networked technologies for information and communication. *Reading Research Quarterly, 35*, 108-127.

Leu, D. J., Kinzer, C. K., Coiro, J. L., & Cammack, D. W. (2004). Toward a theory of new literacies emerging from the internet and other information and communication technologies. In R. B. Ruddell & N. J. Unrau (Eds.), *Theoretical models and processes of reading* (5th ed., pp. 1570-1614). Newark, DE: International Reading Association.

Lewis, C., & Fabos, B. (1999, December). *Chatting on-line: Uses of instant message communication among adolescent girls*. Paper presented at the annual meeting of the National Reading Conference, Orlando, FL.

Lipson, M. Y. (1984). Some unexpected issues in prior knowledge and comprehension. *The Reading Teacher, 37*, 760-764.

Little, J. W. (1982). Norms of collegiality and experimentation: Workplace conditions of school success. *American Educational Research Journal, 19*, 325-340.

Lloyd, C., & Anders, P. (1994). Research-based practices as the content of staff development. In V. Richardson (Ed.), *Staff development and teacher change in reading comprehension instruction: A new generation of programs* (pp. 68-89). New York: Teachers College Press.

Lockhard, J., & Abrams, P. (2004). *Computers for twenty-first century educators* (6th ed.). Boston: Pearson.

Lortie, D. C. (1975). *Schoolteacher*. Chicago: University of Chicago Press.

M

Macrorie, K. (1988). *Searching writing*. New York: Boynton/Cook.

Mallette, M. H., Henk, W. A., & Melnick, S. A. (2004). The influence of *Accelerated Reader* on the affective literacy orientations of intermediate grade students. *Journal of Literacy Research, 36*(1), 73-84.

Mannes, K. (2004). Teaching media-savvy students about the popular media. *English Journal, 93*, 46-51.

Manzo, A. (1969). The ReQuest procedure. *Journal of Reading, 11*, 123-129.

Manzo, A., & Manzo, U. (1990). *Content area reading: A heuristic approach*. Columbus, OH: Merrill.

Maria, K. (1992, December). *The development of scientific concepts: A case Study*. Paper presented at the annual meeting of the National Reading Conference, San Antonio, TX.

Maria, K. (1993, December). *The development of earth concepts*. Paper presented at the annual meeting of the National Reading Conference, Charleston, SC.

Maria, K., & MacGinitie, W. (1987). Learning from texts that refute the reader's prior knowledge. *Reading Research and Instruction, 26,* 222-238.

Marsh, T. (2004). *What WebQuests are (really)?* Retrieved June 10, 2004, from http://www.bestWebQuests.com/what_WebQuests_are.asp

McArthur, K., Penland, T., Spencer, F., & Anders, P. L. (in press). Content area literacy: Focus on students. In D. Lapp & J. Flood, *Content area literacy*. Mahwah, NJ: Lawrence Erlbaum Associates.

McCallister, J. M. (1936). *Remedial and corrective instruction in reading: A program for the upper grades and high school.* New York: Appleton-Century.

McCann, T. M. (1996). A pioneer simulation for writing and for the study of literature. *English Journal, 85,* 62-67.

McKenna, M. C., & Robinson, R. D. (1980). *An introduction to the Cloze Procedure: An annotated bibliography* (2nd ed.). Newark, DE: International Reading Association.

Means, B., & Knapp, M. S. (1991). Cognitive approaches to teaching advanced skills to educationally disadvantaged students. *Phi Delta Kappan, 73,* 282-289.

Meyer, B. J. F., Brandt, D. M., & Bluth, G. J. (1980). Use of top-level structure in text: Key for reading comprehension of ninth-grade students. *Reading Research Quarterly, 16,* 72-103.

Mikulecky, L. J., & Kirkley, J. R. (1998). Changing workplaces, changing classes: The new role of technology in workplace literacy. In D. Reinking, M. C. McKenna, L. D. Labbo, & R. D. Kieffer (Eds.), *Handbook of literacy and technology: Transformations in a post-typographic world* (pp. 303-320). Mahwah, NJ: Lawrence Erlbaum Associates.

Miller, R. (2000). *Creating learning communities*. Boca Raton, FL: Psychology Press.

Mitchell, J. N., & Anders, P. L. (1979, December). *Textbook analysis: The relationship of text questions, prose, and concepts.* Paper presented at the National Reading Conference, San Antonio, TX.

Moje, E. B., Ciechanowski, K. M., Kramer, K. Ellis, L., Carrillo, R., & Collazo, T. (2004). Working toward third space in content area literacy: An examination of everyday funds of knowledge and discourse. *Reading Research Quarterly, 39,* 38-70.

Moje, E. B., Young, J. P., Readence, J. E., & Moore, D.W. (2000). Reinventing adolescent literacy for new times: Perennial and millennial issues. *Journal of Adolescent and Adult Literacy, 43,* 400-411.

Moll, L., & Greenberg, J. (1992). Creating zones of possibilities: Combining social contexts for instruction. In L. Moll (Ed.), *Vygotsky and education* (pp. 319-348). New York: Cambridge University Press.

Moll, L. C., & González, N. (1994). Lessons from research with language minority students. *Journal of Reading Behavior, 26*(4), 439-461.

Montano-Harmon, M. R. (1991). Discourse features of written Mexican Spanish: Current research in contrastive rhetoric and its implications. *Hispanic, 74*(2), 417-425.

Morocco, C. C., & Hindin, A. (2002). The role of conversation in a thematic understanding of literature. *Learning Disabilities Research & Practice, 17,* 144-159.

Muth, D. K. (1987). Teachers' connection questions: Prompting students to organize text ideas. *Journal of Reading, 31,* 254-259.

N

National Middle School Association. (2001). *NMSA research summary #12: Academic achievement.* Retrieved August 16, 2004, from http://www.nmsa.org/services/ressum12.htm

National Reading Panel. (2000). *Report of the National Reading Panel: Teaching children to read.* Washington, DC: National Institute of Child Health and Human Development.

National Society for the Study of Education Committee (W. S Gray, Chair). (1937). *Thirty-Sixth Yearbook of the National Society for the Study of Education.* Chicago: University of Chicago Press.

Neuman, S. B. (2001). Television and reading. In B. J. Guzzetti (Ed.), *Literacy in America: An encyclopedia of history, theory and practice* (pp. 647-648). Santa Barbara, CA: ABC-CLIO.

New London Group. (1996). A pedagogy of multiliteracies: Designing social futures. *Harvard Educational Review, 66,* 60-69.

New London Group. (2000). A pedagogy of multiliteracies: Designing social futures. In B. Cope & M. Kalantzis (Eds.), *Multiliteracies: Literacy learning and the design of social futures* (pp. 17-31). Melbourne: Macmillan.

O

O'Brien, D. (2001). "At-risk" adolescents: Redefining competence through the multiliteracies of intermediality, visual arts, and representation. *Reading Online, 4.* Retrieved June 17, 2004, from http://www.readingonline.org/newliteracies/lit index.asp?HREF=/newliteracies/obrien/index.html

O'Byrne, B. (2003). The paradox of cross-age, multicultural collaboration. *Journal of Adolescent and Adult Literacy, 47,* 50-63.

Odell, L., Goswami, D., & Quick, D. (1983). Writing outside the English composition class: Implications for teaching and for learning. In R. W. Bailey & R. M. Fosheim (Eds.), *Literacy for life: The demand for reading and writing* (pp. 119-134). New York: The Modern Language Association of America.

Osako, G., & Anders, P. L. (1983). The effect of reading interest on comprehension of expository materials with controls for prior knowledge. In J. R. Niles & L. A. Harris (Eds.), *Searches for meaning in reading/language processing and instruction. 32nd Yearbook of the National Reading Conference* (pp. 56-60). Rochester, NY: National Reading Conference.

Ovando, C. J., Collier, V. P., & Combs, M. C. (2003). *Bilingual & ESL classrooms: Teaching in multicultural contexts* (3rd ed.). Boston: McGraw-Hill.

P

Palumbo, D. (1979, October). *The use of comics as an approach to introducing the techniques and terms of narrative to novice readers.* Paper presented at the meeting of the Popular Culture Association in the South, Louisville, KY.

Papert, S. (1980). *Mindstorms: Children computers and powerful ideas.* New York: Basic Books.

Patterson, L., Santa, C. M., Short, K. G., & Smith, K. (Eds). (1993). *Teachers are researchers: Reflection and action.* Newark, DE: International Reading Association.

Pearson, P. D. (1974-1975). The effects of grammatical complexity on children's comprehension, recall, and conception of certain semantic relations. *Reading Research Quarterly, 10,* 155-192.

Pearson, P. D., Hansen, J., & Gordon, C. (1979). The effect of background knowledge on young children's comprehension of explicit and implicit information. *Journal of Reading Behavior, 11,* 201-209.

Pearson, P. D., & Johnson, D. D. (1978). *Teaching reading comprehension.* New York: Holt, Rinehart & Winston.

Pearson, P. D., & Tierney, R. J. (1984). On becoming a thoughtful reader: Learning to read like a writer. In O. Niles (Ed.), *Reading in a complex society* (pp. 144-173). University of Chicago: National Society for the Study of Education.

Pfundt, H., & Duit, R. (1991). *Bibliography: Students' alternative frameworks and science education* (3rd ed.). Kiel, Germany: University of Kiel.

Piaget, J. (1950). *The psychology of intelligence* (M. Percy & D. Berlyne, Trans.). London: Routledge & Kegan Paul. (Original work published 1947)

Posner, G. J., Strike, K. A., Hewson, P. W., & Gertzog, W. A. (1982). Accommodation of a scientific conception: Toward a theory of conceptual change. *Science Education, 67,* 489-508.

R

Raphael, T. (1984). Teaching learners about sources of information for answering comprehension questions. *Journal of Reading, 27,* 303–311.

Readence, J., Bean, T., & Baldwin, S. (1981). *Content area reading: An integrated approach.* Dubuque, IA: Kendall/Hunt.

Readence, J., Rickelman, R. J., & Moore, D. W. (1982). Some historical roots of content area reading instruction. *The Reading Professor, 8,* 5–11.

Reinking, D. (1998). Introduction: Synthesizing technological transformations of literacy in a post-typographical world. In D. Reinking, M. C. McKenna, L. D. Labbo, & R. D. Keiffer (Eds.), *Handbook of literacy and technology: Transformation in a post-typographical world* (pp. xi). Mahwah, NJ: Erlbaum.

Richardson, J. S. (2000). *Read it aloud! Using literature in the secondary content classroom.* Newark, DE: International Reading Association.

Richardson, V. (Ed.). (1994). *Staff development and teacher change in reading comprehension instruction: A new generation of programs.* New York: Teachers College Press.

Richardson, V., & Anders, P. L. (1990). *Final report of the reading instruction study.* Tucson: University of Arizona. (ERIC Document Reproduction Service No. ED 324 655).

Richardson, V., & Anders, P. L. (2005). Professional preparation and development of teachers in literacy instruction for urban settings. In P. L. Anders & J. Flood (Eds.), *The literacy development of students in urban schools.* Newark, DE: The International Reading Association.

Richardson, V., Anders, P. L., Tidwell, D., & Lloyd, C. (1991). The relationship between teachers' beliefs and practices in reading comprehension instruction. *American Educational Research Journal, 28,* 559–586.

Rigg, P. (1985). Petra: Learning to read at forty-five. *Journal of Education, 167*(1), 129–139.

Robb, L. (2000). *Teaching reading in the middle school.* New York: Scholastic.

Robinson, F. (1941). *Diagnostic and remedial techniques for effective study.* New York: Harper.

Roe, B. D., Stoodt, B. D., &, & Burns, P. C. (1991). *Secondary school reading instruction: The content areas.* Boston: Houghton Mifflin.

Rokeach, M. (1968). *Beliefs, attitudes, and values: A theory of organization and change.* San Francisco: Jossey-Bass.

Rosenblatt, L. (1938). *Literature as exploration.* New York: Appleton-Century.

Rosenblatt, L. (1978). *The reader, the text, the poem.* Carbondale, IL: Southern Illinois University Press.

Rubin, D. (1992). *Teaching reading and study skills in content areas* (2nd ed.). Boston: Allyn & Bacon.

Rubinstein-Avila, E. (2003–2004). Conversing with Miguel: An adolescent English language learner struggling with later literacy development. *Journal of Adolescent and Adult Literacy, 47,* 290–300.

Rubinstein-Avila, E. (2003, December). *Staff writers, not at-risk students: Urban youth publishing after school.* Paper presented at the annual meeting of the National Reading Conference, Scottsdale, AZ.

Ruddell, M. R. (1993). *Teaching content reading and writing.* Boston: Allyn & Bacon.

S

Salomon, G. (1994). *Interaction of media, cognition, and learning: An exploration of how symbolic forms cultivate mental skills and affect knowledge acquisition.* Hillsdale, NJ: Lawrence Erlbaum Associates.

Salomon, G., Globerman, T., & Guterman, E. (1989). The computer as a zone of proximal development: Internalizing reading-related metacognitions from a reading partner. *Journal of Educational Psychology, 81*(4), 620–626.

Saulawa, D. (1990). *Instructional strategies and conceptual change.* Unpublished doctoral dissertation, University of Arizona, Tucson.

Schmar-Dobler, E. (2003). Reading on the Internet: The link between literacy and technology. *Journal of Adolescent and Adult Literacy, 47*, 80-87.

Schoenbach, R., Greenleaf, C., Cziko, C., & Hurwitz, L. (1999). *Reading for understanding: A guide to improving reading in middle and high school classrooms*. San Francisco: Jossey-Bass Publishers.

School Renaissance Institute. (2001, January-August). *Supercharge your curriculum with Renaissance!* [Brochure]. Wisconsin Rapids, WI: Author.

Schrock, K. (2004). *Teachers helpers: Assessment and rubric information*. Retrieved August 10, 2004, from <DiscoverySchool.com> at <http://school.discovery.com/schrockguide/assess.html>

Shaw, D. (2003, November 30). A plea for media literacy in our nation's schools. *Los Angeles Times*, pp. x-x. Retrieved September 13, 2004, from http://www.medialit.org/reading_room/article631.html>

Sheingold, K., Hawkins, J., & Char, C. (1984). I'm the thinkist and you're the typist: The interaction of technology and the social life of classrooms. *Journal of Social Issues, 40*(3), 19-23.

Shepard, L. A., & Smith, M. L. (Eds.). (1989). *Flunking grades: Research and policies on retention*. London: Falmer Press.

Shernoff, D. J. (2001). The experience of student engagement. I. High school classrooms: A phenomenological perspective. *Dissertation Abstracts International 62*(7A), 2344. (University Microfilms No. 3019968)

Shneiderman, B. (1998). *Designing the user interface: Strategies for effective human-computer interaction* (3rd ed.). Menlo Park, CA: Addison-Wesley.

Shores, J. H. (1943). Skills related to the ability to read history and science. *Journal of Educational Research, 36*(8), 584-593.

Short, K. G., Schroeder, J., Laird, J., Kauffman, G., Ferguson, M. J., & Crawford, K. M. (1996). *Learning together through inquiry: From Columbus to integrated curriculum*. Portland, ME: Stenhouse.

Shulman, L. S. (1987). Knowledge and teaching: Foundations of the new reform. *Harvard Educational Review, 57*, 1-22.

Smith, F. (1971). *Understanding reading: A psycholinguistic analysis of reading and learning to read*. New York: Holt, Rinehart & Winston.

Smith, F. (1973). *Psycholinguistics and reading*. New York: Holt, Rinehart & Winston.

Smith, F. (1988). *Joining the literacy club*. Portsmouth, NH: Heinemann.

Smith, J. (1992, April). *Old learning mechanisms die hard: The problem of "replacing" student conceptions*. Paper presented at the annual meeting of the American Educational Research Association, San Francisco, CA.

Smith, M. L. (1991). Put to the test: The effects of external testing on teachers. *Educational Researcher, 20*, 8-11.

Smith, M. L., Edelsky, C., Draper, K., Rottenberg, C., & Cherland, M. (1989). *The role of testing in elementary schools*. Los Angeles: University of California, Center for Research on Educational Standards and Student Tests.

Smith, N. B. (1946a). Patterns of writing in different subject areas, part I. *Journal of Reading, 8*, 31-37.

Smith, N. B. (1946b). Patterns of writing in different subject areas, part II. *Journal of Reading, 8*, 97-102.

Smith, N. B. (1963). *Be a better reader*. Englewood Cliffs, NJ: Prentice-Hall.

Spillich, G. J., Vesonder, G. T., Chiesi, H. L., & Voss, J. F. (1979). Text processing of domain-related information for individuals with high- and low-domain knowledge. *Journal of Verbal Learning and Verbal Behavior, 18*, 275-290.

Spiro, R., & Myers, A. (1984). Individual differences and underlying cognitive processes. In P. D. Person (Ed.), *Handbook of reading research* (pp. 471-504). New York: Longman.

Spiro, R., & Taylor, B. M. (1987). On investigating children's transition from narrative to expository discourse: The multidimensional nature of psychological text classification. In R. J. Tierney, P. L. Anders, and J. N. Mitchell (Eds.), *Understanding readers' understanding* (pp. 77-94). Hillsdale, NJ: Lawrence Erlbaum Associates.

Stewart, A. (1989). Structure and organization in instructional text—A cognitive perspective on practice. *Proceedings of selected research papers presented at the association for educational communications and technology.* (ERIC Document Reproduction Service No. ED 308 843)

Stipek, D. (2004). *Engaging schools: Fostering high school students' motivation to learn.* Washington, DC: National Academy Press.

Strang, R. (1938). *Improvement of reading in high school and college*. Lancaster, PA: Science Press.

Street, B. (1995). *Social literacies: Critical approaches to literacy in development, ethnography and education*. New York: Longman.

Street, B. (2003). What's "new" in New Literacy studies? Critical approaches to literacy in theory and practice. *Current Issues in Comparative Education, [online] 5*(2), Retrieved September 9, 2004, from www.tc.columbia.edu

Strike, K. A., & Posner, G. J. (1985). A conceptual change view of learning & understanding. In L. H. T. West and A. L. Pines (Eds.), *Cognitive structure and conceptual change* (pp. 211-231). New York: Academic Press.

Strike, K. A., & Posner, G. J. (1992). A revisionist theory of conceptual change. In R. Duschl and R. Hamilton (Eds.), *Philosophy of science: Cognitive psychology and educational theory and practice.* (pp. 147-176). Albany, NY: State University of New York Press.

Sturtevant, E. (1996). Beyond the content literacy course: Influences on beginning mathematics teachers' use of literacy in student teaching. In D. J. Leu, C. K. Kinzer, & K. A. Hinchman (Eds.), *Literacies for the 21st century: Research and practice. 45th Yearbook of the National Reading Conference* (pp. 146-158). Chicago: National Reading Conference.

Sturtevant, E. G. (2004). *The literacy coach: A key to improving teaching and learning in secondary schools.* Washington. DC: Alliance for Excellent Education.

Swafford, J. D. (1990, July). *Strategy adaptations*. Paper presented at the Thirteenth World Congress on Reading, International Reading Association, Stockholm Sweden.

Swenson, E. J. (1942). A study of the relationships among various types of reading scores on general and science materials. *Journal of Educational Research, 36*(2), 81-90.

T

Tannen, D. (1983). Oral and literate strategies in spoken and written discourse. In R. W. Bailey & R. M. Fosheim (Eds.), *Literacy for life: The demand for reading and writing* (pp. 79-96). New York: Modern Language Association of America.

Taylor, W. (1953). Cloze procedure: A new tool for measuring readability. *Journalism Quarterly, 30*, 415-433.

Thorndike, E. L. (1917). Reading as reasoning: A study of mistakes in paragraph reading. *Journal of Educational Psychology, 8*, 323-332.

Tierney, R. J., & Mosenthal, J. (1980, January). *Discourse comprehension and production: Analyzing text structure and cohesion* (Tech. Rep. No. 152). Urbana: University of Illinois, Center for the Study of Reading.

Tierney, R. J., Mosenthal, J., & Kantor, R. N. (1984). Classroom applications of text analysis: Toward improving text selection and use. In J. Flood (Ed.), *Promoting reading comprehension* (pp. 139-160). Newark, DE: International Reading Association.

Tierney, R. J., Readence, J. E., & Dishner, E. K. (1995). *Reading strategies and practices: A compendium* (3rd ed.). Boston: Allyn & Bacon.

Tobin, J. (Ed.). (2004). *Pikachu's global adventure: The rise and fall of Pokémon*. Durham, NC: Duke University Press.

Toemi, X. (Ed.). (2003). *Challenges of teaching with technology across the curriculum: Issues and solutions*. Hershey, PA: Information Science.

Tomlinson, C. A. (1999). *The differentiated classroom: Responding to the needs of all learners*. Alexandria, VA: Association for Supervision and Curriculum Development.

V

Vacca, R., & Vacca J. (2002). *Content area reading*. Boston: Allyn & Bacon.

Valencia, S. (Forthcoming). *Classroom based literacy assessment*. Mahwah, NJ: Lawrence Erlbaum Associates.

Valencia, S. W., & Stallman, A. C. (1988, December). *Multiple measures of prior knowledge: Comparative predictive validity*. Paper presented at the annual meeting of the National Reading Conference, Tucson, AZ.

Vogt, M. E., & Shearer, B. (2003). *Reading specialists in the real world*. Boston: Allyn & Bacon.

Vosiadou, S., & Brewer, W. F. (1987). Theories of knowledge restructuring in development. *Review of Research in Education, 37*, 51-67.

Vygotsky, L. (1978). *Mind in society*. Cambridge, MA: MIT Press.

W

Wallowitz, L. (2004). Reading as resistance: Gendered messages in literature and media. *English Journal, 93*, 26-31.

Waner, K., Behymer, J., & McCrary, S. (1992). Two points of view on elementary school keyboarding. *Business Education Forum, 47*, 27-35.

Weaver, C. A., & Kintsch, W. (1991). Expository text. In R. Barr, M. L. Kamil, P. B. Mosenthal, & P. D. Pearson (Eds.), *Handbook of reading research* (Vol. 2, pp. 230-245). New York: Longman.

Weisz, P. B. (1983). English and science—symbiosis for survival. In R. W. Bailey & R. M. Fosheim (Eds.), *Literacy for life: The demand for reading and writing* (pp. 125-136). New York: Modern Language Association of America.

Wells, G. (1990). Creating the conditions to encourage literate thinking. *Educational Leadership, 47*(6), 13-17.

Wenger, E., McDermott, R., & Snyder, W. (2002). *Cultivating communities of practice*. Boston, MA: Cambridge Business School Press.

Wertsch, J. V. (1985). *Vygotsky and the social formation of mind*. Cambridge, MA: Harvard University Press.

White, J. B. (1983). The invisible discourse of the law: Reflections on legal literacy and general education. In R. W. Bailey & R. M. Fosheim (Eds.), *Literacy for life: The demand for reading and writing* (pp. 137-150). New York: Modern Language Association of America.

Williams, B. T. (2003). What they see is what we get: Television and middle school writers. *Journal of Adolescent and Adult Literacy, 46*, 546-554.

Wirth, A. G. (1989). The violation of people at work in schools. *Teachers College Record, 90*, 535-549.

Wronkovich, M. (1998). The relationship of early keyboard instruction to computer proficiency. *Educational Technology, 10*, 42-47.

Z

Zhang, Y. (2003). Making meaning in a digital literacy club: Teachers' talk of beliefs about e-mail communication in literacy and learning. In Y. Saito-Abbott, R. Donovan, & T. Abbot (Eds.), *Emerging technologies in teaching language and culture* (Vols. 2 and 3, pp. 129-156). San Diego, CA: Larc Press.

Author Index

Numbers in *italics* indicate pages with complete bibliographic information.

G

H

I

J

K

Subject Index

D

T

CPSIA information can be obtained
at www.ICGtesting.com
Printed in the USA
FSOW02n2150210115
4697FS

9 84340